AAKAR BOOKS CLASSICS

Agrarian India Between the World Wars

A Study of Colonial-Feudal Capitalism

Rostislav A. Ulyanovsky

AGRARIAN INDIA BETWEEN THE WORLD WARS
Rostislav A. Ulyanovsky

First Aakar Edition 2017

ISBN 978-93-5002-480-5

Published by
AAKAR BOOKS
28 E Pocket IV, Mayur Vihar Phase I, Delhi 110 091
Phones : 011 2279 5505, 2279 5641
aakarbooks@gmail.com; www.aakarbooks.com

Printed at
Sapra Brothers, Delhi 110 092

CONTENTS

Foreword

Capitalism began to develop intensively in India after the First World War. According to League of Nations statistics, in the 1920s and 1930s, India was among the top ten countries in the world in terms of its level of industrial development. Sociologists and economists of all schools began to study the country in this context. Several works appeared in the West, written by subjective sociologists and economists, who strove to apply the pattern of capitalist development in the Western countries in order to demonstrate that India would develop in the same way. The facts showed, however, that this was not the case. Although India was, indeed, following a capitalist course of development and advancing faster now than before, although, like all other countries setting out in this direction, it was subject to the natural historical law of socio-economic development discovered by Marxism-Leninism, it was following this course in its own very specific way.

India's capitalist development had inherent specific features. Above all, a particular combination was observed of several economic structures surviving from economic formations of a precapitalist type, with the leading and rapidly developing capitalist structure, the subordination of the whole economy and all its sectors to the world capitalist market and, of course, primarily that of Britain, the metropolitan country. This required comprehensive analysis and consideration of all these specifics, something that could not be achieved by objectivist political economy or bourgeois sociology and the vulgar economics of determinism.

In order to study India, especially its countryside, where about 85 per cent of the population of several hundred million is concentrated, only one methodology could be used at all fruitfully, that is—the Marxist-Leninist methodology of materialist dialectics.

In this book, the author has tried to present an integral work studying one of the most critical periods of and a turning point in the colonial exploitation of India by British imperialism—that of the pre-crisis "flourishing" and the development of the world economic crisis from the end of the 1920s to almost the mid-1930s. The socio-economic analysis in this work discloses the evolution of India's agrarian structure. It covers chiefly the period between the two world wars, which was one of persistent and nation-wide anti-imperialist struggle and, in a number of Indian provinces, also of an anti-feudal movement among the peasantry. It should be noted that it is precisely this period that is covered at best fragmentarily in contemporary socio-economic literature.

The material the author has managed to utilise is, for the most part, unique, especially the many volumes of the British Royal Commission on Agriculture in India (1927) and the research carried out by the Indian Banking Enquiry Committee for the Central Administrated Areas (1931). Extensive use of this material, together with the results of the All-India Population Census of 1931, has made it possible to recreate clear types of representatives of exploitative groups, to show quite clearly the economic policy pursued by British imperialism in the Indian countryside, as well as the differences in the positions of the exploitative strata in India in relation to the peasantry and the land question.

The research is also based on the use of now rare material (with which even experts on the social problems of India are unfamiliar) on the agrarian question and the condition of the peasantry, the development of capitalism and class differentiation in the countryside, the agrarian policy pursued by British imperialism—material that was published by almost all the leading newspapers and journals in India at the time.

The author suggests that considerable interest will be shown in his elaboration of such problems as the development course taken by capitalism, merchant's and usurer's capital, the land-tax systems and the attempts made by the British imperialists to implant junker-type landowner capitalists in India.

The work analyses the impact of the world economic crisis on the position of the immediate producer (cultivator), shows the way Britain robbed agrarian India more and more as the Great Depression of 1929-1933 deepened, and also considers the specific mechanism by which the consequences of the crisis were transferred from the metropolitan country to colonial India.

* * *

The author begins his analysis of India's agrarian structure in the 1920s and 1930s, by considering the evolution of the communal system, which had taken shape long before the British conquered India, suffered greatly at the hands of the conquerors, and began to die out at an accelerating pace in the 19th century. Two authors of the last century carried out classical materialist research into India's communal system. The first was Karl Marx, in his famous letters on India (1858), and the second was M. Kovalevsky, a Russian sociologist, who knew Marx personally and, in 1879, wrote a work on the origins and reasons for the disintegration of communal landownership in India, Ceylon, Algeria, and the Indian commune in Latin America. Kovalevsky's work was studied, in Russian, by Marx, who analysed it in a thorough and friendly way.

A major contribution was made to research into the Indian commune by the book by Prof. I. M. Reisner, which came out in 1932, entitled "Essays on the Class Struggle in India". This book, which soon became a bibliographical rarity, provided a short but deep and comprehensive description of the struggle by the Sikh, Marath and Jat peasantry and touched on the Punjabi, Bombay and Uttar Pradesh peasant communes. The work was based on Marx's approach and, in the main, confirmed his analysis of the evolution of the Indian communal system and the role played by it in India's history. I. M. Reisner was the first to connect the question of the evolution of the Indian peasantry with the mass anti-feudal peasant movements of the 17th and 18th centuries and to carry out logical and historically profound research into the class struggle of commune peasantry against local feudals and Moghul despots, who stood above the commune and exploited it.

Then, roughly 30 years later, a new, postwar generation of Soviet historians of India began to study the Indian peasant commune, the country's feudal agrarian structure, the peasant economy in the late Middle Ages, before India was seized by the British, and during the period of British colonial domination. Interesting new works appeared to enrich the classic conceptions of India provided by the founders of Marxism.

Among the works on the agrarian structure of India and developing countries that came out in the 1970s, worthy of particular note are those by the Soviet experts M. K. Kudryavtsev, V. I. Pavlov, V. G. Rastyannikov, L. B. Alayev, G. K. Shirokov, E. N. Komarov, V. V. Krylov and A. P. Kolontayev. These cover communes and castes, the country's multisectoral socio-economic structures, the historical preconditions for the genesis of capitalism and its typology in the countries of Asia and Africa, the socio-economic development of India in the 18th to 20th centuries, the problems of capitalist development in the countryside of the Orient today, the agrarian evolution of independent India, and the evolution of the market economy in colonial India. A number of works consider the social structure of the Indian countryside, in particular the peasant commune of the 19th century, the chief forms and real content of agrarian relations in India in the 18th and 19th centuries. Other interesting works are those devoted to the specifics of the development of the productive forces and the reproduction process in the developing countries, traditionalism and modernisation of the countryside in these countries during the current scientific and technological revolution, the development of various forms of production, including commodity and capitalist production in Southern and Southeast Asia, and the main stages in the development of the peasant economy. All these works are based on the classical Marxist ones of the 19th century; they develop and enrich our knowledge of the agrarian structure in the East.[1] They all, in one way or another, touch on the specifics of the development of the basis, i.e., the productive forces and relations of production, of the socio-economic, predominantly agrarian structure of India and neighbouring countries.

Many books have been written on the Indian commune, and many more will appear in the future. All Soviet authors carry out their research on the basis of the works of Marx and Engels and their methodology, introducing more and more new factual material, expanding the picture of the social and economic life of the Indian feudal village. Gradually, the problem is arising of defining the specifics not only of production, but also the superstructure in India and the East in general.

In the context of the commune and its specific nature in India and the East, the author considers it necessary to clarify the distinguishing features of the superstructural sphere in the East, as contrasted to Western countries.

* * *

The East and the West really do have their own specifics, ones that are deep and comprehensive. It would be wrong to seek some single key to them, and they certainly cannot be explained in terms of some schema, as this could not cover either history or present reality.

It is, of course, difficult to give a brief but comprehensive study of the specifics of the East and the social structure there. We shall try to focus the reader's attention on just certain major aspects and describe them in condensed form.

It is an indisputable fact that, in economic terms, the countries of Asia and Africa are a whole historical era behind Europe, Japan and North America. A tremendous role here was played by military seizures, foreign enslavement, and the many centuries of colonial oppression. Yet, the economic lag (this being the most evident, so it sometimes conceals the fact that there are spheres in which the East is not behind the West at all) was determined not only by foreign domination. This lag, the scale and nature of which have exerted a fundamental impact on the social structures of the countries of the East, was engendered to a certain extent by superstructure factors, too, and it would be simply impossible to understand the specifics of the East without reference to these.

Let us begin with so-called traditionalism. To this day the East is steeped in traditions. This traditionalism is coming into particularly sharp relief today, against the background of the triumphant advance of socialism throughout the world. The conservative nature of traditions has become an obstacle to progress in the social consciousness and the economic affairs of the peoples of Asia and Africa. Traditions penetrate the entire intellectual and social life of the peoples of the East and of each individual separately. Most recently, of course, the force of conservative, reactionary traditions has been disrupted by capitalist development, and the national and class struggles, but the traditions exist in layers, one on top of the other. Sometimes the leaders of African or Asian countries strive to accelerate the development of their peoples, but their efforts are foiled by the heavy chains of traditions, and the permanent resistance of the social and individual consciousness to anything new. It would be no exaggeration to say that the very deep and comprehensive traditionalism serves as a nutrient medium not only for feudal, but also for national-bourgeois, and often for petty-bourgeois reaction, and that this is precisely what, to a considerable extent, accounts for the low level of consciousness among the rural and the urban working people, and to some degree the contemporary proletariat of Asia and Africa, too.

In many liberated countries, public opinion and even science sing the praises of their past too loudly. This is typical of many countries of Asia and, to a somewhat lesser degree, of Central and Southern Africa. It is also found in the Arab countries of the Middle East. An excessive focusing of public attention on the past, the counterposing of the past to social progress and all-round modernisation, are all manifestations of reaction and nationalistic limitations. One inevitable outcome of this is growing backwardness, lost time, and a slowing down of socio-economic and cultural development.

Traditional living conditions are based on an almost petrified system of morals and social behaviour and, in a number of countries, such as India, they also maintain a strict division of society into castes, which still exist even though the caste system has been officially abolished and has been gradually decaying as a result of capitalist development. For the countries of Africa, the still strong conservative communal structure and tribal links are just as important.

The features of traditionalism mentioned above are immanent not only in the old, but to a considerable extent also in the modern East and, of course, not only in precapitalist structures, but also ones transitional to capitalism and the capitalist structure currently taking shape. They are also manifest in the countries with a socialist orientation.

It is usually asserted that the peoples of Asia and Africa were easy prey for conquerors. One reason for this was that the peasantry of Asia and Africa, which made up 80-90 per cent of the population, were so heavily exploited that they passively accepted almost any conquest or even expected it to bring a change for the better.

The East has always, right from ancient times, everywhere meant the domination of despots. The East is specific in that, in antiquity, the Middle Ages and recently, the age of colonialism, the possession of unlimited power (despotism) made it possible, without personally owning any economic unit or organising any production, to appropriate, through the predominant system of "rent-tax", and the system of private or state feudalism, not only the surplus product, but also a considerable part of the necessary product created by the producers. Colossal wealth, so great that the Europeans who came to the East were astounded, accumulated in the hands of the rulers, usually not connected with economic activities. The colonialists skilfully utilised the lever of extra-economic appropriation for centuries, right up to the collapse of the colonial system this century. The consequences of the parasitic receipt of rents, based on extra-economic coercion, are felt to this day. The East today is distinguished by the survival of extra-economic coercion of the immediate cultivator and non-equivalent exchange.

The bonded peasant, living in terrible poverty and constant hunger and ignorance, had nothing to defend. It is not surprising that, over only 25 years, the Arabs managed, almost without wars, to subject the peoples of North Africa, Iran, Syria, Armenia, Central and Southern Asia. The green banner of Islām at that time bore the ideas of equality and fraternity of all the faithful, these being of tremendous attractive force for the oppressed peasantry. The masses, suffering under the yoke of Oriental despotism, not only did not resist Arab annexation, they even went over to the side of the conquerors.

The specifics of the East today cannot be understood unless the religious factor is taken into account.

The religious systems of the East—Hinduism, Buddhism,

Confucianism, Islam, and the teachings of countless different religious sects—are, of course, diverse, but they do have something in common: not one of these religions, which to this day constitute a major unit linking the entire superstructural sphere, has ever experienced a profound bourgeois reformation like European Christianity has. Not one of them could provide such a powerful spiritual justification for the political and socio-economic activities of society and the individual as European Christianity did at one time, and especially Protestantism, under the protection of which capitalism developed faster and which put the European peasantry and urban population in the foreground of the struggle for a bourgeois system. The religious beliefs of the East, like in the West, too, in the past, do not include just adoration of a deity, but also a "consecrated" way of life and thinking of both society and the individual. What, in European Christianity, may be compared with the all-embracing force of such socio-religious canons as the Rig-Veda, the Laws of Manu, the Dhammapada, with the impact of the moral and ethical code of Confucianism or the iron laws of the Shariat and Adat? There is no doubt that the social structure of the East would have been very different if the envelope of ideas surrounding its material existence had taken some other shape or if it had experienced its own bourgeois Renaissance. The religious systems of the Western world, especially from the 14th and 15th centuries onwards, did much more to promote its social and economic development than the corresponding systems did in the East. It is certainly no chance that the Christian countries of the West, and certainly not the Islamic and Buddhist ones, became the cradle of capitalism.

The lag in the East's economic development meant that proper national, i.e., modern capitalist states began to take shape there later than in the West. Yet, it was national states that, in their turn, acted as powerful accelerators of capitalist development. The delay in the emergence of national states in the East is largely explained, of course, by foreign invasions and domination, but hardly by these alone. A considerable role here was played by the extremely narrow and shallow entrepreneurial and economic base, above all the social division of labour and the development of commodity-money relations. The economic base did not suffice for the formation of a national state, owing to the stagnant nature of the superstructure, too.

National consciousness appeared earlier in the countries of Asia and Africa than did the economic pivot that, in the West, preceded the emergence of a similar consciousness. This pivot was, of course, rapid capitalist development. In the East, national consciousness emerges primarily as a response to aggression, occupation, foreign oppression, to everything that the foreign conqueror and then imperialism brought with them.

It must be admitted that, today too, many peoples that have liberated themselves from colonialism have not yet formed nations, though they have achieved state self-determination. The example of socialist Russia and world socialism indubitably exerted an impact that speeded up the historical process of the formation of national states. The combination of socialism, the international working-class and national liberation movements accelerated this process so much that almost a hundred states in Asia and Africa required only 15 to 25 years to achieve self-determination, while two or three centuries were spent on such processes in the West.

There is one more aspect to the problem. It is said that, for 200 to 300 years, the supremacy of Europe and the United States over their Asian and African colonies consisted in a more advanced mode of production. This is correct, but not an exhaustive explanation. A hundred backward Eastern countries, remaining basically peasant ones, with predominantly pre-capitalist economies whose level of development of production, science and technology was incomparable with that achieved in the Western countries, managed to liberate themselves from the political domination of colonialism. Why did this happen? In what way did these backward nations surpass their oppressors? Not, of course, in the mode of production, nor the productive forces, nor the level of technology and organisation of the economy. It was anti-imperialist, democratic nationalism that aroused the peoples of Asia and Africa, became the organising force behind the struggle waged by hundreds of millions of oppressed people. It was this anti-imperialist nationalism that established close contacts with world socialism, formed a united front with it and, after receiving help from the Soviet Union, the international working-class and communist movements, fell like an avalanche of national revolutionary wars and uprisings on its oppressors, thereby putting imperialism on the defensive.

It is not, therefore, merely a matter of the superiority of the economic basis, but, ultimately, of the balance of world forces, which in one historical era ensured the seizure and protracted oppression of the East by the capitalist West—when there was no force capable of standing up to this hostile West, but in another age provided for the rapid liberation of the East—when such a force appeared and when, after the October Revolution in Russia and the defeat of Nazi Germany in the Second World War, liberation processes throughout the world gained momentum.

The basis and superstructure conditions that had taken shape in the East by the time of its colonial enslavement largely determined the subsequent economic and social development of the colonies and semi-colonies. The invasion of foreign capital undermined the traditional means by which the economy was run and, to some degree, promoted the development of the social division of labour and commodity-money relations. At the same time, colonialism often implanted or conserved precapitalist relations and, on this basis, turned the countries of the East into the outskirts of the world capitalist market. In the East, capitalism could only assume distorted forms, for it satisfied, above all, not the national requirements of the Eastern countries, but those of the capitalist countries of the West. This was capitalism of a specific type, colonial capitalism, dependent, surrounded by a host of precapitalist survivals in both town and countryside, in both production and circulation. It was this that helped preserve, in the East, the relations of production that during the corresponding period in the West had rapidly decayed.

Let us turn to another aspect of the issue. The fact that, for a long time, the East was economically stagnant (in comparison with the West) often influences our ideas about the East today. A superficial look might indicate that the East was still developing slowly, as if this slowness and stagnation constituted a specific feature of this part of the world today, too. But is that the case? First, let us compare growth rates. The actual capitalist structure in Western Europe began to take shape at least five centuries ago, while in the East this structure is still extremely young. It may be confidently stated that in India, for instance, the capitalist sector has existed for about 100-120 years; it arose in the form of the totality of industrial enterprises and railways built in the middle of the last century. Less than 40 of these years have coincided with the country's independent political development, though neocolonial exploitation continues.

The real assistance rendered to India by the socialist states must not, of course, under any circumstances be forgotten, but neocolonialism remains a very powerful, probably the chief force, restraining the country's social progress and keeping it within the framework of the capitalist system. Yet, even under these conditions, when mighty internal and external factors of a conservative nature continue to operate, India has managed to join the ten most industrially developed countries in the world. A trend towards accelerated development of capitalism—a deformed capitalism, in many ways meeting the interests of monopoly capitalism, yet still developing at an accelerating rate—is also observed in other countries of Asia and Africa following the capitalist course of development: Malaysia, Thailand, Singapore, the Philippines, Indonesia, Iran, Turkey, Saudi Arabia, Tunisia, Nigeria, Senegal, Cameroon, Zaire, Kenya, and so on.

The following paradox may, therefore, be formulated: the specific nature of the economic development of the East today consists in a fantastic intertwining of basis and superstructure conservatism and dynamism, profound backwardness and social progress. Meanwhile, bourgeois dynamism, which for a long time was considered to be inherent chiefly in Western countries, is growing in strength in the East, too. In this connection, the national capitalist sector is obviously playing an increasingly negative role from the point of view of the development prospects of the countries of the East. The ruling classes linked with this sector, their parties and leaders are demonstrating a growing inclination towards compromise with foreign private capital, though, of course, they uphold state independence and often both anti-imperialist and anti-colonialist positions.

Many of the specific features of the political and economic structures of the liberated countries are of quite independent significance and cannot be understood without an analysis of superstructure phenomena and institutions, and their interaction with the basis, without a study of the particular impact exerted by capitalism and imperialism on the developing bourgeois society, without account of the combination of the transplantation to the East of the developed Western forms of capitalism and, at the same time, the conservation or extremely slow ousting of the precapitalist relations that remain in a number of countries and regions, and often even predominate. The specific nature of the social structure of the developing countries cannot be understood unless attention is focused first on the dependent, subordinate, peripheral position in the world capitalist economy allotted by imperialism to the developing countries, the former countries of colonial-feudal capitalism. Further, to clarify these specifics full account must be taken of the impact exerted on the developing countries by the two opposing socio-economic systems in the world today. While the socialist community renders them help in strengthening their political sovereignty, achieving economic independence and social progress, the actions of world imperialism are designed to undermine their political independence, maintain and strengthen the economic exploitation of these countries and preserve outdated economic forms.

The symbol of our times is the fact that, in the East, a mighty trend has emerged towards a socialist orientation in a large group of states. This trend is encountering difficulties on its way, sometimes serious ones, as well as political and social disruptions, but it is breaking through the oppression of the conservative superstructure receiving help from the socialist countries, and borrowing in some positive form certain elementary principles of scientific socialism, especially in the economy. A new non-capitalist economic structure is taking shape, so the fundamentally new prospect of socialist development is opening up before the East.

The matter consists, therefore, not in an interaction of a multitude of sectors that supposedly determines the current situation and the prospects for the liberated countries' development, but in the fact that, in the course of the national liberation revolution, an opportunity is created for choosing a non-capitalist development course, a socialist orientation. The West never had this choice; it had only one possible course—that of capitalist development. In this sense, the East is in a completely different position, which, it must be said, gives it major advantages.

Chapter One

The Evolution of India's Agrarian System

India's Agrarian System Before Colonial Seizure

At the time when British merchant's capital, in the form of the East-India Company, was making its first experiments at colonial seizures, the Moghul Empire was already living through its last decades. The disintegration of the empire of the Great Moghuls, which was the last centralised eastern despotic state in India, was manifested mainly in the feudalisation of the country's agrarian system, i.e., the establishment of private feudal landed property, in the history of which state feudal and private feudal ownership often replaced each other, but these processes eventually came to a halt under the impact of a number of internal and external factors.

In the process of the feudalisation of India's agrarian system, accompanied by peasant rebellions against the feudals, who seized communal and peasant land (the Marath, Sikh, and other uprisings), the centralised state links established by the swords of the Moghul conquerors were greatly weakened. The zamindars and jagirdars—the agents of the centralised eastern despotic state for collecting taxes and rents, who had turned, over several hundred years, from being officials paid by the state into the hereditary holders of their posts, had, by the end of the age of the Great Moghuls, become private feudal lords of huge territories in India. The loss of individual parts of the Moghul Empire, the unprecedented growth of feudal separatism, the weakening of the central state power as a result of the increasing role and influence of the former deputies of the central government, the change in the direction of the chief trade routes connecting the East with Europe, the decline of the once vital caravan routes after the discovery of the sea route to India—all these factors furthered the formation of a number of virtually independent feudal states both in the south of India and on the Indo-Ganges plain (the Audh and Bengal princedoms, the state of Ahmed-Shah Durrani and the states of the Sikhs and Maraths).

The relative state unity of India achieved by the Moghuls was totally destroyed by the development and consolidation of private feudal property and the formation, on this basis, of local feudal-state entities. Thus, by the beginning of the period of colonialism, British merchant's capital acquired an opportunity for making extensive colonial seizures, especially by swallowing up local feudal states that had broken away from the Great Moghuls.

The basis of the socio-economic system in agrarian India at that time was the land commune, which constituted a result, of different degrees, of the disintegration of the patriarchal-tribal system. This disintegration was so significant that, by the end of the age of the Great Moghuls, there were virtually no more full tribal communes practising communal production and consumption in India. Moreover, the next stage in the disintegration of the patriarchal system—the commune as a group of united families with its natural inequality and the systematic redivision of the land, with contracting communal production within the framework of a large, united family—was also on the way out. The social form of the organisation of farming was the simple agricultural commune with the usual farmstead-hereditary ownership of the land, while the forms connected with family and blood ties and an annual redivision of the land were receding into the past. Once economic inequality had arisen on the grounds of the inequality in large united families, on the basis of the growth of the productive force of labour and under the conditions of the caste system with its harsh exploitation, it engendered a certain differentiation of the property, and then the socio-economic level of the peasantry. Communal land tenure was replaced by private peasant farmstead-hereditary farming and, for this to be turned into private landed property, an all-out expansion was required of the commodity economy, a total separation of crafts from farming and, on this basis, the gradual destruction of the commune-type organisation. Indian farming at that time was, from the point of view of development trends, already beginning to go over to the primitive commodity economy. It might be said,

2*

however, that this transition could itself only be achieved over a long period of time. The Indian commune remained a major brake on the commercialisation of the peasant economy, as it was based on subsistence production.

The restraining influence of the commune on the centrifugal social forces that arose within the commune and led it ultimately to its disintegration was considerable. It must be taken into account for an understanding of the significance of the social revolution that the British were compelled to accomplish before giving an impetus to the development of India's home market. The strength of the land commune lay in it being the chief socio-labour unit, the initial social form of the organisation of the production process. The commune's exceptional importance in this respect arose from "that peculiar combination of hand-weaving, hand-spinning and hand-tilling agriculture which gave them self-supporting power".[1]

For this sort of commune the outside world simply did not exist. Its entire socio-economic life fitted into prepared, ready forms that served, at any moment, as a ready-made schema sanctified by the economic experience of generations. The individual peasant household, being a sort of atom of the commune and satisfying its requirements within the commune and through it, operated, until the British conquest, on a fundamentally subsistence basis. This does not exclude the fact that India, before the arrival of the British colonisers, has gone through several periods of intensive growth of both home and foreign trade (the ages of the Mauria and Moghuls) which, however, could not change the subsistence nature of farming, since all this commodity turnover was based on the sale of the peasants' surplus product, coming partially or in its entirety in the form of rent and tax to the central government through its local deputies. Even the reform introduced by Akbar of the tax exploitation of the peasantry, replacing the tax in kind with a money tax, was unable to change the profoundly subsistence nature of the Indian peasant economy. Previously, before the Akbar reform, the peasantry's surplus product entered commodity turnover through the government local deputy, who was on his way to becoming a feudal, through the feudal state, or the merchant tax-farmer; after the reform the realisation of this surplus product was carried out partly by the peasant himself. The peasant began to take his own product to the market, but only the amount necessary to pay his taxes.

This could not but contribute to the further decay of the commune and was naturally accompanied by painful processes: a rise in the degree of feudal exploitation of the peasantry and a drop in its miserly standard of living. Yet, the peasant's farming remained basically subsistence, closed farming, and all his requirements continued to be met by means of the joint farming and industrial production within the commune.

Commodity production was preceded by commodity circulation, but Indian farming production, until the arrival of the British colonisers, not only was not commodity production, it was not even involved in commodity circulation on any large scale, though elements of commercialisation had already appeared.

There can be no doubt that the introduction of money rents promoted the growth of trade, expanded the volume of commodity turnover, strengthened money circulation and thereby brought Indian subsistence farming closer to its logical end. Since, however, the only form of capital at the time was merchant's and usurer's capital, which could not, on its own, engender any radical change in the economic system, and since the relations of production within the commune remained unchanged, i.e., based on united craft production and farming, agricultural production remained subsistence farming, while the land commune continued to exist as the chief social unit.

Such was the social system that, based on communal land tenure and the subsistence economy, on united craft production and farming, served as the passive subject of the historical forces operating in the sphere of Indian politics. Such was the society, based on "a sort of equilibrium, resulting from a general repulsion and constitutional exclusiveness between all its members".[2]

The zamindars and jagirdars, who were the local agents of the central Moghul government, in spite of being only government tax-collectors, went far beyond their official powers in their exploitative activities. They not only increased land taxes at will or introduced new taxes (on the roads, water, marriage, pilgrimage, etc.) but also, and this is particularly important, since they were far from the central government, virtually owned the land belonging to the peasant commune. By seizing non-cultivated land and the local irrigation network, levying extra taxes, and expanding their own lands, the zamindars changed from being just government tax-collectors into a force opposing Moghul centralisation and striving to gain possession of the land for the purposes of the feudal exploitation of the peasant commune.

The end of the centralised Moghul state was already predetermined when the Moghuls, without departing in the slightest from the land policy of their predecessors, left whole districts and provinces in the hands of the former Hindu Rajahs, merely taking tribute from them, or set up their own institution of government deputies and generously handed over jagirs—huge part of the country—to their attendants. Over time; the landed property of the zamindars and jagirdars became hereditary and each new emperor usually confirmed the hereditary rights of the zamindar and his heir. Even if the zamindar was lax in paying taxes into the central treasury, he was usually replaced by a relative, but retained the land he had seized, including uncultivated land (nankar).

The process of the "feudal emancipation" of the zamindars dealt a heavy blow to the commune, especially when the zamindars and jagirdars found it more profitable not to collect the taxes themselves, but to allow third persons to purchase this privilege in individual parts of the district. The zamindars farmed out whole groups of villages, cultivated and unused lands, often constituting an entire district, or taluq. The rulers of the taluqs, in turn, farmed out part of their rights to others, thereby forming a parasitic stratum of landowners participating in the plunder of the peasants' surplus product. This naturally entailed the fiercest exploitation of the land commune. Districts ceased to be integral tax units, and became groups by categories of separate hereditary tax-collecting owners.[3] Being a tax-farmer, the zamindar here played the part of the founder of the multi-storey structure of parasites, which was, to a certain extent, modernised by the British.

Thus, the outdated communal land tenure began to be replaced within the framework of communal landownership by hereditary, farmstead-peasant farming, as a precursor of the future private landed property, while state landownership of the Great Moghuls began to be replaced by the feudal property of the zamindars. These were two inseparable socio-economic processes, one of which worked from below, within the exploited commune, and the other from above, in the exploiting class.

The transition to land belonging to local feudal zamindars did not mean any fundamental change in the mode of production or the forms of exploitation compared with those of the period of the centralised Moghul despotic state. This process could not result in the dispossession of the peasants' land or a transition to feudal unpaid work (corvée) and serfdom, because the zamindar, now becoming a feudal, did not, in contrast to his European or Russian counterparts, support serfdom or have his own independent landowner economy. The peasant continued to own the chief production factors as he had under the Moghuls, when the land belonged to the state. The mode of production and the relations of exploitation remained unchanged. Instead of landed property concentrated on the national scale, property by local feudals began to emerge. The economic system based on the commune remained as before.

In *Capital,* Marx wrote in the chapter "The Genesis of Capitalist Ground-Rent", concerning this sort of land relations: "The direct producer . . . is to be found here in possession of his own means of production, the necessary material labour conditions required for the realisation of his labour and the production of his means of subsistence. He conducts his agricultural activity and the rural home industries connected with it independently. . . Under such conditions the surplus-labour for the nominal owner of the land can only be extorted from them by other than economic pressure, whatever the form assumed may be."[4]

The First Period of British Rule (the Period of the Primitive Accumulation of Capital)

This period, which coincided, in the main, with domination by the East-India Company, occurred at the end of the 18th century. It was characterised by an exceptionally powerful process of plunder, stopping at nothing, which was either connected or, more frequently, not connected, with trade. Trade was the mask concealing the piracy practised on dry land by the British colonisers who, by means of their theft, created the base without which Britain's rapid industrial capitalist development would have been impossible. This open or concealed robbery brought Bengal's agriculture to an unprecedented state of depletion (at the end of the 18th century). The merchant's capital that plundered India was, in the metropolitan country, only just setting about creating industrial capitalist production. It had not yet become industrial capital, which is inevitably faced with solving the problems of its survival—those of raw materials and markets. Unless these problems are solved, neither cheap mass production, nor the more profitable sale of the output, or a growth of surplus value is possible. Here are a few illustrations of the activities of the British colonisers in Bengal and certain other parts of India, which were the first to come under British influence.[5]

—In the first 18 years of its existence, the East-India Company made an annual profit of 175 per cent.

—The seizure of Bengal (1757) was accompanied by the expropriation of the ruling classes, the theft of treasure, precious metals and stones, and the confiscation of the princedoms of Satara, Jhansi and Gandota (the treaty between Clive and Mir-Jafar).

—Tax-collectors used terrorist methods. Before British rule was established, the total sum of land tax levied in Bengal was 14,245 thousand rupees in 1748, and 14,704 thousand in 1757, but in 1777, under the British, the sum was 28,181 thousand rupees.

—From 1765 to 1771, tax collection alone in Bengal provided the East-India Company with an income of 40 million rupees.

—In the Najandabad and Leoni districts of the former Central Province, under the Maraths 22,770 rupees had been collected in land taxes, but under the British, in 1821—103,000 and in 1825—138,000 rupees.

—87 per cent of the incomes of the British East-India Company consisted of land taxes.

The degree of exploitation of the peasantry was naturally

reflected not only in these figures. The actual tax burden was much greater than they indicate, since the collection of the land tax was carried out by tax-farmers, who were undoubtedly not particularly honest.[6] This was the basis on which the mass peasant movement arose (the uprising of 1768-1780). The plunderous policy objectively conflicted with the desire to maintain the constant exploitation of India, which was impossible without the support of the former dominant classes. The creation of a new Bengal landed aristocracy, consisting mainly of tax-farmers, was a result of the need to accomplish a profound strategic step in land policy in order to set up, in this exploited colonial country, a class support for the foreign exploiters. The replacement of one governor-general, Hastings, by another, Cornwallis, of the policy of expropriation of the landed aristocracy by their restoration did not indicate any fundamentally new attitude on the part of Britain to its new colony; it was merely designed to change the methods of exploitation, which had been disrupted by frequent wars and uprisings, to accomplish a transition to exploitation of a relatively more considered kind, relying on allies from among the Indian ruling classes.

According to some calculations, the total sum of values exported from India to Britain over the century from 1757 to 1857 was £1 billion, and according to others—£723 million.

In a word, the policy pursued by British merchant's capital at this stage of its domination in India may be briefly formulated thus: robbery, seizure of territories and unbridled exploitation of the immediate producers on the basis of non-economic coercion. The exploitation of the immediate producer during this period was based chiefly on robbery by means of taxes.

The Second Period of British Rule (the Period of Industrial Capitalism)

This was the decisive stage in the industrialisation of Britain itself. At the same time, it was accompanied by a growth of British colonial might. All the chief colonial acquisitions in India were made at precisely this time. The land policy as a lever in the hands of the dominant class always served, in spite of all its contradictoriness at individual stages, as a most reliable instrument for the exploitation and bondage of the immediate producer. The British land policy in India in the age of merchant's capital was essentially a plunderous tax policy, but the land policy of industrial capital went far beyond the bounds of just robbery by means of taxation.

The objective result of the economic policy of British industrial capital in India consisted in the destruction of the commune, the breaking off of the links between farming and craft production, and the rapid commercialisation of agriculture—in a word, the formation of a colony as a raw material base and a sales market for the metropolitan country. This does not mean that British industrial capital pursued a direct policy of eliminating precapitalist relations in India. British capital was always, in its approach to the old agrarian system, governed by specific considerations and conditions in the given period of its domination. The ways in which this old system was broken down did not run straight, but zigzagged. In just the same way, the results of the destructive work were extremely contradictory, limited and conditional. From the abstract theoretical point of view, it would seem that the historical mission of British industrial capital in India was to eliminate the subsistence economy and its foundations—the unification of craft production and farming in the form of the peasant commune—and to rearrange land relations thoroughly in preparation for the development of capitalism.

Yet, nowhere did British industrial capital fulfil this historical mission. On the contrary, everywhere under the influence of various factors (the political and economic situation in the metropolitan country and in the colony, a number of military reasons, and so on), the adjustment of land relations for the development of capitalism ended in agreements with the feudal classes. British colonialism strove to set up modern private landed property, but was forced to compromise with those who previously received land rent, on the one hand, and with the peasantry, who considered the land as an essential condition for their survival, on the other.

Instead of the complete destruction of the precapitalist system, there was only a partial purge of it (the elimination of the commune) and the retention or creation, from among the former rent-receivers, tax-farmers, merchant capitalists, of its foundations, i.e., feudal landed property in one or another somewhat modernised form, subordinate to British capital. That is why, as Marx put it, the result of this extremely contradictory land policy of the British was that "in Bengal they created a caricature of large-scale English landed estates; in southeastern India a caricature of small parcelled property; in the north-west they did all they could to transform the Indian economic community with common ownership of the soil into a caricature of itself."[7]

The possibility of the dominance of capital given the presence of precapitalist relations of production in the country's agrarian system has been proved by history. Marx wrote on this that only the emerging capitalist mode of production could itself create the form corresponding to it, subordinating farming to capital, "it thus transforms feudal landed property, clan property, small-peasant property in mark communes—no matter how divergent their juristic forms may be—into the economic form corresponding to the requirements of this mode of production."[8]

The fact is that the industrial capital of the metropolitan country set up or maintained feudal receivers of rent, thereby obtaining in the colony its own loyal class allies, and then used them not only as a political support in the exploitation of the colony, but also as the most reliable obstacle to any free development of national capitalism.

The Colonial Transformation of India's Land System

The results of the land policy pursued by the British in India may be set out briefly in the four following points:

— Replacement of the old feudal aristocracy by new landlords from among the merchant bourgeoisie, tax-farmers, (Bengal, Bihar and Orissa—permanently settled zamindars).

— Subordination and subsequent adaptation of the old feudal lords to the dominance of British capital (the United Provinces—temporarily settled zamindars).

— Removal of the feudals and communal landed property, and the establishment, on this basis, of direct contacts between the state and the producers that used to belong to communes (Bombay, Madras—ryotwari).

— Transformation of the commune into a fiscal unit or an organisation for mutual guarantees, with direct contacts being established on this basis between the state and the peasant commune (the Punjab).

Let us look more closely at each in turn of these forms of landed property created by the British.

Permanently Settled Zamindars (Bengal, Bihar, Orissa)

The reform of Bengal landed property was carried out by the British landed aristocracy and constituted a compromise with the feudal classes of Bengal. The need for it arose from a desire to avert a union between the country's increasingly dissatisfied landowners and French colonial capital, which, being in contact with certain Persian, Afghan and Indian princes, was, at that time, a real threat to British rule in Bengal. The reform was introduced in 1794 (and supplemented in 1812) under Governor-General Cornwallis, who, when he left for India in 1784, received from the British parliament instructions to restore the landed aristocracy.

The provision on the reform stipulated: permanently fixed land-tax rates from the zamindars, at 90 per cent of the sum they collected in rent from the peasants in 1794; the right of the zamindars to drive the peasants from the land and raise rents at will; the zamindars' right to judge peasant matters.

As a result of this act, the peasants, who were the actual owners of the land, became tenant-farmers without rights, while the zamindars became the owners of the land. The division of the Bengal peasantry within the commune into full members of the commune and members without full rights lost its significance after the introduction of the act, since both groups became defenceless tenant-farmers. The peasants' deprival of their right to perpetual hereditary landownership and their transformation into tenants without rights, who could be driven from the land at the will of the zamindar, undermined the peasant commune. Yet, neither did the peasant become a serf nor the zamindar a serfowner. By not setting up a landlord's farm, or acting as a feudal serfowner cultivating his own land by means of serf labour, the new Bengali landlord was very similar to the type of zamindar that had existed at the end of the Moghul Empire; he farmed out the collection of rents and thereby laid the foundations for the formation of a hierarchy of parasitic rent-receivers. As a consequence, in Bengal the hierarchy of subzamindars had up to twenty rungs. By the 1930s, there were about 8 million rent-collectors, while in 1794 the land was given over to 46,000 zamindar tax-farmers. Below the zamindar, as the hereditary owner of all the given land, came the first tax-farmer, second, third, and so on.[9]

The system of subzamindars naturally led to additional exploitation of the peasantry since, when he farmed out rent collection, the chief zamindar made no reduction in the rent that he himself had previously collected from the peasants of the given region. Thus, any new middleman between the peasants and the zamindar resulted in higher rents levied on the peasants and an increase in the tax burden. This, besides, explains why, after the introduction of the act on this, the invariable tax rates payable to the government meant a rise in the incomes of the permanent zamindars alone by 300 per cent. Ninety per cent of the rent of 1794, fixed under the act and handed over to the British imperialists, was in the final count only 22 per cent of the rents levied on the peasants by the landlords. The incomes of the zamindars also went up extraordinarily, because, in 1828, the Anglo-Indian government issued a special decree declaring all uncultivated land (meadows, pastures and forests) state property. In just the same way, the zamindars appropriated the uncultivated land of their region as their own personal property.

The objective significance of this form of landed property was that the substantial capitals of the Indian merchant bourgeoisie at the end of the 18th century and the subsequent Indian capital accumulations went into agriculture, the purchase of the profitable titles of subzamindars, the purchase and leasing of the land of tenant-farmers who had been driven off their plots, usury and so on, rather than into industry. This naturally led to the creation of a class that, throughout its historical existence right up to the mid-20th century, constituted a major back-up for and ally of British colonialism.

The next stage in Britain's policy in Bengal was the adoption of two acts (1859 and 1885) introducing major amendments to the form of landed property, engendered by the need to satisfy the growing requirements of British industrial capital for raw materials within the British Empire. Bengal had a monopoly of the supply of jute. Up to 1830, jute exports were insignificant. The rapid development of jute production began in the second half of last century. The export of jute from Bengal up to 1860 is shown by the following figures (tonnes)[10]:

1828-1833	1,200	1843-1848	23,800
1833-1838	6,700	1848-1853	73,900
1838-1843	11,700	1853-1858	71,000

The enormous demand for raw jute was rising as a result, first, of the solution of the problems involved in the spinning of jute by machine (1833) and, second, of the impossibility of exporting Russian hemp on to the world market owing to the Crimean War (1853-1856). In spite of this increase in the demand for jute, the Bengali peasant, mercilessly exploited by the zamindars, could not expand his jute output rapidly enough to satisfy the market demand, especially since this crop required extremely intensive labour, special preparation of the soil and a number of farming improvements that, by raising the price of land, allowed the zamindars to drive the tenants without rights from the land and receive differential rent for the improvements made by the peasant. Under the circumstances, the Bengali peasant lacked the necessary incentive to engage in the mass production of jute. The 1859 Act is usually interpreted as being in defence of the cultivating tenants but, in fact, it was based on the creation of the preconditions for supplying British industrial capital with raw material, rather than the protection of the peasants against the zamindars.

It is indicative that, when feudal landed property became an obstacle to the development of British industrial capital, British capital restricted feudal exploitation precisely to the extent required, on the one hand, to retain the political support of the zamindars while, on the other, guaranteeing at least the minimum amount of raw material required.

The Bengal Tenancy Act of 1859 cancelled out all laws issued from 1799 to 1812, and prohibited the Bengali zamindars from driving the peasants from the land or raising rents. This law was an attempt to create the minimum necessary conditions for the development of jute production. The establishment of relatively stable rents on the peasants' plots of land, the possibility of raising them only by decision of the courts, the recognition of peasants who had possessed one and the same plot of land for 12 consecutive years as the hereditary and perpetual tenants, the possibility of selling the right of perpetual leasing on the market—such were the chief provisions of this law. The rise in jute exports after the law came out confirms all this (tonnes)[11]:

1858-1863	97,000	1883-1888	822,400
1863-1868	262,800	1888-1893	1,037,300
1868-1873	485,800	1893-1898	1,208,400
1873-1878	536,200	1898-1903	1,195,900
1878-1883	727,400		

Over 45 years, jute exports went up 12-13-fold. It must be recalled that the 1859 law limiting the landowners' rights was issued as a follow-up to the Sipai rebellion of 1857/59.

The reform of Bengali landed property did not end there, however. In practice, the act of 1859 was applied as a law "defending" not the peasant tenants, but the landlord tenants (the multitiered hierarchy of subzamindars). Its primary goal was to limit the rights of the big landowners in relation to the peasants, but this was to the benefit of the intermediate holders of the land, who were included in the term "tenants", and whose rights in relation to the actual cultivators were not limited at all. Thus, the peasantry was done out of its share in favour of the prosperous intermediate stratum of landholders —the big tenants.

In 1885, this situation forced the Anglo-Indian government to pass a detailed law enumerating the rights of all sorts of landholders in Bengal. The law established the following levels of land tenure: first rank—subzamindars, second rank—peasant tenants, and third rank—peasant subtenants. The first rank covered various categories of subzamindars, whom this law entitled to retain 10 per cent of the rent received from the peasants. The chief zamindar could not demand an increase in his share through a reduction in the 10-per cent rent received by the subzamindar. The second rank included so-called perpetual tenants, whose rent could be raised only once every 15 years and by not more than 2 annas on the rupee. The rights of perpetual leasing included the right of inheritance, mortgaging and sale of the land. The sale of the right to perpetual leasing on the market could only be carried out with the permission of the landlord, who received 25 per cent of the purchase price. Only the peasant tenant who had worked and held his plot, belonging to one and the same zamindar, for 12 consecutive years received the right of perpetual leasing. This law also provided for the legal position of a substantial group of landless peasants and subtenants.

The legal position of this stratum of landless peasants, subletting their plots, came down to the following: the perpetual tenant could charge his subtenant 50 per cent more rent than he himself paid. The rent the peasant subtenant was charged could only be raised, by court decision, once every 5 years.

In no other province did the British introduce any regulation of peasant subtenancy, and that in Bengal merely served to increase the number of moneylenders among the perpetual tenants and the pauperisation of the peasant subtenants.

Temporarily Settled Zamindars (the United Provinces)

Britain's demand for Indian raw materials increased particularly when it seized new colonial markets and the country's industrial production began to develop rapidly. As early as the 1820s, British industrial capital came up against the problem of a shortage of raw materials for British industry. This was inevitable, since the immediate producer of the raw materials—the Indian ryot—remained under the pressure of feudal exploitation. Moreover, the economy was still far from commercialised. Under these conditions, the task facing British industrial capital was to introduce changes into the agrarian system in the newly acquired provinces of India that would allow it to make it easier for the Indian ryot to produce industrial raw materials. This is why the systems of land tenure, introduced in all areas conquered after 1800 and especially after 1815, differed from those in Bengal. The system of temporary zamindars established by the British demonstrated all the duality and historically limited nature of the land policy pursued by British capital, which was then undertaking large-scale territorial seizures in India and, on the one hand, needed feudal support in the newly acquired areas but, on the other, was striving to implement the rapid commercialisation of the peasant economy. British industrial capital, considering its experience in Bengal, and regardless of a multitude of demands, did not introduce the Bengali system of land tenure in the United and Central Provinces.

In Audh, the big feudals, or taluqdars, were recognised as the owners of the land. The middle and lower links in the chain of feudal landed property were abolished. This explains the presence of exceptionally large-scale landed property in Audh, which took shape as a result of the elimination of the smaller feudal landowners. Two-thirds of Audh was occupied by 300 estates. All the taluqdars were recognised as hereditary owners, by primogeniture.

In Agra, it was the middle-level feudals who were recognised as the landowners. The upper-rank feudals were partly expropriated, and partly put on pensions paid out of additional taxes on the peasants. In spite of these differences, the overall landed property system was unified in that it was not an individual landlord but a group of them, a landlord "commune", that enjoyed the right to the land. This group of landlords provided mutual guarantees in the payment of revenues to the government. This was the first, (though not the main) difference between this system and the Bengali one; the sum of taxes levied by the government on the temporary zamindars was not stable, but reset every 10, 30 or 50 years, after which time the tax rates were reviewed. This was the second difference between the two systems.

The landlords' mutual guarantees were introduced only later, when it turned out that the old feudal aristocrats (the Audh taluqdars-rajputi) could not pay the taxes and were going bankrupt, and their lands sold by auction. To prevent this happening in the future, the mutual guarantee system was introduced.

The collective, joint ownership of the land was an interesting specimen of the extremely confused land relations in India. In fact, each estate was partly owned by an individual, and partly by all those who had, as it were, a right to a share of the rent levied on the given estate. Since they were collectively responsible to the government for the payment of taxes, each individual co-owner contributed the part of the tax corresponding to his share in the income received from the estate as a whole. In this sense, the estate was not an integral territorial unit of several villages; it could consist of parts of different villages. One and the same village could be divided up between several landlords. This situation naturally made mutual guarantees necessary in relation to the payment of taxes. The law that introduced the system of temporary zamindars provided for the transfer to the government of 85 per cent of the total rent collected by the zamindar from the peasants. Subsequently, the government's share dropped to 40-50 per cent. Since, however, the rents increased, the absolute tax revenues of the government from this sort of landed property also grew.

This system of land tenure also underwent several additional transformations, chiefly in the sphere of the relations between the zamindars and the peasants. The 1887 Law for Audh, for instance, allowed for rents to be raised only once every 7 years and then by not more than 6.5 per cent. The landlords easily got round this, however. They increased their incomes by another 25 per cent from meadows, open land, pasture, craftsmen, temples, tributes, and so on. As for Agra, the 1859 Law issued for Bengal was applied to this province, too. As in Bengal, however, it was systematically violated by the zamindars and a new law was required.

This last law (1881) set three levels of tenant:

— Tenants from among the former lower feudal owners and subowners (in the south-east of the United Provinces), paying a constant rent.

— Tenants from among the former lower levels of the feudal hierarchy, paying a constant rent on the rest of the territory of the United Provinces, where the rent for other forms of land tenure was systematically rising.

— Perpetual tenants—peasants who acquired this right by renting the land from one and the same landlord for 12 consecutive years. The rent they had to pay could be raised every 10 years. The right to lifelong leasing could not be acquired by peasants who were subtenant share-croppers. This right was hereditary. In 1926, a law was passed allowing the Audh perpetual tenants to mortgage and sell their rights. The same law entitled them to redeem the land held on lease as their own property for four times the rent.

In this context, note should be made of the role of perpetual tenure. The fact is that the British imperialists used this system as a sort of safety valve: by opening it slightly, they could temporarily relieve peasant dissatisfaction in individual regions. Perpetual tenure did not further the penetration of capitalist methods of production into agriculture. The perpetual tenant usually used his own accumulations for moneylending, trade, and the nonproductive leasing of land for the purpose of subletting it on binding terms. The position of the perpetual tenants differed between the provinces of India. In Bengal, for instance, most of them were economically very similar to most of the cultivating subtenants, though even there an upper crust of rich peasants and moneylenders emerged.

The creation of the institute of perpetual tenure did not have the desired results; instead, it further intensified the semi-feudal exploitation of the ordinary peasant tenants at will. A substantial proportion of the perpetual tenants themselves fell into the paws of money-lenders and merchants, and dropped to the status of cultivating tenants without rights. I. M. Reisner wrote on this: "Since the perpetual tenant remained a small peasant, the old landholder usually got round the law by the levying of illegal taxes and thousands of other means. Since the right of perpetual tenure was farmed out to a new stratum of exploiters, yet another level of landholders took shape, that between the former owners and the peasantry. In this way, the old owners would receive the same or slightly less rent, but the total ruinous rent charged to the peasantry would rise, in order to satisfy the new exploiters in the shape of the perpetual tenants."[12]

The Central Provinces, annexed by the British in the course of the ceaseless struggle waged by the Marath state, were also among those where the system of temporary zamindars was instituted. Here, British capital made the village elders its political allies, by turning them into landowners, or malguzars, and empowering them to collect taxes. The entire village in which the malguzar previously enjoyed only certain privileges was now his own estate. The peasants, who actually worked the land, became merely tenants. In this province, four categories of cultivating tenant emerged:

— Absolute perpetual tenants. This right was enjoyed by the higher castes and certain old feudal lords. The law provided for the right to sell, mortgage and sublet the land.

— Perpetual tenants. This right was acquired on the basis of twelve-year tenancy, as in Bengal. The perpetual tenant enjoyed the right to inherit, sell, mortgage and sublet the land. The last three rights could not be exercised without the consent of the malguzar and unless he was given presents—salami. The rent paid to the malguzar by these two types of perpetual tenant was set by the British officials.

— Simple tenants. They could be thrown off the land only by decision of the courts. The rent was raised systematically, once every seven years.

— Subtenants. There were no laws governing subletting. Most of the peasants belonged to this category of subtenants without any rights.

Ryotwari and the Punjabi Property System (Bombay, Madras, the Punjab)

The ryotwari system was the most developed that British capital was capable of instituting during the transformation of India's agrarian structure. This system is put forward as a model one by British and Indian bourgeois writers on the subject. British capital worked persistently and long to introduce the system, especially from the time when it became clear that the country could not be constantly flooded with British-made goods unless it was also allowed to produce something, i.e., unless an active enough home market was created. This fact, noted by Marx, began to be understood by the British politicians when the cotton industry began to acquire vital importance for Britain's entire social structure and the East India Company for the British cotton industry.

The British cotton industry, which provided Britain with a twelfth of its national income, and delivered an eighth of all exports to India, and a fourth of cotton fabric, was closely linked with India's position as a solvent market and source of raw materials. The demands of the British cotton industry for Indian cotton were fully manifested at the time of the 1845 crisis, and especially during the cotton crop failure in the USA in 1850, let alone the period of the American Civil War, when the British had to begin seriously developing cotton-growing in India. The development of cotton-growing was accompanied by railway construction, too. During this period, British industrial capital had a vested interest in India also as a sales market, especially since the commodity turnover and export of fabrics to India began to demonstrate a downward trend. Britain's economic ties with India, in which primarily the British cotton industry was interested, were not firm enough, mainly because the Indian population's effective demand was hardly growing at all. At this time, British policy in India became the object of a struggle between the financial oligarchy, which continued to conquer and rob the country, and the British industrialists, who, as Marx put it, felt the need to create new productive forces in India to replace the local industry they had detroyed.

The industrialists were influential in Britain, and demanded now the destruction of the financial oligarchy that, in conjunction with the Indian feudals, did what it liked with India, as if it were its own personal estate. As early as 1824, the British industrial bourgeoisie assumed predominant significance in the British parliament, and, through the 1832 reforms, established once and for all its position as the politically dominant class. The growing political might of the British industrial bourgeoisie in the metropolitan country could not but reflect on the land policy pursued by the British in India, since their plunderous policy conflicted directly with the interests of the industrial bourgeoisie, who felt their economic dependence both on the solvency of the Indian market and on the need to meet their own raw material requirements. The British industrial bourgeoisie was once more faced with the task of transferring Indian agriculture onto the lines of the maximum possible commercialisation and specialisation and the production of industrial raw material crops. The ryotwari system was precisely an attempt to fulfil these tasks.

The system was set up in Madras in 1820 and in Bombay in 1825. Frightened of losing its profits as a result of the inevitable rapid ruin of the Indian peasantry if the old land policy was continued, British industrial capital made certain reforms, the first of which were: the introduction of the ryotwari system, the system of Punjabi property and a certain cut in the taxes levied on the peasants. The essence of the ryotwari system consisted in the following:

—There was no middleman between the state authorities and the former full commune members and the immediate producers; the colonial state received the entire rent, leaving nothing for any zamindars.

—Each ryot was taxable personally without any mutual guarantees.

—The ryot had the right to alienate his land without asking government permission.

—The land could be confiscated for non-payment of tax rental.

—The tax rates were periodically reviewed, with the peasants having the right to refuse to use the land both during the time of the review of the tax contract and at any other time.

This list of the provisions of the ryotwari system reveals its sense, role and significance and shows that it undoubtedly provided greater opportunities for capitalist development than the other systems of land tenure did. The introduction of this system was also explained by certain historical preconditions characteristic of the southern provinces of India. First, the south of India was the territory most affected by maritime trade and began to establish links with the foreign market before many other parts of the country did; second, before British rule was established in the south of India, feudal exploitation had been fairly well exhausted by powerful peasant movements, so British industrial capital found no landholder here apart from the peasants themselves. Third, the activities of the East-India Company in the south tied it to collecting taxes directly from the peasantry.[13]

Initially, under this system, which later underwent certain changes, the state removed from the peasant holding about two-thirds of the gross product from irrigated land and half of it from arid land. In the 1840s, taxes dropped somewhat to about a quarter and then a tenth of the gross product. In exactly the same way, certain conditions hampering the penetration of commodity-money relations into the peasant economy (the ban on leaving the land at any time, the compulsory cultivation of non-irrigated lands, however unprofitable it might be, and the like) were soon amended. Thus, the ryotwari system eventually led, after a number of amendments, to the creation of a sort of peasant property, limited by two conditions: payment of the land tax on time and the impossibility of utilising the land for anything but harvesting.

This system could not create a stratum of prosperous peasants that was equal in might and size everywhere. It proved to be a mightly lever for transferring the subsistence peasant economy to the production of commercial crops, which was precisely what British industrial capital required. The main mass of the peasantry in the countryside of this region still remained poor peasants and agricultural labourers, hired temporarily by a rich peasant and combining work for wages with the cultivation of his own miniscule plot of land. Under this system, the farmer paid the government a tax that coincided with the rent.

The fact must be noted that even here, where British capital was, as it were, radical, the old feudal estates were still retained in the form of gift lands, temples or inams, as happened in the Bombay Presidency, where, in 1888, large-scale landed property occupied, in the form of 3 thousand estates, over 8 million acres or 35 per cent of the land, while 1,300 thousand peasant holdings occupied only 65 per cent of the total area. In precisely the same way, in the Madras Presidency 460,000 holdings belonging to exploiting classes accounted, in 1888, for over 24 million acres, i.e., 60 per cent of the land, while the 2,500 thousand peasant holdings occupied only 18 million acres, or 40 per cent of the land.[14]

Let us proceed to the system of Punjabi peasant property. Its historical roots go far back into the peasant movement of the Sikhs, which resulted in the restoration of the communal organisation in the countryside and the elimination of the dominance of the Moghul feudals. The Punjab was annexed by Britain in 1849 and, in 1854, the first law was issued on the organisation of the land in the Punjab, according to which the

Sikh feudals who had reemerged on the basis of the peasant commune were not deprived of their feudal rights. The Punjabi peasantry demonstrated all signs of a dissatisfaction with the retention of feudal property and the British, considering the possibility of joint actions between them and the unsubdued Afghan tribes, had to eliminate the Sikh landed estates. This helped the British subsequently in the sense that the Punjabi peasantry, satisfied by the elimination of the Sikh feudals, not only did not take part in the Sipai rebellion, but even helped to put it down. There were special cases even here, however. In 1865, the British government passed the law on the restoration of the Punjabi landed aristocracy, though in a conditional and compromise form. The essence of the law was that it ensured the former feudals the opportunity to receive 10 per cent more from the peasants, over and above the sum the peasants were paying to the government as money rent. The former feudals were a type of classical parasites, deprived of even the usual landlord rights, including that to sell their illusory domains.

The land order established by the British in the Punjab differed somewhat from that in the ryotwari areas. The first fundamental difference consisted in the fact that the Punjabi peasant was tied by the payment of taxes to the mutual guarantees of the commune. Taxes were collected within the commune, on the basis of the economic prosperity of each peasant household, but the tax was paid on behalf of the commune as a whole and, from this point of view, the British government was faced not with the individual producer, but the commune. Yet, by setting up this caricature of a peasant commune, based on the collective and simultaneous payment of taxes, the British could not, of course, prevent its rapid disappearance. It was Marx who called this fiscal commune a caricature.

Not wishing to hold back the formation of a stratum of prosperous holdings by mutual guarantees, the British later passed a number of laws allowing family and individual plots to break away from the communal landed property. This meant that British industrial capital, while appreciating the traditional Sikh commune and pursuing a policy of the commercialisation of the peasant economy in the Punjab, as an area of export grain crops (wheat), did everything possible to deliver this commune from both the ruined peasantry and the prosperous peasant stratum. As a result, the peasant commune in the Punjab gradually became a total fiction. The ruined and almost ruined peasant became more tied up in the nets of the moneylenders in the Punjab than anywhere else. The transfer of a substantial quantity of communal land into the hands of the moneylenders took place so rapidly that the Anglo-Indian government passed a special law in 1901 prohibiting the non-farming castes from acquiring land. Even so, landed property continued to be concentrated in the hands of moneylenders.

Under the 1867 and 1887 laws, the Punjabi peasants were recognised as fourth category perpetual tenants, with the right to sell, mortgage and sublet their land. Subletting was permitted for a period of 7 years. Moreover, in the Punjab the group of peasants not covered by the institute of tenure in perpetuity and constituting the most exploited stratum was growing. The land relations between this stratum of the peasantry and the perpetual tenants were determined by a so-called free contract. In 1888, there were 2,500 thousand such holdings, covering 7,500 thousand acres of land.

The Nature of Peasant Tenancy, Share-Cropping and Rent

Perpetual tenancy hampers the broad introduction of the capitalist mode of production in agriculture. It can conceal the following types of relations of exploitation:

—The perpetual tenant sublets his land, in return for a rent in money or in kind, thereby becoming a parasitic receiver of rent.

—The perpetual tenant sublets part of his land on shackling terms and cultivates the rest of it himself.

—The perpetual tenant leases out all his land on a share-cropping basis, participating partially in agricultural production by furnishing land or implements. It is the landless share-cropper who is the cultivator.

—The perpetual tenant is a capitalist entrepreneur who receives profits and differential rent.

—The perpetual tenant is a peasant who is himself a cultivator and is exploited by either the landowner or the state, or by both.

Of these five types of relations of exploitation, concealed in the form of perpetual tenure, three should be included among precapitalist and transitional ones, as Marx's analysis shows.

Marx considered share-cropping as a transitory form in the period of transition from feudalism to capitalism. He wrote: "As a transitory form from the original form of rent to capitalist rent, we may consider the metayer system, or share-cropping, under which the manager (farmer) furnishes labour (his own or another's), and also a portion of working capital, and the landlord furnishes, aside from land, another portion of working capital (e.g., cattle), and the product is divided between tenant and landlord in definite proportions which vary from country to country . . . essentially, rent no longer appears here as the normal form of surplus-value in general."[15]

This transitory form of share-cropping includes that which was found, to some small extent, mainly in the Central Provinces, Assam and the United Provinces, where the actual owner provided not only the land, but also some capital (buildings, seeds, cattle), while the share-cropper furnished tools in addition to his labour-power. Under these conditions, the output was divided between them in a ratio of 6:4 or 5:5.

Here, the share-cropper is a "capitalist" in himself, for he claimed a certain part of the product not because he was a labourer, but because he owned part of the tools. In the same way, the farmer claimed the surplus product not only as the owner of the land, but also as the person advancing capital. Under such share-cropping conditions, the rent does not coincide with the entire mass of the surplus product, for the owner, for example, receives interest on the capital advanced, just as the share-cropper may, in addition to the necessary product, receive part of the surplus product, thereby drawing closer to the status of farmer, if he uses the labour of others.

All other forms of share-cropping, in contrast to this one established by Marx, were varieties of subletting, where the owner provided only the land and the rest of the capital and labour-power came only from the subtenant. The most widespread form of such subletting was the leasing for payment of a share of the product or so-called batai (division). Its essence was as follows: the farmer furnished the land for subletting, while the subtenant provided all the other elements of production. The ratio in which the product was divided was 7:3, 6:4 or 5:5. Out of the gross product collected, the tenant share-cropper paid 8 or 9 per cent to village craftsmen and 2 or 3 per cent to officials.

It is quite clear that this is not the transitory-type share-cropping as defined by Marx, for the rent here acted, to a considerable extent, as "the normal form of surplus-value in general". The subtenant received only the necessary product, out of which, by means of additional levies (in Bihar there were 12 of them), a further sum equal to as much as 25 per cent of the rent was removed. It is interesting that the owner of the land was able, under the impact of British capital, to adapt even this type of precapitalist relations, which were widespread in the past in India, to the demands of the commodity-money market.

The entire system of monetary payments by the lower land-holder to higher levels, from the ordinary peasant to the government, had one and the same basis—appropriation of the peasants' surplus product, chiefly by means of extra-economic coercion. The size of the incomes of all the landowning classes in India was, to a considerable extent, arbitrary, reflecting the dominance of feudal survivals. The rent paid to the zamindar or directly to the state was not capitalist rent, i.e., the income of the landowner over and above the average profit, which remained with the tenant. The rent also swallowed up the "average profit" and differential rent of the peasant tenant and even a substantial part of his necessary product. As Marx put it, the rent still remained the "normal form of surplus-value in general".

Money rent in no way presupposes the domination of capitalist relations in a country's agrarian system. Being only a transmuted form of rent in kind, money rent, as Marx noted, constitutes a serious threat to the reproduction of the working conditions and the means of subsistence themselves. It makes it more or less impossible to expand production and forces the immediate producer to restrict his means of subsistence to the physical minimum.[16] This is all the more true when money rent in the hands of the colonialists becomes a major lever for exploiting the enslaved masses of immediate producers. It is not the size of average profits that determines the limits to the rent paid by the cultivating tenant to the landlord, but that of the surplus and necessary product that he retains, are determined entirely by rent as their limit. This was one of the decisive features of the domination of precapitalist survivals in Indian agriculture.[17]

Chapter Two

The Main Features of India's Agrarian System After the First World War

Imperialist Domination and the Countryside

The objective consequences of British colonial rule in India were the gradual penetration of capitalism into the Indian countryside, with imperialism helping maintain feudal survivals, India's involvement in the world capitalist economy, the development of commodity-money relations, and gradually increasing property and class differentiation of the Indian peasantry. The evolution of the agrarian system, determined, by the mid-1930s, by the still dominant feudal survivals, was proceeding anyway, in some form or another and to some degree or another, in the direction of capitalism. Lenin wrote on Russian serfdom in the countryside: "The replacement coming about in Russia had long since occurred in the advanced countries of the West: it is the replacement of a feudal by a capitalist economy.

"It is, and can only be, a question of the forms, conditions, rapidity and circumstances of *this* replacement; all *other* considerations, which are not infrequently put in the forefront, are no more than an *unwitting* beating about the bush, the 'bush' being precisely this replacement."[1]

The forms, conditions, rapidity and circumstances of the gradual replacement of the feudal by the capitalist economy were, of course, different in India not only from the advanced countries of the West, but also tsarist Russia, since the shifts in the course of India's capitalist development were taking place in a colonial country and, moreover, under the conditions of the general crisis and disintegration of capitalism. Yet, the assertions that no replacement took place in the economy of the Indian countryside, that there was a complete stagnation of economic relations there, that the agrarian evolution in India was an exception to the general rules of the development of capitalism in agriculture, are nothing but an historically belated restoration of the ideas of populism, an attempt to reverse the order of the historical process in India, particularly the evolution of the agrarian system. In the sphere of politics and the class struggle, such claims objectively lead, in essence, to a rejection of the anti-imperialist and anti-feudal revolution, the strength of which grows precisely in connection with the development of capitalism, no matter how slowly this process advances and however capitalist relations might intertwine with precapitalist ones.

The development of the commodity-money economy and the gradual penetration of capitalist relations into the Indian countryside intensified the burden of feudal and usury exploitation and the exploitation of the toiling peasantry, and thus exacerbated and raised the class struggle to a new and higher level. They did this by forcing the main mass of the peasantry to set about overthrowing the domination of imperialism and the survivals of precapitalist relations, imperialism's retention of and support for which led to a growing conflict between the trends in the development of the productive forces and the existing relations of production.

As soon as neo-populist concepts are accepted concerning the domination in India of pure or almost pure and unchanged feudalism, and the stagnation of the Indian rural economy, the reverse order of agrarian evolution and the inapplicability to India of the laws governing capitalist development in agriculture, one of the objective economic foundations for the intensification of the class struggle and one of the preconditions for the development of the agrarian crisis—India's chief problem, disappears.

There is also a danger that the major specifics of India's agrarian evolution, the specifics and consequences of the penetration and development of capitalism within the country, the dominant role of feudal survivals in the countryside, gradually taking the course of capitalist development, and the strengthening, in this connection, of the colonial-feudal exploitation of the main mass of the peasantry, might all be forgotten.

As we have already shown, while gradually developing commodity-money and capitalist relations under their own control and promoting India's involvement in the system of the world capitalist market and the world social division of labour, the British capitalists were compelled, in order to strengthen their own domination in India, to compromise with the feudal landowners, which had previously and under the British, too, dominated over the millions of bonded peasant holdings. Moreover, it might be said that, in a number of regions, the British furthered the development and strengthening of the domination of the landlords, who exploited the peasants by feudal or semi-feudal methods. Suffice it to point to the permanent and temporary zamindars, taluqdars and malguzars, these owners of feudal latifundia, in order to realise that this really was the case. The British consolidated the landlord system wherever it had existed before their arrival and furthered its development wherever there had been no landed estates. In order to step up the exploitation of the peasantry, the British capitalists created various sorts of hereditary perpetual and lifelong leases with different rights as to their sale. The capitalism of the metropolitan country, functioning in the colony in the first stages of its domination chiefly as merchant's and usurer's capitalism and only subsequently partially as industrial, even by the time of its final development stage not only did not change the entire precapitalist mode of production in India, but consolidated feudal and semi-feudal relations in various forms, having destroyed the chief pivot of the old Indian society—the subsistence commune.

British capital also used the commercial apparatus in India. It expanded it, giving it a national scale, greatly strengthened the already developed usury, subordinating both these forms of capital—merchant's and usurer's—to its monopolistic firms and banks. In spite of a number of uprisings, India's oppressed classes—the peasantry and urban poor—lacked the strength for a successful revolution in order to divert India's development from the extremely torturous colonial course to that of free independent national development. The gradual development of the precapitalist agrarian system towards capitalism was taking place under conditions of the domination of foreign capital, which operated in India primarily not as industrial, but as merchant's and loan capital, relying on the

Indian feudals and adapting the old agrarian structure to the needs of the metropolitan country's industrial and finance capital. "Capitalism, which has included the colonial village into its system of taxation and trade apparatus, and which has overturned precapitalist relations (for instance, the destruction of the village commune), does not thereby liberate the peasants from the yoke of precapitalist forms of bondage and exploitation, but only gives the latter a monetary expression . . . which still more increases the suffering of the peasantry."[2]

This is why feudal and semi-feudal relations of exploitation predominated in agrarian India in the 1920s and 1930s, in spite of the substantial shifts in the direction of the development of commodity-money and capitalist relations.

British capital in India was increasingly drawing the land, means of production and peasant output into commodity turnover and thereby opening up broad opportunities for the expropriation of the poor and medium peasant economies, having subordinated them to the market. Having maintained and consolidated the domination of the semi-feudal landowner, moneylender and merchant, however, it did its best to slow down and hamper the gradual transformation of agricultural production into commodity and then capitalist production. The domination of British imperialism held back the expansion of the home market, which, in spite of the imperialist monopoly, was still taking shape.

Given the systematic hampering of the development of the capitalist productive forces, the domination of the imperialists and feudals led to a degradation of the main mass of peasant holdings. At a given stage in its domination in the colony, imperialism came up against a protracted crisis of the home market, connected with a sharp drop in the toiling masses' purchasing power in both town and countryside.

The contradiction of the capitalist mode of production consisting in the way it undermines its own market by the same methods as it creates it, was manifested particularly clearly during the worldwide Great Depression of 1929-1933. The growth of the commodity economy, the destruction of the commune and the ruin of the peasantry were utilised almost entirely by British capital, which held back internal capital accumulation in India and the development of national industrial capitalism in the towns and capitalist farms in the countryside in the interests of the capitalist development of the metropolitan country itself. A rapid growth of the productive forces based on the destruction of India's subsistence economy took place not in India itself, but in Britain. This means, however, that the ruined Indian peasantry mostly remained in the villages, transferring to the status of landless peasant tenants or share-croppers and forming huge numbers of coolies and paupers. The number of landless peasants was constantly growing: 8 million in 1875, 34 million in 1901, 50 million in 1911 and 37 million in 1921.

The opposite process, which had also taken place previously but gained momentum in connection with the world crisis, was a rapid concentration of the land in the hands of landlords and rent-receivers from among the merchants and moneylenders. Landlord landed property increased, while peasant land tenure diminished. Over 50 years, the number of parasitic rent-receivers increased 10-fold (million)[3]:

1872	1	1901	6
1881	2.5	1911	8.5
1891	4	1921	10

The average area of peasant holdings was falling rapidly and was, per capita of the agricultural population (acres)[4]:

1891	1.28	1911	1.00
1901	1.24	1921	0.86

The ruin of the toiling masses in the countryside could only take place in such an acute form and over such an extended period of time because the economic advantages of the transition to capitalism were seized by another, oppressing country, leaving the oppressed country only the negative factors connected with the transition to the capitalist mode of production.

In the process of India's transition to capitalism, the countryside did not lose any of its population. Moreover, up to 1931, increasing numbers of the population were winning their livelihood from agriculture, while the absolute and relative increases in the population were greater in the countryside than in the towns (Table 1).

Class differentiation increased in the villages. In 1921, there

Table 1

The Growth of the Relative Rural Overpopulation*

Year	Total population, millions	Rural population, millions	% increase in total population	% increase in rural population	% of able-bodied population living off agriculture
1891	287	175	—	—	61
1901	284	195	5	7	66
1911	315	224	7.1	9	71
1921	319	233	1.2	3	73
1931	352	314	10.6	9.6	66

* *Census of India 1931,* Vol. 1, Calcutta, 1932-1933.

were 3.7 million able-bodied rent-receivers (10 million together with dependants) in British India, 74.7 (173.1) million peasants, and 21.7 (37.9) million farm servants and field labourers.

The class differentiation in the Indian countryside can be seen even more clearly from the following. The overall domination is quite obvious, in all parts of India, of the parasitic rent-receiver, landowner-merchant and moneylender, who did not set up landed estates of any substantial size or share in the country's economy, and who used their accumulations for the purposes of feudal, semi-feudal and commercial-usurious robbery of the toiling peasantry. The landed estates were different primarily in area, the amount of rent charged, and the number of bonded peasant tenants, rather than the way the agricultural production was organised. A clear idea of landownership is provided by the following data for the Belar district of the Madras Presidency[5]:

	1901	1921
Non-cultivating landowners	13,108	35,920
Tenant landowners (subzamindars, i.e., non-cultivating tenants)	256	28,298
Cultivating tenants	43,655	113,168
Peasant landowners	451,035	315,949

The situation in the Belar district reflected a phenomenon common to all India, the specific evolution of the agrarian system of a colonial country: a rapid growth of the feudal and semi-feudal upper crust under imperialist patronage, which supported imperialism. Most of these landowners were not engaged in farming at all. They distributed their right to collect rents, on certain conditions, to a vast and rapidly growing stratum of middlemen non-cultivating tenants. All this took place against a background of the rapid ruin of the small (parcelled) cultivating landowners and their transition to the status of tenant share-croppers without rights.

Taking the Madras Presidency as a whole, this description is still applicable. For every 1,000 of the rural population, there were:

	1901	1921
Non-cultivating landowners	30	56
Non-cultivating tenants	2	32
Peasant landowners	512	398
Cultivating tenants	167	240
Debt slaves	289	97[6]
Farm servants and field labourers	—	177

A similar picture and the same sort of evolution are seen if we take data for India as a whole. Throughout India, for every 1,000 principals of the rural population, according to Padmanabha Pillai there were[7]:

	1901	1911	1921
Non-cultivating landowners	19	23	49
Non-cultivating tenants	1	4	28
Peasant landowners	484	426	381
Cultivating tenants	151	207	225
Farm servants and field labourers	345	340	317

According to data for the whole country, over 20 years there was a rapid growth of the parasitic upper crust: of landowners by 2.5 times, of tenant landowners—28-fold. At the same time, there was a drop in the number of peasant landowners; they were stratified, a substantial proportion of them dropping to the status of share-croppers without rights. The number of farm servants and field labourers also dropped, partly as a result of mass epidemics and famine.

Data for the comparatively limited district-size territory, for whole provinces and for India in general indicate one and the same process. It is characteristic that even the numerical ratio between the different socio-class strata was basically of the same type and homogeneous during the evolution of the agrarian structure.

Land Distribution

The poverty of the Indian peasantry was not a result of the shortage of land in general, as some bourgeois British and Indian economists believe, but stemmed from the colonial and semi-feudal social system, which lay as a heavy burden on the toiling peasantry. In 1927/28, 223.8 million acres (Table 2) in British India were cultivated, while 206.3 million acres of arable and fallow land were not. Given that the Indian countryside was suffocating from an enormous rural overpopulation and the peasants' land was divided up into extremely small plots, the chief obstacle to the development of all cultivable land was the landed estate, the monopoly of the feudals and imperialism over the land and water. There can be no doubt that the chief precondition for the use of the enormous area of suitable but uncultivated land was abolition of the large landed estates and, thereby, the release of the small (parcelled) holding from the oppression of feudal survivals.

The landowners' latifundia exerted the most detrimental effect on India's entire social development, on the level of agricultural machinery and farming, on the standard of living of hundreds of millions of peasants and, to no lesser degree, on that of the working class. The attempts by British and Indian bourgeois economists to present the shortage of land as the main reason for the sufferings of the peasantry are, therefore, unfounded. The land-starvation of the peasants in India was not a consequence of natural conditions, but a result of the landed property predominance and the large areas of land in the hands of the big landowners.

Table 2

Area of Land in India,*
million acres

	1915/16	1918/19	1921/22	1924/25	1927/28	1932/33
Total area	619	627	667.3	668	669.9	667.0
Forests	85	87	85.4	87	88.9	88.4
Unsuitable for cultivation	144	147	153.4	154	143.6	145.0
Suitable but uncultivated	114	114	151.2	153	155.4	154.0
Fallow	52	73	54.5	47	50.9	50.4
Cultivated area	222	201	223.4	227	223.8	232.0
Irrigated area	47	47	—	45	43.2	49.6

* Compiled from: *Indian Yearbook 1924,* Bombay and Calcutta, Benneth, Coleman and Co., p. 268; *Statistical Abstract for British India.* 1915/16-1924/25; *Yearbook of the World Economy,* Moscow, 1930 (in Russian); *Labour Monthly,* III, 1935; *Civil and Military Gazette,* May 12, 1935.

Abolition of landed estates does not, of course, immediately resolve the problem of the peasants' land shortage, resulting from the agrarian system. This is particularly true in India, where, as a general rule, the landowner himself had no large cultivated area of his own as a possible major additional land fund for distribution among the peasantry directly after an agrarian revolution. The elimination of the predominant agrarian relations in the countryside would, however, having liberated the toiling masses from imperialist and feudal exploitation, have been the first major and decisive precondition for the development, on a mass scale, of new fertile and other cultivable lands.

The British imperialists persistently pointed out the possibility of colonising new parts of the country (Sind, Rajputana, etc.), thereby deceiving the Indian peasantry, since the colonisation of unsettled lands could not eliminate the peasants' land shortage. The practice of colonising individual regions of India in most cases showed that, in time, on the newly settled land agrarian relations developed that were similar to those that existed in the country's main districts.

The strength of landlordism is revealed quite thoroughly by a comparison of the average size of peasant holdings with that of landed estates in the country's chief provinces (see Table 3).

Table 3

Peasant Land Tenure and Landed Estates*

	Average peasant holding, acres	Average holding of permanent zamindars, acres	Average holding of temporary zamindars, acres	Number of landlords permanent zamindars	Number of landlords temporary zamindars
Assam	2.96	210,500	141	19	12,027
Bengal	2.59	425	813	92,508	3,886
Bihar and Orissa	3.09	402	924	103,211	12,269
Central Provinces	8.48	—	480	—	80,000
Madras	4.91	16,000	80	300	306,000
United Provinces, Agra	2.51	200	117	3,500	400,000
Audh	—	65,000	140	20	140,000
British India	4.6	426	188	231,093	1,146,535

* *Agrarian Problems,* No. 3, 1928; A. Mukerjee, *Agrarian India,* Moscow, 1929, pp. 108-09 (in Russian).

The data in Table 3 are averaged so they naturally conceal the extremes and somewhat blur the true situation, which is much more multifaceted. Yet, even these data reveal the monstrous burden of the landlord latifundia.

According to data for the end of last century, compiled by one of the most outstanding British economists and historians, Baden-Powell, almost all the land in Bengal was monopolised by big landowners (Table 4).

Table 4

Landed Estates in Bengal*

Area, acres	Number of estates	Average area, acres	Total area, million acres
Less than 500	85,500	216	18.5
500 to 20,000	10,000	1,000	10.0
Over 20,000	500	25,000	12.5
	96,000		41.0

* B. H. Baden-Powell, *The Landed Systems of British India,* Vol. 1, Oxford, 1892.

The other aspect of this colossal excess of land in the hands of the landlords was the shortage of land in those of the masses of the peasantry. Most of the peasants were not the owners of land parcels, but bonded or semi-bonded tenants cultivating land belonging to feudal landowners and British imperialists. Moreover, the area leased by poor to middle peasants from the landowners averaged 2.05 acres, which did not usually provide even the minimum means of subsistence. The size of the plots of land rented by the peasants in the chief regions of Bengal was as follows (acres):

Bankura	1.86	Dacca	1.52
Midnapur	1.29	Mymensingh	2.67
Jessur	1.78	Rajshahi	2.20
Backerganj	25.1	Noakhali	2.30
Faridpur	1.39	Tippera	1.90

The influence of the dominant feudal survivals in Bengal's agrarian system was expressed not only in the very small amounts of land held by the main masses of the peasantry, but also in the extreme overlapping of peasant holdings, unsurpassed anywhere else in India.

Feudal survivals were strong, however, not just in those parts where large landed property indubitably predominated (Bengal, the United Provinces, and others). The fact is that even in the regions of so-called small-scale peasant landownership, alongside the rich peasants (kulaks) a new stratum of semi-feudal owners took shape, who gradually brought the land into cultivation and leased it to the peasants on the basis of rent bondage—share-cropping. For example, in the Punjab in 1927, 16.5 of the 30 million cultivated acres were leased for fettering rent in money or in kind. Less than half the cultivated land belonged to the peasants, who had been ruined by usury and semi-feudal exploitation.

In a number of Punjabi villages, the moneylender became the new landowner, merging with the landowning stratum, personifying landlord's and usurer's functions and taking more than half the land into his own hands. It is not surprising, therefore, that, in the Punjab, 18 per cent of all the peasants owned plots of less than an acre, 25.5 per cent of them—from 1 to 3 acres, and 15 per cent—from 3 to 5 acres. In a word, 58.5 per cent of the peasants owned from less than an acre to 5 acres each, which was below the starvation level. Out of all the land leased out in the Punjab (16.5 million acres), 85 per cent was rented by tenants without any rights. Even in this region of so-called small-scale peasant landownership, the distribution of the land was such that 53 per cent of all holdings from 1 to 5 acres accounted for 10 per cent of the total area of land, while 4 per cent of the holdings, with over 50 acres, accounted for 25 per cent of the area of the province, or half the cultivated land there.

Data published in the *Bombay Chronicle* in 1930 on the nature of landed property in the Punjab further confirmed the concentration of land by landlords. The total cultivated area in the Punjab was 29 million acres, distributed among 3.5 million holdings as follows: peasants, making up 84.5 per cent of the total rural population of the province, held only 38.6 per cent of the cultivated land, while non-cultivating landowners, 15.5 per cent of the rural population, held 61.4 per cent of it.

Feudal survivals were still strong even in the parts of India that were more developed in commodity-money terms. One of the experts on the Banking Committee carried out the following quite interesting calculations for the Punjab, a region of wheat monoculture. The rents in this province were so high that, in 1928, the price of land for the province as a whole was 245 times higher than the net annual agricultural income, and in 1929—273 times higher. There are two reasons for this:

the exceptionally high rent paid to the landlord and the extremely low income received by the peasant from the land.

The immediate producer, who farmed the landlord's land, was thus compelled to hand over such large quantities of his produce that he had trouble reproducing his labour-power, and lived at the lowest, most poverty-stricken, below-starvation level.

In this light, the high degree of commercialisation and specialisation of the peasant economy both acquire a specific hue. A more decisive factor in such colonial commercialisation and specialisation than the development of capitalism was the use of feudal and semi-feudal survivals for involving the peasant economy in market turnover.

In Bombay and Madras, where a similar tax system dominated for the ownership and tenure of the land, the peasantry was just as oppressed by the feudal-usury yoke as in the regions where, right from the beginning of British rule, the land had been in the hands of landlords. In these regions, the concentration of the land by merchant's and usurer's capital was carried on at accelerated rates, and the moneylending landowner, merchant landowner and ryot landowner or rich peasant who appeared on this basis personified, in addition to capitalist methods of exploitation, all the worst aspects of the dominant precapitalist survivals.

Table 5

The Nature and Dynamics of Landownership in the Bombay Province (ryotwari region)*

Area of holding, acres	Number of holdings		Change in number of holdings
	1916/17	1921/22	
Less than 5	991,234	1,041,245	+50,011
5-15	610,851	640,236	+29,385
15-25	269,652	266,378	— 3,274
25-100	269,710	260,559	— 9,151
100-500	34,391	34,117	— 274
Over 500	3,207	3,369	+ 162

* *Census of India 1921*, Vol. VIII. Calcutta, 1923, p. 215.

Table 6

The Distribution of Landed Property in the Bombay Province in 1921/22*

Area of holdings, acres	Total cultivated area		Total number of landowners	
	Area of cultivated land, acres	%%	Number	%%
Less than 5	2,024,461	8.6	872,485	46
5-15	4,932,266	21.0	529,649	29
15-25	4,337,143	18.4	221,449	12
25-100	8,854,114	37.7	206,143	11
100-500	3,333,598	14.3	18,824	2
Total	23,486,612	100.0	1,848,450	100

* *Census of India 1921,* Vol. VIII. Calcutta, 1923, p. 216.

The chief question of agrarian evolution is that of the land, not only in regions of traditional landlordism, but also in ones where the British, right from the beginning of their rule, promoted the creation of a caricature of parcel landholding. By the 1930s, as we have shown from the example of the Punjab and other provinces, the agrarian system in these parts had undergone major changes that brought the problem of abolishing all feudal survivals, especially landed estates, right to the fore.

Proof of the concentration of the land in the hands of landlords in regions of peasant farming is provided by the data in Table 5 and 6. Although the data in Table 5 cover only a five-year period, they still reveal the process of the concentration of land by big landowners clearly enough. A growing number of middle links of the peasantry, medium and small landowners were washed away. There were, on the one hand, more and more miniscule peasant holdings, and, on the other, big landed estates, whose owners leased out the land primarily on rent bondage terms.

In this way, ideas to the effect that the spheres of the system of ryotwari were really spheres of peasant land tenure were already fundamentally wrong in the 1920s and 1930s. About 50 per cent of the land in Bombay province was in the hands of big and medium landowners, who to a greater or lesser degree reproduced the agrarian relations characteristic of the regions where the systems of permanent or temporary zamindars predominated. This did not, of course, remove the specifics of the agrarian evolution in these regions, nor those connected with the deeper differentiation of the peasantry there. It merely showed that even here only radical agrarian transformations could solve the problem of the land.

A similar process took place in Madras province, the second biggest region of peasant land tenure. Over a period of 20 years (1901-1921), the number of big landowners here out of every 1,000 of the rural population increased from 19 to 49, i.e., by 150 per cent, the number of non-cultivating tenants who sublet their land on rent bondage terms increased from 1 to 28, i.e., by 2,700 per cent, the number of bonded tenant share-croppers rose from 151 to 225, i.e., by 50 per cent, and the number of peasant landowners farming mainly by means of their own labour dropped from 484 to 381 in the 1,000, i.e., by almost 22 per cent. Polarisation increased in this province, too: big landowners and parasitic tenants (including some of the rich peasants), on the one hand, and the tenant share-croppers without rights, on the other (Table 7).

As we can see from the table, in the ryotwari regions of Madras province, the first group (no more than 3 acres)—71 per cent of holdings—accounted for about 34 per cent of the cultivated land, the second group (from 7 to 12 acres)—22.6 per cent of holdings—had 38 per cent of the land, and the third group (20 acres or more)—about 6 per cent of holdings—owned about 30 per cent of the cultivated land. The third group of holdings, being about only a twelfth of the size of the first, in terms of the number of holdings, occupied a similar area. Thus, the process of the distribution of the land between owners took place here extremely rapidly in favour of the upper group of landowners. The rightless tenant share-cropper was increasingly becoming the central figure in Indian farming. The domination of the feudals and British imperialists hampered the development of the productive forces.

Table 7

The Distribution of Landed Property in the Ryotwari Regions of Madras Province in 1920/21*

Average area of holding, acres	Number of holdings	%%	Land area, acres	%%
Less than 1	508,620	16	310,142	2.0
3	1,679,176	55	5,065,178	31.6
7	574,975	18	4,361,262	27.2
12	140,892	4.6	1,805,280	11.1
20	83,940	2.7	1,699,766	10.6
40	33,293	1	1,320,250	8.2
87	6,761	Less than 1	592,471	3.7
200	2,143	Less than 1	441,711	2.7
Over 500	782	—	413,663	4.6
Total	3,030,582	100	16,020,931	100

* *Census of India 1921*, Vol. VIII. Calcutta, 1923, p. 217.

All these data together are best at explaining the extremely acute contradiction in the socio-economic life of India before the Second World War: the semi-feudal, degenerating village with a multitude of small and big exploiters sitting on the extremely broken up peasant strip, and the most "advanced" (decaying) British finance capital, maintaining the precapitalist agrarian order beneficial to it.

Usury and Commercial Exploitation of the Peasantry

The laws of capitalist credit could not operate in Indian agriculture, oppressed by the yoke of feudal survivals. Instead of the average interest rate of the money capitalist, it was the compound usurious interest that dominated in the Indian countryside. Usury existed in India even before the arrival of the British, but it had never dominated in the sphere of village life, and such perfect conditions had never been created for it to flourish as after the colonial enslavement of the country. The absolute sum of peasant indebtedness to moneylenders had topped the 22-billion-rupee mark by 1932. About 80 per cent of the peasants were in debt to moneylenders. The business of the village moneylender was the most important one in India. In comparison, the liberal professions had no major role to play. The significance of even merchants and craftsmen, to say nothing of the industrial classes, was in the comparative background.

If the reasons for the enormous expansion of usury are sought, it is essential to bear in mind the anti-industrialisation policy pursued by Britain, which forced local accumulations into the sphere of the commercial and usurious exploitation of the toiling peasantry. The most important condition for the flourishing of usury is the existence of small holdings, which, by their very nature, preclude the free and rapid development of the productive forces of labour, of their social form, and the concentration of capital, and which inevitably lead the peasant to beg help from moneylenders, regardless of the size of the harvest. Under conditions of comparatively high commodity farming combined with the domination of landlords' property, as soon as the peasant resorts to usury credit, the small peasant holding falls firmly into the clutches of the creditor. It sinks in the process of ruin as far as the debt slavery of the cultivator and his dependants for many years, often for life, and equally frequently, the payment of the deceased peasant's debts devolves on his relatives, so they form the basis of debt slavery. These were not just individual cases. The situation lasted until the 1970s, in spite of all the reforms, decrees and transformations. It was most widespread among the harijans, the lowest untouchable caste of field labourers, farm servants and share-croppers.

With developed capitalist credit, too, of course, in the absence of landlord, the Indian small peasant would soon have lost his property, for, in the final analysis, large-scale capitalist production inevitably ousted small-scale. The difference, however, consisted in the fact that, being deprived of the land and means of production by the moneylender, the peasant usually became a pauper or subtenant share-cropper without any rights, since the usurer did not usally organise or carry on any large-scale farming activities. The transition of part of the ruined peasantry to the status of hired workers of a big capitalist businessman, who gradually emerged from among the ranks of the landlords, merchant moneylenders, and upper echelons of the peasantry, took place extremely slowly and on an insignificant scale. This is why the picture of the Indian countryside would be totally incomplete unless we pointed out the exceptionally powerful parasitic figure, oppressing by his exploitation the overwhelming majority of the poor and middle peasants—the figure of the moneylender.

Let us present certain material on the scale of mortgage indebtedness of the peasantry in individual regions of India in the 1930s. Data on the usurious exploitation of the Mysore peasantry is interesting. The peasant holding here was 6.5 acres of land on average, while its mortgage indebtedness was forty times greater than the sum of the land tax. Considering that, in the form of land tax, the peasant handed over a fifth of his net income from the land, the average mortgage indebtedness of the peasants worked out at a sum equal to their net income over an 8-year period. The mean annual income of the Mysore peasant, according to one set of calculations, was roughly 35 rupees, while another set put it at 56 rupees. Taking the median between them, 45 rupees, however, it turns out that there were 360-400 rupees of mortgage indebtedness for every peasant holding, to say nothing of other forms of agricultural debt (land and water taxes, etc.).

In the Punjab, just the annual interest rates on mortgages were treble the total sum of the land tax levied on the peasants of this province. This means that, while handing over a fifth of his annual income in land tax, the Punjabi peasant immediately handed over another three-fifths to the money-lender, thereby leaving himself only a fifth of the income. There were 31 rupees of mortgage debt per acre of cultivated land, meaning, with the average peasant holding in the Punjab of 9 acres, 280 rupees of mortgage indebtedness per holding. Another reservation should be introduced here: in fact, the position of the toiling peasantry was even worse for, first, a substantial part of the poor and middle peasants stood below the average level in terms of the size of land tenure and, second, the main amount of the mortgage debt was placed precisely among this part of the peasantry that was going to ruin. The average figures naturally conceal the extremes and distort the true, class sense of the economic phenomena under consideration.

The situation with mortgage debt in Bombay province was extremely serious. The Bombay peasants' total indebtedness was 810 million rupees, which is 15 times greater than the total sum of the land tax and roughly 55 per cent of the value of the entire annual agricultural output of the province. The average debt of the peasant household was 329 rupees. In Sind 13 per cent of the peasants were completely free of debt; in Northern Gujarat—21 per cent, in Southern Gujarat—23 per cent and in Konkan—29 per cent. Thus, no less than three-quarters of all the peasant landholders were in debt and, naturally, it was those who were least economically viable that fell into debt first. The peasant population, forced to turn to credit, provided chiefly by moneylenders, reached 84 per cent in Sind, and 66 per cent in Broche (a region of high quality cotton production). This confirms once more that the reasons for the developed peasant indebtedness lay primarily in India's agrarian system itself, in the domination of imperialism and feudal survivals.[8]

The Indian usurer, however, exploited the peasant economy not only through the system of usury bondage. Being a merchant and often a comprador of foreign and Indian trading firms, at the same time, he exploited the Indian poor and middle peasant without restraint both as the seller of agricultural output and the purchaser of industrial goods. Let us give an example of this sphere of the Indian usurer's activities. According to sample data collected by the Indian Central Cotton Committee, the conditions for the financing and trade in cotton in the Punjab were as follows:

1. Out of the 1,820 cotton producers 51.3 per cent resorted to loans before and at the beginning of the cultivation period.

2. The sum of indebtedness of each peasant resorting to loans was equal to 628 rupees.

3. As other research has shown, too, it was established that cultivating landowners found it easier to obtain credit and the sum of the debt was much higher among them than among cultivating tenants. The sum of the debt of the peasant land-

owner was 818 rupees, while that of the peasant tenant was 412 rupees.

4. Sowcars (moneylenders) loaned 68 per cent; 8.8 per cent came from co-operative societies, 16.9 per cent from landlords, 3 per cent from relatives and 3 per cent from trading middlemen.

5. The loans granted on terms of 20-per cent annual interest or less accounted for 67 per cent, of 20- to 30-per cent interest —27 per cent, and over 30-per cent a year—6 per cent.

6. The cotton harvest sold directly in the villages accounted for 72 per cent. The chief purchaser was the village merchant moneylender from the Bania caste, who bought up 83.4 per cent of the cotton sold in the village.

7. Immediate producers took 26 per cent of the cartloads of cotton to the town market and village usurers and merchants—74 per cent.

One witness before the Royal Commission on Agriculture in India said that the Punjabi peasant was under the power of small merchants even in the central part of the province, where communications were good. The same witness asserted that the peasant could sell his output usually only through the local merchants, the travelling merchant or an agent of town-based firms or through the commissioner for the local town market, if he was selling cotton—to the cotton-ginning plant, if wheat —to the brokers of big wholesale purchasing firms. The peasant preferred to sell his output to village or travelling merchants, though they paid less, since they supplied him with town-made commodities, on credit, throughout the year.

A similar situation was observed in the United Provinces: under the system of usurious advances, the peasant received for his maund[9] of sugar juice not 8 annas, but 6.5, and for sugarcane from an acre not 173 but 144 rupees. For 100 maunds of cotton, the peasant received 80 rupees, while the merchant moneylender—236.

The moneylender not only oppressed the main mass of the cultivators forced to resort to credit, thereby ruining their economies and collecting debts even from their descendants (in India in the 1930s, there were about 6 million debt slaves), but also deprived most of the peasants of free access to the town market and, in conjunction with the monopolistic purchasing agencies, took advantage of the enormous difference between the prices in the village and town market. Thus, they appropriated, on average, 20 to 50 per cent and sometimes even more than 50 per cent of the price of agricultural output, and established in the villages usurious contracts for the peasants' harvest, buying it up for monopoly low prices. This made the Indian merchant moneylender, together with the landlord, the enemy of the toiling peasantry and a most influential ally of British imperialism. This exploiting threesome, often combined in one or two individuals, being the specific bearer of the archaic relations predominant in the Indian countryside, ensured, by its very existence and the methods by which it exploited the peasant, that British imperialism would receive high colonial superprofits. Colonial superprofits are based on non-equivalent exchange between the metropolitan country and the colony. A substantial share of colonial superprofits comes from direct robbery, deceit, short measure, and usurious bondage, which were characteristic methods of initial capitalist exploitation.

The most eminent Indian financiers and industrialists, who sat on the Banking Committee specially set up in 1930, understood that the impoverishment of the main mass of the Indian rural population, the extremely narrow domestic market, the rapacious exploitation of the peasantry by the excessively bloated lower and worst forms of capital, and the tax pressure of imperialism did not create a favourable situation for the development of modern capitalist credit. In relation to the latter, British imperialism pursued a restrictive policy, just as it held back the industrial development of India. Stating that the banks could not grant credit under conditions of universal impoverishent, ignorance and helplessness, the Committee modestly reminded the colonial administration of the desirability of measures to industrialise the country, while resolutely demanding that a policy be pursued of implanting a system of junkers and rich peasants from above, by driving the bankrupt tenant-farmer from the land.

British and Indian bourgeois economists, when analysing the problems involved in the loan debt, almost always see the main reason for it as "the Indians' natural idleness", "extravagance", wastefulness, big outlays on weddings, funerals, and various religious ceremonies. In fact, it is quite obvious that the oppression of the small peasant property by the landlords' latifundia, the imperialist tax pressure, and the extreme poverty of the small producer as a result of feudal-imperialist exploitation, were the real reasons for the peasants' enormous mortgage indebtedness.

Table 8

The Reasons for Indebtedness in Madras Province
% %*

	Belar district (red earth)	Anantapur district (red earth)	Regions on the deltas of the Kistna and Godavari rivers	Regions of the upper reaches of the Kistna and Godavari rivers
Non-productive purposes				
Purchase of land (payment of rent and taxes)	23	16	28	18
Legal costs	3	2	1	2
Payment on advances and the like	10	10	3	1
Payment of old debts	3	6	8	24
Total	39	34	40	45
Productive purposes				
Soil improvement	7	13	24	29
Purchase of live or inanimate stocks	22	17	—	—
House-building	3	2	8	6
Total	32	32	32	35

* *Madras Provincial Banking Enquiry Committee,* Vol. 1, Madras, 1930, p. 284.

The data of special research in a number of districts of Madras province (Table 8), carried out during the reconclusion of rent agreements, reveal the true reasons for indebtedness—the necessity of covering non-productive costs, i.e., the payment of feudal rents and taxes, the paying off of old debts to moneylenders, payment to merchants, legal costs with moneylenders and landlords. At the same time, loans for a number of productive purposes indicate the gradual emergence of a small group of rich peasant holdings. Small and medium-size landholders partly take loans for productive purposes, too. They are forced to resort to credit in order to provide themselves with the most elementary conditions of production, of which they had been deprived as a result of feudal-imperialist exploitation. Virtually as soon as they acquire certain elements necessary for the production process, they are again deprived of them, and fall more and more into the clutches of the moneylender, having to hand over a growing proportion of their output, and transferring, on a considerable scale, to the status of unpaid debt slaves of usurer's capital.

British imperialism supported and consolidated the bearers of outdated land orders and, in turn, enjoyed their support. Over a long period of time, Indian usurer's and merchant's capital reproduced on a constantly expanding basis the totality of the most plunderous methods of primitive accumulation. It merged in a particular form, on the one hand, with the system of feudal and landlord exploitation, and on the other, with the system of colonial domination, both being chief conditions for the maintenance of its profits. This is why we can talk about a colonial-feudal regime in India; this is why agrarian transformations geared against the landlord and moneylender were inseparable from the overthrow of the power of British imperialism.

Differentiation of the Peasantry

In spite of the all-oppressing merchant's, moneylender's and landlord's yoke, the Indian peasantry was still not homogeneous in the class sense. It did not consist of peasants of a single type, oppressed by need. Account must be taken of the fact that, under the burden of precapitalist relations, in connection with them, relations of a capitalist type were taking shape in a very contradictory intertwining of capitalist and precapitalist relations. Lenin wrote: "*Inasmuch* as in our countryside serf-owning society is being eliminated by 'present-day' (bourgeois) society, *insomuch* the peasantry ceases to be a class and becomes divided into the rural proletariat and the rural bourgeoisie (big, middle, petty, and very small). *Inasmuch* as serf-owning relationships still exist, *insomuch* the 'peasantry' still continues to be a class, i.e., we repeat, a class of serf-owning society rather than of bourgeois society. This 'inasmuch-insomuch' exists in real life in the form of an *extremely complex* web of serf-owning and bourgeois relationship, in the Russian countryside today."[10] Lenin's famous "inasmuch-insomuch", covering the process, dynamics and dialectics of the transition by feudal society to a bourgeois one, considering the conditions determined by the colonial nature of the country, was undoubtedly applicable to India, too.

It is true that the entire history of British colonial rule in India was one of robbery of the peasantry, epidemics and chronic famines. It is true that this entire history was one of the "depeasantisation" and pauperisation of the peasant and craftsman. Yet, it is also true that it was precisely during this age that the power of money was not only slowly oppressing, but also splitting the peasantry and strengthening its property and social differentiation in a way that was very painful for the masses.

The peasants' output was increasingly becoming a commodity, By means of taxes, the forced spread of commercial crops, forward contracting by moneylenders, by means of the use of large landed property, the leasing of the land on the conditions that a specific commercial crop be grown and a number of other measures, imperialism turned the peasant economy into one that could not survive without selling its output. Imperialism made use of the destruction of cottage industry connected with farming, of its partial transformation into cottage-type capitalist industry, the development of a commodity-money economy, the creation of at least a caricature of semi-bourgeois semi-feudal private ownership of the land and its involvement in commodity turnover, the organisation of enormous plantation latifundia and promotion of the development of landowners and moneylenders along capitalist lines, in order to introduce into India's agrarian system a quite powerful stream of capitalist relations, which existed, struggled and intertwined with the dominant survivals of the precapitalist agrarian system.

In the 1930s, there were about 36 million agricultural workers, field labourers and farm servants in India. Many of them were still far from real proletarians, working not for a capitalist-type entrepreneur, but for a representative of initial capitalist profit—the rich peasant engaged in moneylending, trade and so on. Many of them retained their own minute strips of land as they feared a final break with the land. Capitalism, however, develops in such specific forms in agriculture, especially in a colony, that it would be wrong to suppose that it would inevitably require a pure, landless worker. Lenin included a considerable part of the Russian peasantry (hired agricultural workers with some land) among representatives of the rural proletariat. In addition to the transformation of the peasants' output into a commodity, the peasants' labour-power, too, did become a commodity in some regions, though on an incomparably smaller scale and much more slowly.

Three inseparable processes—specialisation of agricultural areas, the increase of the production of commercial crops and the commercialisation of the peasant economy—formed an integral process reflecting, above all, the penetration of capitalism into the Indian countryside and its adaptation to serving the raw material requirements of the metropolitan country. From 1895 to 1913/14 inclusively, the sown area under all industrial crops increased by 62 per cent, that under cotton by 63 per cent, under jute by 38 per cent, while that under cereals rose by 37.4 per cent. Correspondingly there was a rise in the harvest of industrial crops (Table 9) and their export on to the world market.

The penetration of foreign capital restructured Indian agriculture along colonial, semi-feudal, semi-capitalist lines. Where previously wheat had been grown, there was now a change over to cotton, jute and rice. Areas where cereal crops had predominated began to produce sugar cane, oil-bearing crops, and so on. All these major changes in Indian agriculture were made at the expense of the peasant masses, the result often being the extinction of the toiling peasantry, especially at the end of the 18th century and during the first half of the 19th. At

Table 9

Yield of Industrial Crops*

Year	Cotton	Jute	Sugar cane	Tea	Coffee	Rubber
	million bales		thousand tonnes	million lbs		
1904/05	3.9	7.4	2,170	220	29	—
1914/15	4.9	10.4	2,443	3	—	—
1929/30	7.0	10.3	2,752	433	39	28
1933/34	6.5	8.0	4,896	384	35	12.9

* *The Agricultural Question and the Peasant Movement. Handbook,* Vol. 4, Moscow, 1937, p. 105 (in Russian).

the same time, not only did agricultural production methods and technology remain unchanged; the majority of peasant holdings were ruined as a result of the survival of the feudal oppression, coupled with a high level of enforced commercialisation and specialisation of agriculture.

Share-cropping predominated in India, and in some regions even rent in kind rather than in money prevailed. The documents of the Royal Commission on Agriculture in India confirm this. Rent in kind was naturally more of a burden than money rent. It was the last resort of the very poor majority in the village, while the middle and prosperous strata paid in money. The prosperous peasants with more money at their disposal tried to use money rents to free themselves from the landlord bondage.

Under the system of share-cropping with rent in kind (batai), "the tenant makes Rs. 19 profit per acre only, whereas the landlord makes Rs. 30 . . . *Batai* tenancy is usually found where the landlord is dominant. It is not the choice of the tenant; it is due to the power of the landlord to insist on it."[11]

Most of the Indian peasantry rented land on harsh terms out of need and hunger, for the sake of the food to be obtained. There was increasing stratification among the tenants, too, with capitalist tenants gradually growing in numbers, as well as bonded tenants. The rich peasant was not only engaged in moneylending and leased out his land, though these were his main sources of income; he also himself rented land for capitalist enterprise.

India was not a country of "levelling poverty". A differentiation was taking place among the peasantry there. Oversimplification on this issue might lead to errors just as great as underestimating the influence and strength of the feudal survivals, if the laws and development course of capitalism of politically and economically independent country are applied mechanically and indiscriminately to India. The Indian peasant economy was, after all, subordinate to the commodity and money market and, therefore, to capital, so populist arguments to the effect that the economy was not heading for capitalism were unfounded. Yet, any arguments concerning the dominance of the capitalist mode of production and the relations of production corresponding to it in the Indian countryside are equally mistaken. The predominance of feudal-landlord exploitation, merged with merchant's and usurer's capital, in a situation of relatively high commercialisation and relatively developed money relations—such was the specific nature of the Indian countryside in the 1930s. The colonial development of capitalism in India was carried out by foreign imperialism relying on the support of the feudal and moneylending class. While bringing the Indian countryside into contact with capitalist relations, it did not radically renew the productive forces and relations of production, it brought the decay of a number of the chief supports of the feudal system (the commune, the subsistence economy, the links between crafts and farming), and engendered, on the basis of enforced commercialisation, an accelerated ruin of the peasant masses.

Lenin wrote: "Small producers are tied and subjected to the market. Out of the exchange of products arises the power of money; the conversion of agricultural produce into money is followed by the conversion of labour-power into money. Commodity production becomes capitalist production... The freer that farming [peasant—*R. U.*] is from land congestion, landlord oppression, the pressure of medieval relations and system of landownership, bondage, and tyranny, the more strongly do capitalist relationships develop within that peasant farming."[12]

Lenin's point is fully confirmed by India's agrarian evolution. In addition, account must be taken of the fact that commodity-money relations in India were indubitably tending towards a transition to capitalist relations. Under the predominance of the feudal-colonial regime, however, such trends were interrupted daily and hourly and were paralysed by the very fact of the domination of colonial monopoly and semi-feudal exploitation.

Chapter Three

The Landed Estate in India and New Features in British Imperialism's Agrarian Policy

The question of the landed estate in India, of the attempts made by imperialism to turn the parasitic receivers of rent—its feudal support in the countryside—into the organisers of large-scale capitalist, junker-type farming was at one time of considerable interest and topical political significance. In its altered form, this question is still of importance today, in independent India.

The ultimate goal of British imperialism's attempts in India was, by reformist means, to solve the agrarian question from above, at the expense of the peasant masses, to expand its own social base in the countryside, to transform the system of agraiian relations and Indian agriculture itself, and to tie Indian agriculture more closely to the industry of the metropolitan country, on a new basis of large-scale capitalist landed estates. All these attempts by British imperialism were in vain, but why exactly?

During the 1930s and 1940s, an agrarian crisis developed in India along with the anti-imperialist revolutionary movement which was gaining momentum and revealing new aspects and features indicating its greater maturity and transition to a higher level. This was connected with the continuing and deepening economic crisis. This was against the background, in India, of a protracted degradation of agriculture, a degradation that was a specific expression of the general crisis of capitalism on its colonial outskirts.

The attitude of British imperialism to the Indian peasants, who increasingly frequently expressed their dissatisfaction, was not exhausted by just a big stick policy, punitive detachments, and the practice of putting down the peasant movement.

The question arises concerning the type of agrarian programme and the kind of economic measures employed by British imperialism to penetrate the Indian countryside; and the essence of its attempts at a reformist solution to the agrarian question in order to find a way out of the impasse of degradation and crisis in Indian agriculture.

* * *

In the early 1930s, the British government published the multivolume report of the Royal Commission on Agriculture in India.[1] The Commission was set up in connection with the serious crisis in the Indian countryside and was intended to provide a true picture of agrarian relations and establish any possibility of restructuring them on the basis of a further bourgeoisification through the enforced creation of a landed estate-type of economy and the organisation of capitalist credit.

The Royal Commission on Agriculture in India heard a considerable evidence from the biggest landlords, concerning the economy of the Indian feudal estate. We shall now present and analyse this information.

The Central Provinces

The estate of Rao Bahadur M. G. Deshpande. The landowner was a malguzar (temporarily settled zamindar) of country stock, born 32 miles from Nagpur. His estate included 22 villages. He said that at the time of the co-operative movement he was the Secretary of the Central Bank. The villages belonging to him had no agricultural co-operative credit societies. He said that there were none "because we advance them at the same rate at which the banks also advance them.

"Who is we?

"I myself, because I have also got a moneylending business."[2]

Here is a typical absentee moneylending landlord. His loan operations were not confined to money. The landless peasant tenants to whom he leased his estate lands[3] were provided with seed on loan. Here, the seed loan was not only a loaning operation in kind, but also a lever by which the landowner, and with him the British trade monopolies, enforced their own choice of crop rotation on most peasants. Seed loans by landowners to bonded tenant farmers transformed the economy of the immediate producer into an agrarian-raw material appendage of the British trade monopolies: "I advance seed and take cotton in return. Supposing I advance four *khandis*[4] of seed, and get two *khandis* of cotton in return." We can calculate what this means in money terms. Four khandis of seed cost 4 × 28 = 112 to 4 × 40 = 160 rupees; 2 khandis of cotton are worth 2 × 115 = 230 rupees. Thus, the short-term loan (4 to 6 months) brings in a money income for the moneylending landlord of 230 rupees minus 112 or 160 rupees, i.e., from 50 to 100 per cent or more on the "capital invested". "Then I am not wrong in saying that you advance Rs. 112 and recover Rs. 230?

"No, that is always the case in the moneylending business."

In winter, when the peasant's miserable remains of the harvest run out, after he has been robbed of his output by the moneylending landlord, the latter, a type so widespread in India, also provides grain on a loan basis according to the sawai system, on which he earns a more than 25 per cent return. The extent to which this landlord engages in moneylending and to which his peasants are bound by debts can be seen from the fact that the land revenue they pay to the government under the malguzari system stands at 5,000 rupees, while the income tax paid by the landlord on his moneylending activities amounts to 2.5 thousand rupees.[5]

It is hard to pinpoint the main source of this landlord's money income. It is not surprising that he testified that "land does not pay" (as if he engaged in farming, rather than causing its collapse) and that the source of his income was "land and moneylending".[6]

Here, we have a typical representative of the class of parasitic rent-collectors, a representative of landowning and moneylending exploiters, drawing off the peasant's surplus product, binding the cultivator with a net of debt fetters, using every available opportunity to get rich from the calamities, need and sufferings that befell the people, and engaged in farming on his own estate through exploitation of debt slaves he himself created.

It is interesting that the British official C. M. Trivedy, the Registrar of Co-operative Societies in the very province where this particular landowner prospered, wrote in his testimony to the Royal Commission that the poverty and indebtedness of the rural population was growing largely as a result of the fact that many villages were in the power of the malguzars, who had no interest in the rural population and considered their dependent villages and tenant farmers as a possible source of income from moneylending. In other words, they used these villages merely to the extent that was necessary for their moneylending operations. Villages where malguzars were resident landlords and ones belonging to absentee landlords of a moneylender type differed greatly from one another. Abuse of the malguzar system was one, if not the chief reason for the unprofitability and backwardness of agriculture, a slow rate of agricultural development, and overall indebtedness.

British capital, which had turned India into its own estate, implanted in the Central Provinces a large stratum of landowning malguzars. The malguzar was the offspring of British capital and its direct feudal support. Trivedy recommended, after British capital had already exploited India for a hundred years, first, that the malguzars should develop along the lines of the British landlord and, second, that their children should be provided with a broad agronomic education.

The estate of B. G. Khaparde, a member of the Land Council in the Amraoti district. Khaparde was an ardent supporter of the creation of an industry in India to produce agricultural machinery and equipment, which is evidently why he acted as agent for Kirloskar Brothers, India's biggest farm machinery firm. He believed India should "be taught to make her own tools and use them, and not depend on other countries to manufacture tools for her".[7]

How did this supporter of mechanised farming run his own estate? He was a malguzar owning 1,500 acres, as well as renting an additional 500 acres from the government officially, under the ryotwari system. He also acted as an advocate. From 1911 onwards he lived permanently in the town, while his estate was run on his behalf by his brother. The land was leased to local peasants. He was engaged in moneylending, providing his tenants with money loans as an advance on the harvest of the crop dictated by him and most profitable to himself (cotton).

F. J. Plymen, Director of Agriculture, Central Provinces and Barar, wrote in his testimony that the landlord predominated, he "aims at getting his tenant as completely as possible into debt and then, taking all his produce, either leaves him just sufficient for bare maintenance or actually deprives him of his land. This class of moneylending landlord is a curse. He represents one of the chief obstacles to agricultural and economic advance. He is prevalent in many parts of the wheat and rice tracts."[8]

The North-West Frontier Province

Here is another interesting example of a moneylending landlord.

The estate of Sayard Pir Kamal Gilani (from Kohat) was of 1,100 acres in area, of which 100 were irrigated. All the land was leased out on batai, i.e., half-and-half share-cropping. The tenant did not enjoy freedom of crop rotation, but was compelled to sow his plot as dictated by the landowner.

"Has the proprietor any right to insist that his tenants shall follow rotations or other practices laid down by him?

"He cannot insist, but if they resist they can be turned out."[9]

Thus, although the rights of the landlord to enforce a given crop rotation were not officially recognised (there was no need for this), being land monopolists the landlords resorted to more radical and simple means for ensuring themselves the most favourable provision of raw materials for the monopolies, i.e., they evicted the tenants from the land if they refused to grow the crops the landlord wanted.

According to this landlord's testimony, the price of an acre of irrigated land in the Kohat district was from 600 to 2,000 rupees. The rent charged was, of course, equally monstrous. As the landlord himself often let slip, the rent was far more than half the gross product usually taken under the batai system.

W. Robertson-Brown, Agricultural Officer in the North-West Frontier Province, who studied 30 villages in the irrigated zone of the Peshawar district, came to the following conclusions: "Every landholder, big or small, was deep in debt . . . generally to those whose land they cultivate. . . the tenant giving half the produce as rent cannot live decently on five or even ten acres: he would be better off if he were regularly employed on even so little as 10 annas per day... The rent charged for the bare irrigated land without a steading or even a dwelling throughout the Peshawar District is about double that demanded for the best arable land in England with a house and steading on the farm. On the rents now prevailing no farmer with capital, however enterprising and experienced he may be, can farm a reasonably big area of land at a profit."

This "enlightened" official made an interesting proposal: "It would seem better to let the failures drop out and encourage men with ability and capital to farm in a progressive way. Where almost every small cultivator is in distress, how can relief be given without inflicting hardship on others?"[10]

Thus, the idea was to provide men with ability and capital with the opportunity to evict the bankrupt peasants from the land in order to organise capitalist farm estates.

F. V. Wylie, Settlement Officer in the North-West Frontier Province, was asked about the attitude shown by big landlords towards the running of large farms: "The wealthy man in this district, without exception practically, takes no interest whatsoever in his land; he simply eats up the profits." This official showed a certain wit. When asked by the Chairman of the Commission "whether the margin left to a farmer is on the side of surplus or on the side of deficit", he replied that "on general grounds it must be on the side of surplus, because he exists".[11]

Wylie could not have imagined in 1927 that, a few years later, the North-West Frontier Province peasants would remind the British authorities of their existence. They were to wage an armed struggle that, in the mid-1930s, grew into a partisan war that literally exhausted the British government. This war would make it necessary to mobilise the best of the Anglo-Indian army and air squadrons against the rebels and to drop incendiaries on the "red-shirts'" villages.

The Madras Presidency

The estate of M. T. Subramanya Mudaliyar. This moneylending landlord owned 700 acres of irrigated land on the deltas of the rivers Godawari and Tungabhadra. He had a special

60-acre farm worked by 10 share-croppers. When this was profitable, he sometimes paid them money. The farm was used to grow selected seed for the Department of Agriculture. In 1895, Mudaliyar graduated from an agricultural college, so was an agriculturally educated landholder. How, then, did he use the over 700 acres of irrigated land in the regions of the labour-intensive tropical cultivation of rice? He testified before the Royal Commission as follows:

"You are living on the produce of your land?

"Yes.

"You depend chiefly on the income derived from your ryots?

"Yes.

"And you are a ryotwari landholder?

"Yes.

" . . . What is your arrangement?

"In some places I get a fixed rent, and in some places I get a crop share.

"What is your crop share?

"In some cases, it is two-thirds, in others it is half.

". . .Do I understand that the cost of cultivation, except the water rate, is deducted from the tenant's share?

"Yes.

" . . . Suppose a tenant does not give you satisfaction, are you able to eject him?

"Yes, I can eject him at my will.

"Supposing he has improved the fertility of the land, you say you can eject him at your will?

"Yes.

" . . . Without giving him any compensation for the improvements?

"Yes.

"You advance money?

"Yes.

"How is the loan realised?

"I will take it from him as soon as the harvest is over; if he is able to sell the grain at the market rate he will do so and return the money to me, or he will give me grain to the value of the amount, according to the price of the market.

"When the harvest time is over, you get two-thirds of the crop, and out of the one-third, you take the cost of cultivation, and from what little is left you hope to get back your loan; is that the position?

"Yes."[12]

Thus, having grabbed most of the land in one of India's most densely populated regions, the semi-feudal landlord exploited the tenant, who had no rights, on the basis of a starvation-level bonded rent, usury interest and the debt slavery of the share-croppers. The landlord grabbed the miserable harvest even before it was brought in, leaving the peasant just enough, with difficulty, to reproduce his labour-power.

Another typical example in this connection: landowner *Dr. P. Subbarayan from the Kumaramangalam district of Madras.* He owned 83 villages, 40,000 acres of land, of which 35,000 were dry, 3,500 garden and 1,500 wet land. He had his own steading of 156 acres and received annual rents to the sum of 80,000 rupees. Like the multitude of moneylenders living on his land, he himself also advanced loans. Here is part of his evidence:

"Would you mind telling us what the rent is on your estates?...

"The dry rate on my estate is Rs. 1-10-0 [1 rupee 10 annas—*R. U.*] per acre on an average; the garden rate is Rs. 4-12-0 and the wet rate, Rs. 6-12-0.

"Would you say that they [the farmers—*R. U.*] are heavily indebted . . . on your estate?

"Yes, I think they are very heavily indebted at present because I find there are lots of money decrees against them; they are selling their land and these moneylenders really become holders under them instead of the tenants whose land they have bought up."[13]

The Punjab

One of those best informed concerning the agrarian question in India was M. L. Darling, a representative of the British authorities, who wrote several major works on the peasants of the Punjab. In his evidence before the Commission he proposed: "An effort should be made to get the larger landlords to realize their obligation to give a lead on their own estates in the matter of agricultural improvement... At present there are very few landlords who do anything at all. This is one of the crying needs of the Province."[14]

Darling was obviously determined to bring Indian agriculture out of its chronic crisis and to expand the domestic market for commodities from the metropolitan country by creating a class of capitalist landlords through expropriation of the ryots. Below we present an interesting dialogue between him and the Chairman of the Royal Commission, which reveals the essence of the policy of implanting junker-type landlords:

"Turning for a moment to the existing landlord class, do they show any signs of wishing to take a lead in progressive agriculture?—I made certain inquiries on that point in connection with my book, and the result was most disappointing. There is this to be said for the Punjab landlord, that there are only a few countries in the world where the landlord has shown any sense of social obligation... It seems to me of great importance that they should be roused to a sense of their obligations, because in reading of agricultural progress in Europe one is very much impressed by the part played by the landlord in Germany... Looking to a progressive future for the Punjab, one must emphasise the importance of landlords."[15]

They were thus staking on the Indian junker-type landlord.

The estate of Khan Bagadur Said Shiramekhdi consisted of 40 "squares" (1 square = 25 acres), i.e., a thousand acres of land, received as a reward from the government. He was himself a descendant of the old Moghul aristocracy, expropriated by the Sikh revolution, and was given land by the British authorities for his "good services". All but two of his "quarters" were leased out for bonded rent according to the batai system—share-cropping. He was a moneylender and often gave seed loans on the security of the harvest.

Sardar Sampuran Singh, the Honorary Secretary of the Lyallpur Central Co-operative Bank (the Punjab) gave the following assessment of the Lyallpur landlords in his written testimony on the position of agriculture in this granary of the Punjab, an area with a predominance of canal irrigation (Chenab, Ravi) and the production of irrigated wheat: "Their policy has been in the direction of expansion of their holdings, and not of effective agriculture.

"Owners of large areas of agricultural lands, when they get rich, go to live in towns ... and lose touch with real agriculture."[16]

W. R. Wilson, Deputy Commissioner, Jhelum district, where canal irrigation and the production of irrigated wheat predominated, also said that the junker-type landlords had "a perfect passion for consolidating large estates. . . But as these 'Junkers' help to form the Government's body-guard on the Council, this ever growing *latifundia* 'which ruined Rome and the Provinces' is not likely to receive any check."[17]

Another official of the Gujarat Central Co-operative Bank, Khan Bahadur Chaudhri Fazl Ali, was equally decisive on this issue: "At present, the non-agriculturist landholders are not working on their lands themselves, but the agriculturists are doing every work for them. These latter will become coolies, and consequently their interest in land will lapse, as the cultivators do not know any other art, and thus they will have to work under such capitalists. The result will be that instead of cultivators, a class of slaves will be produced."[18]

Let us note, in passing, that the evidences given by the officials of the Punjabi agricultural and credit co-operative, which included the most well-off upper crust of the villages in their ranks, were full of dissatisfaction over the parasitism and absenteeism of landlords. There were quite substantial contradictions between the feudal landlords who monopolised the mass of the land and the rich Punjab peasants, the most mature in this province, striving towards a free capitalist farming and to rob the peasants not only on a feudal but also a capitalist basis.

The United Provinces

The estate of Raja Kushal Pal Singh, a major landowner, taluqdar, member of the province's Legislative Council, and Chairman of the Agra District Board. He did not live on his estate, but in Agra, the province's central town. The size of his estate is idicated by the amount he paid the government in land tax—90,000 rupees a year. He is easy to describe:

"You are a landowner, I suppose?

"Yes, landowner in the sense that I collect rent from the tenants."[19]

Bombay

The situation was the same in Bombay. Two tax-collectors from different districts of Bombay gave the Royal Commission a clear picture of landlord parasitism. H. F. Knight, collector of West Khandesh, a cotton-growing area, pointed out the tremendous growth of the agricultural population surplus and stressed the need to eliminate the fragmentation of the land and speed up the transition to large-scale farms: "I would like to try the experiment of removing land in some areas from the operation of Hindu law, making fragmentary cultivation a criminal offence involving forfeiture of the land. This sounds excessively Draconian, but obviously land cannot increase *pari passu* with the population and unless fragmentation or the increase of population is stopped, we must everywhere reach eventually the condition . . . where the bulk of the population cannot support themselves on their land, and the possession of this land prevents them ever becoming a permanent and efficient industrial labour force elsewhere. Unless the land can support the agricultural population, the population must be reduced by pestilence or famine or birth control; in the present state of Indian opinion the last named remedy seems unlikely."[20]

To expropriate the immediate producer, eject him from the land, consolidate holdings at his expense, thereby turning the feudal into a junker—such was this official's actual programme. And this at a time when 50 per cent of the land suitable for cultivation (206 million acres in 1927/28) could not, in spite of the enormous agricultural population surplus, be developed by the landless bonded peasants. Even those who, at the price of poverty and indescribable suffering, managed to get hold of this land, had to part with 60-70 per cent of their harvest, swallowed up by rent, interest and commercial profits. The movement of the holdings of the rural masses—the middle and poor colonial peasantry—was more often governed by increasingly contracting, rather than simple, reproduction. The consequences of the 1929-1933 economic crisis and growing colonial-feudal exploitation made it absolutely impossible to maintain the farmed and cultivated land at the same level or on the same scale. The sown area dropped and this, under one-crop conditions, especially the production of industrial crops, doomed the peasantry to famine and pestilence.

Another Bombay tax-collector from the Kaira district, R. M. Maxwell, believed that, as a result of prevalence of landlordism, "most of the profits of agriculture go into the pockets of persons, largely non-agriculturists, who regard the land mainly as a safe investment for their capital".[21]

S. S. Salimath, Deputy Director of Agriculture in Dharwar (Bombay), proposed discouraging absentee landlordism either by law or other means, in order to force the landlords to engage in large-scale farming and invest capital not in landownership for the sake of the rent, but in agriculture itself, for the purpose of obtaining a capitalist profit. He wrote: "I have observed that lands are being purchased by absentee landlords to a great extent. They earn money from other professions and invest it into lands at any cost. To discourage absentee landlordship either by law or by other means may go a long way to help the matter."[22]

Salimath forgot that the famous draft Bombay act on small holdings, as a result of which up to 3.5 million tiny peasant holdings should have been expropriated to the benefit of the Bombay rich peasant and landlord in order to encourage them to farm on a large scale, had been dropped in 1928, for hundreds of thousands of cultivators forced the Bombay authorities to give up the idea of passing this act and conceal it carefully from the peasants, who did not use petitions but threats, demonstrations and the burning of landlords' property to back up their arguments.

Yet, such acts had already been passed in the United Provinces, Bengal and the Central Provinces, but they did not have the desired results, and could not do so, given the growing crisis and rising dissatisfaction among the peasants. Besides, this was expressed well by one of the witnesses to the Royal Commission in the North-West Frontier Province, which had been, taken over by the red-shirt agro-peasant tribal movement. A certain Khan Bahadur Sadullah Khan declared: "In this Province, there is no impetus to take to agriculture for the capitalist class, because they feel insecure outside the urban area."[23]

The growing revolutionary pressure of the peasant masses and the crisis, which exacerbated all class contradictions in the country and raised them to a new and higher level of maturity, were ultimately behind the certain timidity and confusion demonstrated by the representatives of British imperialism in implementing the "prussianisation" of the Indian agrarian system. These factors also accounted for the weak response shown by the feudal landlords to the new trends in the British colonisers' agrarian policy. The correlation of the class forces and the resultant of the class struggle in India were such that they fettered British imperialism, reducing its room for manoeuvre in transforming the agrarian system and dooming even its partial measures in this direction to failure.

We have already pointed out that the prevalence of big landed estates was reproduced relatively rapidly in newly colonised and irrigated areas, where the land was sometimes sold initially to urban capitalists who settled the land in order to run a big capitalist farm, and then began to lease it out increasingly "successfully" for bonded rents to landless peasants. In his testimony on this account, the former temporary manager of the Indian Central Cotton Committee noted that, although the actual cultivators of the land did not have enough land at their disposal, areas of a thousand acres were sold in Nizam, Gwalior and near the Sukkur dam to the holders of capital, instead of being distributed in small plots suitable for efficient farming by small farmers. He said that these capitalists, who were not genuine cultivators of the land, divided up their huge areas into small plots, which they then sold or leased out, while they themselves enjoyed an idle life. Most often, the land belonged to landholders who were more rentiers than agriculturists.

A representative of the Irrigators' Central Committee, Deccan Canals, took an interesting stand on the question of setting up big junker estates. This was evidently a semi-feudal, semi-capitalist enterprise, making enormous profits (37 per cent) from charging the peasant tenants a high water rate, for they had virtually no irrigation facilities of their own capable of providing them with even relative "water independence", and were, therefore, mercilessly exploited by the monopolists of irrigation sources. This representative had a vested interest in the existence of the tenant farmers, oppressed by the feudal yoke, so he naturally defended them. After all, the retention of the tenants' impoverished level of existence guaranteed him high profits. He said that if the proposal was for farming to be handed over to big capitalists, he was naturally against it. He came out against industrialisation of the country's agriculture. He wanted the peasants, the true backbone of the country, as he put it, to remain in the future, too, and the agricultural nature of the country to stay unchanged. He did not mean by this, of course, or so he said, anything with respect to the preferability of big farmers. Maybe both systems were necessary, but he felt that their further survival should take its natural course.

The retention of bonded tenants as an object for the most profitable exploitation, bringing in unprecedented profits to the water monopolists—such was the theme of this speech. Moreover, this representative of the Irrigators' Central Committee evidently understood the historically conditioned limitations on the British authorities' vain reformist attempts, so he was not against big junker farms provided everything was allowed to take its natural course.

British imperialism attempted to consolidate and expand its social support in the Indian countryside, but these attempts involved a battle with the peasant masses. From the formal, legal point of view, they were usually concealed behind the verbiage of acts on consolidation of estates. In 1928, for example, an act was passed on the consolidation of holdings in the Central Provinces, but it was initially implemented experimentally in one part of this province—Chatisgarha. The Royal Commission on Agriculture in India noted that it allowed a certain part, almost half of all holdings occupying not less than two-thirds of all the village's land, to work out a plan for consolidation. Once confirmed, it would become mandatory for all.

The Royal Commission praised this act, its directness and simplicity and, although the consolidation of holdings is not the same thing as expropriation, it does lay the foundations for it, for, in the process of consolidation, it is primarily the more prosperous strata who benefit and consolidate the best land in their own hands. In general, references to the legality of the expropriation of land parcels by finance capital, the ejection of tenants, ruined in advance by feudal-landlord exploitation, for the purpose of clearing the land for a growth of the Indian junker and rich peasant classes, are, of course, references to class legality. Here is what the Royal Commission itself had to say on legality: "We recognise that the introduction of an element of compulsion may be inevitable, but compulsion should not be regarded as dispensing with the need for the most scrupulous attention to the wishes of the people... In view of the novelty of such a scheme in present circumstances, we think that the element of compulsion should be reserved till the latest possible stage, and it will probably be found that the most suitable time to resort to this step is when the scheme for consolidation has been fully worked out in the closest consultation with the right-holders and when every reasonable attempt has been made to reconcile conflicting interests and wishes. When all that persuasion, perseverance and skill can do has been exhausted and a beneficial scheme of consolidation has been completed, we think that compulsion may be applied to secure for the majority advantages which an obstinate minority might otherwise withhold."[24] British law in the Indian countryside was naturally presented as defence of the interests of the majority, but there can be no doubt that the act on consolidation of holdings was used primarily by the rich strata in the village. They always won the support of the majority, since the latter were dependent on them.

The prospects for the development of the Indian countryside from the point of view of the class struggle became more and more complex for both the implementation of the programme for land consolidation and the eviction of the peasants, and for mass compulsion. In practice, it was the class struggle waged by the peasants that decided the fate of the attempts to consolidate the land.

Throughout the period of British rule in India, an anti-industrialisation policy was pursued there. This policy of holding back and slowing down the country's industrial capitalist development was the cornerstone supporting the colonial monopoly of imperialism. It complied fully with imperialism's historical mission in the colony—to turn India into an agrarian-raw material appendage of the industrial metropolitan country. The unprecedented agricultural population surplus and the absolute growth of this population through the ruin of urban artisans, the drop in the population of medium-sized towns that had previously been trade and craft centres, the impossibility of the ruined peasant masses being absorbed by the towns—all these factors resulting from the domination of the colonial monopoly led to a retention, under the conditions of relatively high commodity and money relations in the countryside, of the dominant role of the feudal survivals, in the context of the protracted pursuance of an anti-industrialisation policy. It is natural, therefore, that the problem of implanting junker estates from above in India cannot be regarded in isolation from the issue of industry, the question of where the dozens of millions of peasants evicted from the land would be employed. This was obviously a very pressing problem. Let us mention just Germany in the second half of the 19th century, where the capitalist development of agriculture was accompanied by a rapid development of industry, which more or less swallowed up the expropriated peasantry.

What did the Royal Commission have to say about the problem of the junker progress? Here is an excerpt from speeches by two of India's leading economists. A liberal, reformist economist was asked by the Commission what was his opinion on the fact that it had been suggested that all small holdings be eliminated and large ones be set up in their place in order that the landholders might hire the current small tenants to work for them as labourers, and might introduce better cultivation methods and set firm wages for the small land cultivators; the idea behind this proposal was to improve the situation for everyone, increase the income from the land and, consequently, bring a rise in the wages.

Radhakamal Mukerjee replied that such a proposal would suit a country with huge tracts of land and a small population to work it; India's industry was not developed enough to employ all the agricultural labour-power released.

A representative of the Madras Board of Revenue formulated the same idea thus: "The Bill . . . must tend to create a landless proletariat which is always a danger and doubly so in a country where industries are so little developed that they cannot absorb the surplus agricultural population."[25]

The Indian bourgeoisie's agrarian programme as it appeared in the 1930s was set out in a number of documents of the National Congress and the League of Independence. It differed from the imperialist policy of implanting Indian junkers in that the economists from among the local bourgeoisie, like Mukerjee, also stressed the need for India's more rapid industrial development as a means for absorbing at least part of the expropriated peasants.

Sam Higginbottom, Principal of the Allahabad Agricultural Institute, posed the question in this way: "The Indian farmer is in a vicious circle, far too many men work on and must live off the same small piece of land. Human life and labour is the cheapest and least efficient of all commodities sold in India. To get some of it off the soil and into productive industry is of the first importance in agricultural progress in India...

"At least thirty per cent of [India's—*R.U.*] population must be diverted to industry, commerce and transportation if agriculture is to be profitable in India."[26] This would have meant a work force of 20 to 25 million people, or about 90 to 100 million including their dependents.

However much the opinions expressed by the colonisers exacting tribute from the peasants might differ in their wording the proposals made by the "specialists" were essentially the same. Imperialism was intending to clear the land for the junker landlord, ejecting the impoverished, ruined small peasants, who pressed with amazing force on the land monopolised by the landlords, moneylenders and merchants—and this at a time when 70 per cent of the harvest was taken away from the Indian peasantry without any equivalent, as a result of the sway of the landlords and the trade and finance monopoly of the moneylender and merchant.

The historical need to eliminate this crying system of feudal-imperialist exploitation was dictated by the inevitable development course of the economy itself and the class struggle. The retention of this system or the meagre attempts to reform it along the lines of the Stolypin reform in Russia inevitably aroused the colonial peasant masses to the struggle. This colonial reactionary agrarian programme was revoked and its advocates hushed up, for imperialism was unable to initiate it on any broad scale right up to the collapse of British rule in India in 1947.

* * *

Let us turn to landlord tenure, which by the 1930s was already beginning to set up large-scale junker farms in Indian agriculture. The Royal Commission on Agriculture in India loudly praised the "successes" scored by the British authorities in setting up large-scale farming. The Commission heard the evidence of quite a few of these home-grown junker landlords. We shall present some of the evidence given to the Royal Commission by these specific representatives of the tendency towards Prussian-type development.

The Central Provinces

The estate of Rao Sahib T. S. Korde (Murtizapur in the Akola district). The total estate consisted of 600 acres, 400 of which were the landlord's personal holding. The area included three villages in which the ryotwari system prevailed.[27] The creation of an enterprise-type farm on this estate began with the organisation of a special farm of 20 acres (a thirtieth of the total area), where four wells were digged for irrigation purposes, at a cost of 22,000 rupees. The remaining 580 acres, including the farmstead land, was leased out to local landless peasants.

Rent was paid in kind, though money was charged on some plots. Half-and-half share-cropping—batai—predominated here, too, and 95 per cent of the land was cultivated on this basis. Yet, a start had been made and the development trend was clear. The owner of just a special farm was also a member of the Legislative Council and of the Nationalist Party, and wanted to become a big junker. He stressed this himself. A careful study of the structure of his estate reveals an interesting feature: for the land rented from the government, the owner paid a land tax of 2-3 rupees an acre, while the rent he charged the bonded share-croppers amounted to 20 rupees an acre. The rate of "profit" (or "rate" of feudal rent, to be more precise) was 1,000 per cent (20:2). Not a bad income, received, moreover, without any capital being invested.[28]

It is clear that this landowner, like the entire landowning class, was ensured unprecedentedly high money incomes precisely by this possibility of appropriating the surplus product of the cultivator on the basis of extra-economic coercion, as a result of his monopoly of the land and water and the virtual tying of the peasants to their tiny plots combined with merchant's and usurer's bondage. This bondage was also a result of the pressure exerted by the constantly growing agricultural population surplus, the impossibility of peasants becoming, on any mass scale, an agricultural or industrial proletariat. Without any substantial investment of capital in agricultural production, without any transition to capitalist farming on the basis of the exploitation of hired labour, the feudal and semi-feudal incomes were extremely high.

In this way, at one pole there was extended reproduction of landlord landownership and money incomes of semi-feudal exploiters in the village, while at the other there was the continually narrowing reproduction of peasant farming, the rise in the mortgage debt and the ruin of the rural masses.

The estate of the landlord Amanat Ali (Burhanpur). A total of 950 acres was cultivated in two areas: 800 acres in one and 150 in the other. In addition to the cultivated land, the landowner rented another 300 acres of barren land from the government, which he was ploughing up by tractor. At the time of giving evidence to the Royal Commission, 80 acres had been brought under the plough. An area of 800 acres was worked by hired labour. There were two people employed specifically to oversee the wage labourers. The owner himself ran the farm. The labourers were paid in money and the servants partly in kind and partly in cash.

The farm had already been operating for five years. The main crops were cotton, wheat and chickpeas, the first two for sale and the third to pay the estate servants. Most of the land was not irrigated, with sugar cane, vegetables and irrigated wheat being grown on the part that was irrigated. An oil-engine and a centrifugal pump were used to raise the water to the surface of the wells.

The three-field system and alternating crop rotation predominated on the estate. The landlord did not engage in moneylending. He had organised a cattle farm with 60 pairs of bullocks and about 80 cows. Dairy cattle were bred primarily for fertiliser. The sown area was ploughed once every three years, but was broken up by a disk harrow six times before each sowing of wheat and four times for cotton.

The landlord did not make use of the services of middlemen

or brokers, but used his own transport to take his produce the fifty miles to the market to sell. First, samples of the output were brought to the market, a price was agreed and then the produce was sold directly to wholesale firms or cotton gins and sugar refineries. The owner kept a careful watch on price movements and if, for some reason, prices were not profitable, he stored the output in his own warehouses at the market and waited for a change in the market situation. As a result, he received at least one rupee more for a maund of cotton than the ordinary farmer did.[29]

Such was the farm belonging to this landlord, who was undoubtedly almost a junker already, having five years previously evicted the tenant farmers he himself had ruined and having started to implement the colonisers' agrarian programme. Yet, even here, incidental use had to be made of feudal methods for exploiting the peasants. In addition to this capitalist farm, the owner also owned land in "several nearby villages", which was leased out to local peasants on the basis of bonded share-cropping. Unfortunately, it is not possible to determine the scale of the leasing operations engaged in by this junker of feudal exploiter stock. He himself modestly kept quiet about this side of his activities. There can be no doubt, however, that this landed estate, too, functioned in a constant intertwining with feudal exploitation.

The capitalist profit of a junker, which is based on exploitation of hired labour, is backed up and supplemented by the landlord's rent, charged on the basis of extra-economic exploitation and bonded share-cropping. Such is this type of comparatively more developed junker, in contrast to the landlord previously mentioned, who had only just started developing in the Prussian way.

The estate of Chandrabhan Behari Lall (Jubbulpore). According to the managing proprietor, Shyam Sundar Bhargava, the estate consisted of 60 villages with a total area of about 60,000 acres. The landlord acted as a malguzar in relation to the tenants living in these villages, who were almost all occupancy ones, or enjoying no rights at all. An area of 5,000 acres was cultivated by hired labour. The landowner's father was a big feudal landlord. This latifundia had already existed for 90 years by the time the Commission heard the evidence.

The introduction of a big farm began with an experimental station established in 1913 on an area of 90 acres. The workers were paid mainly in kind. The landlord advanced money loans at an interest rate of 12 to 15 per cent and seed loans for 25 per cent per annum. There were two agronomists and one assistant working on the experimental farm.

The chief crop was wheat, though sugar cane had also begun to be grown on the land which was irrigated by canal. Only the estate used the water from the canal; the surrounding villages did not receive water from it. No fertilisers were used on the estate and the soil was becoming exhausted. The farm was run in a wasteful manner. The crop rotation was 5-6 years under wheat, followed by some other crop. There were also paddy fields, where rice was grown as payment in kind for the workers, not for sale.

Funds provided by the provincial authorities had been used to purchase a steam plough for ploughing not the lanlord's land, but that of the share-croppers in the surrounding villages, for which they had to pay 17 rupees per acre. The estate had its own grain shops at the railway stations and the wheat was transported straight to Bombay, without the services of local middlemen or the local market.

In order to sell his own output and that of his tenants, the landowner had organised a big trading firm that also bought up the produce of other, smaller landlords and their tenants:

"We have got our own grain shops at the railway stations, and along with the grain shops we have got our own firm. . .

"Do you forward the wheat from other cultivators?

"Yes.

"So that you are, in fact, merchants?

"We are merchants also. We always get much better prices in Bombay. The name of our firm is well known down there for quality."

The estate had 400 pairs of bullocks, and an annual 2,000 maunds of silo feed was prepared. A dairy farm of 60 head of cattle had been organised to carry out experiments in cross-breeding. Sixty thousand rupees had been invested in these experiments.

Here is a characteristic quote: "A sort of feudal relation exists between them [tenants—*R. U.*] and you?

"Yes. Most of the villages are under us for the last 80 or 100 years.

"So that there is a feeling of personal attachment always between the tenants and the landlords?

"Yes."

In the season, an average of up to 400 workers were hired. Permanent workers were paid 7 rupees 8 annas a month, only 2 rupees being in money and the rest in rice. It is interesting that the 5,000 acres worked by hired labour were scattered all over the estate and the most compact plots under wheat were of no more than 90 acres.

The manager said: "On our own farm we consider ourselves in two capacities: one as the landlord of the village and the other as the farm manager."[30] In a word, in relation to the rightless occupancy tenants he was the landlord, the "landlord of others", and from these "others" received a precapitalist rent, in contrast to being a "landlord for himself" on his own farm where, in addition to enterprise profit, he also realised absolute and differential rent as capitalist categories that were already beginning to take shape.

Such was this capitalist estate, somewhat similar to that of a British landlord. The former elder of the village commune, who, after the colonisation of India by British capital, had been turned into a malguzar landlord, the owner of the land in the village, who by means of trade and moneylending had subjugated over fifty other villages, had become a hereditary feudal. After the First World War, he began to organise a large junker-type farm on a thirteenth of his land, worked by hired labour for a miserly remuneration in kind, and organised a trading firm for the wholesale of the output. Thus, we have here not only a junker landlord, but also a merchant moneylender, on whose estate, as social relations became capitalised but precapitalist rent in kind survived, the categories of capitalist relations appeared—absolute and differential rent as the surplus over the average rate of profit that he received as the capitalist landlord.

The still dominant role of feudal survivals on this estate is obvious, but a new economic process was beginning to emerge there, too—a tendency towards the Prussian course of development, with all its consequences for the surrounding land parcels of the rightless and landless tenants.

The estate of M. R. Dokras (Amraoti district). This "liberal" landlord, who was a lawyer by profession, owned 200 acres of land and rented another 200 from the government. All 400 acres were cultivated by hired labour. He began running a consolidated farm in 1916. Ploughing was carried out by mechanical plough. The chief crops were cotton and millet, the latter for paymet to the labourers in kind:

"What do you pay the labourer?

"Rs. 150 per year. I pay them in kind and the value of it comes to Rs. 150 per year."[31]

The Punjab

The estate of Col. E. H. Cole. This estate consisted of 7,500 acres, a thousand of which were cultivated by hired labour. The estate had six tractors, a farm-machinery repair shop, and a stud farm. The rest of the land (6,500 acres) was leased on the batai system, the crop rotation being dictated to the tenants. For the sale of the wheat grown on the estate and harvested by the tenants, stores had been built in Okara, and from there the produce was sent to the seaport of Karachi.[32]

The tendency in the economic development of this estate is clear. There was hired labour, capitalist use of farm machinery and capital investment to obtain profit. The tremendous weight of feudal and semi-feudal farming methods also pressed on this estate, however. The relations of capitalist hire and feudal exploitation of the rightless tenants interwove, forming such a contradictory whole that it is even difficult to say where the bonded share-cropping ended and capitalist wage slavery began.

The estate of Ujjal Singh. This landowner was a member of the Punjabi Legislative Council. He had 1,700 acres worked by hired labour. On his own farm, he used 40 pairs of bullocks to pull primitive wooden ploughs. He kept 200 pairs of sheep for fertilisation purposes and intended to bring their numbers up to a thousand. The land was situated on the lower Bari Doab Canal. The landowner had priority irrigation rights. In the first four years during which a big farm was run, he was exempted from land tax. From the fifth to the eighth year, he paid from a quarter to a half of the normal tax rate. At the end of the eighth year, having paid the government 25 rupees per acre, he acquired property rights over all the cultivated land.[33] The chief crops were wheat and cotton.

The following feature was extremely characteristic. A few years before the survey, this landlord acquired a mechanical plough, but not for use on his own farm. From 1926 onwards he began to use it to plough up barren land. This land (25 squares or 625 acres) he leased out on batai to landless and ruined peasants, tying them to the land, thereby creating for himself a precapitalist environment and source of cheap labour-power and entwining his share-croppers with moneylending and trading operations. It is indicative that the barren land he ploughed up by mechanical plough could not have been developed previously by the local ruined peasants, for they had lost not only their land, but also all their means of production.[34]

This estate thus presents an interesting example of the "inventive" landlord-capitalist, who began to run a big farm on still uncultivated land and realised that it was profitable not only to receive capitalist profit, but also semi-feudal rent; so he created a growing precapitalist appendage to his capitalist farm.

It is not out of the question that the "taste" for capitalist enterprise developed in this landlord at the same time as, so to say, a desire to back up capitalist profit with a constantly rising "rate" of semi-feudal share-cropping.

The United Provinces

The estate of Raja Jagannath Baksh Singh (Rae-Bareli district). This landlord was a member of the Legislative Council, representing the taluqdars of Audh. His estate consisted of twenty villages. His own farm land, the exact area of which is unknown, had been run on a consolidated scale since 1917. The estate had a manager. All the land on the big farm was irrigated, for which purpose about twenty wells had been sunk. Each well gave 60,000 litres of water an hour and irrigated an area of about 70 bighas (1 bigha = 5/8 acre or 0.25 hectares).

From these data it may be established that the approximate size of his farm was about 900 acres.

The chief crop was irrigated wheat. Mineral fertilisers were used extensively, as well as manure. Fertilised land yielded 24 maunds of wheat per acre, while unfertilised yielded 16. This was double the yield on the peasants' plots. Almost the entire area under wheat was sown with selected seed and the output sold to the Department of Agriculture.

Twenty pairs of bullocks and iron ploughs were used for ploughing. Fifty bighas were under rice and yielded a double harvest. The landlord wanted to expand his farm. In his written testimony he demanded the accelerated introduction of new machinery in Indian agriculture.

The labourers were paid partly in money and partly in kind, the latter usually during the wheat harvest at a rate of one-seventeenth of the grain collected by the labourers. All the labourers were conscripted from the villages on the estate. The money wage of an adult labourer was, at the rupee rate then in force, an unprecedentedly low—1.5 to 4 annas a day.

As a result of this high exploitation of the hired labourers, the junker landlord received extraordinary revenues:

"This year you have had a profit of about 75 per cent?

"Yes, I think it is more.

"Was this the case in previous years also, or is it a special case this year?

"The profit has been quite good in the previous years, but it has been on the increase, and the figures which I gave are for the last year."[35]

This barbaric exploitation of hired labour on a big capitalist estate weighed down by semi-feudal survivals combined with extra-economic appropriation of the tenants' surplus product, provided the source of the semi-feudal, semi-capitalist accumulation of this descendant of the Audh hereditary landed aristocracy.

The estate of Sardar Kirpal Singh (Gorakhpur district). This estate consisted of 10,000 acres, with one big farm, worked by hired labour occupying 600 of them. The main crops were sugar cane and wheat. The land was worked by iron ploughs and the draught power provided by bullocks. A tractor had been purchased. Two 200-foot wells had been sunk and equipped with hose pumps and a gas engine for lifting the water. Another three such wells were under construction. Wages were paid in money. A new labourer received 4 annas a day and one with at least two-year service behind him—from 6 to 8 annas. At the beginning of the working season, the landlord advanced the labourers half their wages at an interest rate of 9 or 10 per cent per annum, thereby drawing them into his moneylending net and binding them to his estate.

There was a factory for processing the sugar cane, producing 400 to 600 tonnes a day. It operated 90 to 100 days a year and gave a total of 80,000 maunds of sugar. The landlord was engaged in large-scale trading operations, buying up sugar cane from the peasants in surrounding villages. Often, the sugar cane was given to the peasants to process at home. Day labourers were also employed in the sugar refinery, which opened immediately after the sugar cane harvest. Hence the estate had permanent reserves of farm labourers.[36]

Such were the various types of capitalist landlord presented to the Royal Commission, but there were only a few of them[37] and they did not determine the social structure of the countryside in the 1930s. They were mere drops in the ocean of the prevailing feudal and semi-feudal relations, which penetrated deeply into the economies of these historically late representatives of the Indian junker class encouraged by British imperialism. The contradictory intertwining of capitalist and precapitalist exploitation methods, the former, on the whole, being in the lead while the latter still predominated, was felt everywhere: the barbaric exploitation of hired labour, the incredibly low wages, mostly in kind or mixed, the long working day in tropical conditions, the comparatively primitive machinery and farming methods and the mainly rapacious exploitation of the land, leading to soil erosion, together with exhaustion of people's labour-power. The junker did not need to bother about any reasonable reproduction of labour-power because the growing agricultural population surplus, meant, he knew in advance, that thousands of landless peasants, impoverished people, coolies and paupers, expropriated by moneylenders, merchants or he himself and ejected from the production process, would always be available, for under threat of starvation, at least some of them would always be willing to labour on the estate of the landlord or rich peasant, on whatever terms—this was characteristic of the landed estate.[38]

It is quite evident that however weak the stratum of capitalist landlords, however minor their role in Indian agriculture in the 1930s, however painful this slow crystallisation of the large landed estate might have been for the peasant masses, the class of Indian landlords, as a rule acting as both merchants and moneylenders, was already breaking down into different groups according to the "exploitation methods" they used. Some were becoming parasitic rent receivers, who did not run any farm of their own and leased their latifundia to the peasants in various forms of subletting, while others were already applying modern capitalist forms of farming, existing in an infinity of different versions and interwoven with precapitalist forms.

The capitalist landlords were in the minority, but being a live embodiment of the new line in the agrarian policy pursued by British imperialism in India, they heralded a historically delayed, extremely weak trend, overwhelmed by the pressure of feudal and imperialist exploitation, towards Prussian capitalist development. Even so, they constituted a real economic phenomenon that had never (especially in the colony) existed in a pure form anywhere, but was only very strongly linked and joined with the economic forms of the obsolete mode of production, which, in India, had been subordinated to and used by imperialism to derive a class support from the former owners of money and land.

The predominance of small-scale farming on big latifundia, the struggle between the small landholders, who were striving to obtain land, and the feudal latifundia, which monopolised the mass of the land, constituted the basis of the agrarian problem in India, the objective economic reason for the rise of the peasant masses to struggle against the landlord and imperialism.

It would, of course, be equally wrong to either exaggerate or underestimate the significance of capitalist landlord elements in India's rural economy in the 1930s. One might argue about the extent, and the conditions of this development at that time, but it is an indisputable fact that feudal survivals prevailed in the agrarian system of the country as a whole and that

7*

a capitalist landlord system was taking shape. Even so, "the basis of exploitation is not the separation of the worker from the land, but the compulsory attachment of the ruined peasant to it; not the proprietor's capital but his land; not the implements belonging to the owner of latifundia, but the age-old wooden plough of the peasant; not the progress of agriculture but ancient, centuries-old routine; not 'freely hired labour', but enslavement to the moneylender."[39]

As we can see, all these "new" trends in British imperialism's agrarian policy achieved no real success. The capitalist landlord was still a rarity and played no major role even in the mid-1940s, just before India's independence. In this connection, mention should be made of the Torrens system, which was characteristic of Indian landed property. Under this system, which was implemented and most widespread in the colonies, all feudal titles, privileges and rights of landlords, princes, permanent and life-long tenants, etc., were not a thing of the past, destroyed by imperialism; on the contrary, they were, one might say, "capitalised" in the sense that each owner of money had the right to acquire any titles, privileges or rights. The refuse of the feudal Middle Ages was not washed away but retained and acted its part in the feudal exploitation of the peasantry, as an object for sale and purchase, as a share of land rent, which could be extracted from the peasants by anyone with money enough to purchase this "right". Thus, the acquisition of land by the money capitalist and moneylender, industrial capitalist and the bourgeois intellectual was an extremely deep-running process, though permanent links were maintained at the same time between the main mass of the bourgeoisie and big landowners, this being mostly conditioned by social origins.

This system was an imperialist invention and it underlined the extent to which the obsolete feudal classes were the allies of imperialism and how much imperialist domination in the colonies itself acted as a major obstacle to the capitalist development of agriculture.

In this way, imperialism's agrarian policy in the colonies differed little from that pursued in the previous period. Imperialism was trying, by reform means, to expand the capitalist development of farming through speeding up the formation of the rich peasant stratum and the transformation of the landlords into capitalist landlords. In real economic life, this policy was represented as a manifestation of the Prussian bourgeois development course, largely paralysed by the remaining colonial-feudal regime. The main factor hampering Prussian bourgeois development of Indian agriculture was, therefore, the imperialist monopoly itself.

The historical age of attempts at reformist solutions to the agrarian problem in the colonies coincided with that of the general crisis of capitalism, intensified by the economic crisis of 1929-1933 and characterised by an exacerbation of imperialist contradictions throughout the world, a new rise in the revolutionary movement in the metropolitan countries and the unleashing of anti-imperialist agrarian revolutions in the colonies, which found an ally and support in the proletariat everywhere. This historical era was distinguished by the collapse of imperialists' efforts to solve the agrarian question by means of reforms and thereby consolidate their social base in the colonial countryside, the reason for their failure being the revolutionary struggle waged by the proletariat and the peasantry.

Even so, the agrarian system of India had specific historical features distinguishing it from Germany at the end of the 19th century and from Russia at the end of last and the beginning of this century, which were then following the Prussian course of capitalist development. What were these specifics? Lenin wrote the following on the agrarian system in Russia: "There can be no doubt that during the past half-century [following the 1861 reform—*R. U.*] capitalism has paved the way for itself *through* landlord farming."[40]

In India, capitalism did not do this, for its agrarian system did not include landlord farming on any large scale. Ownership of the land by landlords, without any landlord farming, constituted one of the specific features of the agrarian system in India. For most Indian landlords, ownership of the land did not involve ownership of means for farming, but merely a bare feudal or semi-feudal title, allowing them to charge the tenant peasants, who were precapitalist share-croppers, a land rent. As a rule, all or almost all the land was leased out in small plots to peasants. This explains why the penetration of capitalist elements into the countryside through landlord farming did not take place on a large scale in India and, at least, did not play the same role as it did in Russia and Germany.

The transition to the capitalist mode of production on the basis of the Prussian course put the landed estate at the head of this process, so painful for the masses. The fact that, in India, no such landlord-junker estates were created was weighty evidence that all imperialism's attempts to turn the landowner into a capitalist entrepreneur were in vain, for large-scale landed property was here virtually unconnected with large-scale farming, and was merely a means for squeezing rent out of the peasants.

Concerning the results of imperialism's reformist attempts to solve the agrarian question from above, the Sixth World Congress of the Communist International had the following to say: "The pitiful attempts at carrying through agrarian reforms without damaging the colonial regime are intended to facilitate the gradual conversion of semi-feudal landownership into capitalist landlordism, and in certain cases to establish a narrow stratum of kulak peasants. In practice this only leads to an ever-increasing pauperisation of the overwhelming majority of the peasants, which again, in its turn, paralyses the development of the internal market."[41]

It was not so much the policy of converting the landowner into an agricultural capitalist or the policy of establishing a narrow stratum of rich peasants, that was decisive for the type of the colonial regime in India, as that of allying with the landowner for the purpose of the joint exploitation of the peasants on the basis of the continuing dominance of precapitalist relations of production, assuming a commodity-money form.

Even when the landlord with capitalist pretensions made use of freely hired labour or that of the peasants, in the form of semi-capitalist, semi-bonded labour in India, this was never on a scale allowing him to manage and successfully put the capitalist development of agriculture on Prussian lines. The colonial regime assumed and consolidated this specific feature of India, which had to be taken into account. In precolonial India, the feudal landownership that had gradually taken shape did not get as far as developed serf forms or corvée, as had happened, for example, in Russia. There was no corvée or landlord farming in India, no division of the land, as there had been in Russia, into that of the peasants and that of the landlord, though feudal landlordism did and still does exist there as an expression of the feudals' monopoly of the land.

In postreform Russia, part of the land on the landlord's farm was cultivated on the basis of small-scale bonded share-cropping, and the rest on that of freely hired labour, but in India all the land on the estate was worked on the basis of precapitalist and semi-feudal share-cropping, while the peasant tenant was economically a semi-slave share-cropper.

In all, these social conditions in Indian agriculture proved less favourable for the penetration of capitalism into farming than those when the landlord himself (for example under the conditions in postreform Russia) often initiated certain progressive farming methods, the hiring of labour-power, and commercialisation, thereby increasingly becoming a capitalist landlord.

Finally, given the extremely low consumption level of the peasant masses and the extraordinarily high rate of exploitation and corresponding extra-economic appropriation of almost all the surplus product of the peasantry, and given the constantly growing land tenure by the ruined strata of the population, who rented land on terms ensuring them no more than literally a starvation level of subsistence, there was no economic incentive to the landlord to go over to capitalist-type farming or to industrial capitalist enterprise in agriculture.

At the beginning of his work "The Agrarian Question in Russia Towards the Close of the Nineteenth Century", Lenin gives a short list of the results of postreform development in Russian agriculture. We present this here, as it gives a general picture of the direction, course and nature of the development of Russian agriculture for comparison with that of Indian agriculture.[42]

Russia

1. a) "The trend of development is towards a decline in landownership by the nobility. Landownership by people irrespective of the social-estate they belong to is increasing, and increasing very rapidly."

India

The trend of development is towards an increase in landownership by landlords. Landownership by people irrespective of the social-estate they belong to is increasing; the right to practise exploitation as a landlord can be enjoyed by anyone with enough money or belonging mainly to the upper castes.

b) *Russia*

Peasant landownership increased "more than twofold".

India

Peasant landownership (peasant landowners in general, including permanent and lifelong tenants) is falling.

c) *Russia*

Landownership by "other social-estates" multiplied eightfold over 28 years.

India

Landownership by "other social-estates"—the bourgeoisie, intelligentsia, officials, upper echelons of the petty bourgeoisie in the towns—grows as a manifestation of the increase in landownership by people irrespective of the social-estate they belong to. People with money acquire land on a mass scale.

2. *Russia*

"The peasants are consequently increasingly crystallising out social elements which are turning into private owners of land. This is a general fact."

India

The chief process is for the peasants to crystallise out social elements that are transformed from being peasant landowners into tenant share-croppers, and then landless paupers; at the same time, a narrow stratum of landowners is crystallising out (a rich, prosperous peasant group), but this process is subordinate and secondary.

3. *Russia*

"The power of the land is declining, the power of money is growing. Land is being drawn more and more into the stream of commerce."

India
The power of money is growing as a converted form of feudal and semi-feudal power of the land. The land is being drawn more than ever into commerce, but this is primarily an expression of the sale and purchase of a share of land rent. Money is going into landownership not for the purposes of capitalist farming, but for the purchase of feudal privileges to charge rent.

Such are the chief specifics of the evolution of the agrarian system in India in the 1930s, compared with those of Russia at the end of the 19th century.

The question of landlord economy in India could also be considered from a somewhat different angle. It might be imagined that all the land leased out by the Indian landlord on a share basis consisted of the landed estate worked by share-croppers, i.e., on the basis of labour service, for Lenin believed that the half-and-half share-cropping system was one form of labour service, while "labour service is the transition from the corvée to capitalism".[43] Further, Lenin pointed out that, in Russia at the end of the 19th century, a large share of landed estate land was leased to the peasants on a share-cropping-cum-labour service basis. It would seem that no grounds existed for denying, therefore, the presence of landlord farming in India, since all the land belonging to landlords may be considered as constituting their farms, worked by share-croppers, i.e., on the labour service basis. But Lenin said that "the landlord economy based on labour service *requires* a peasant who has an allotment, as well as implements and livestock if only of the poorest kind",[44] and receiving "wages" in the form of the necessary product put out by the peasant on his own plot of land. In India, however, there were no peasants with an allotment producing a surplus product on the landlord's field part of the time, and the necessary product on his own land the rest of the time; nor was there any distinction between land belonging to landlords and peasants.

When we speak of landlord economy in India, account must be taken of the fact that, in a number of regions, it existed or was beginning to be created on the basis of a combination of freely hired labour and labour service. It was not a typical, mass-scale, decisive phenomenon in the country's agrarian system.

This did not, however, conflict with the fact that, in many regions, there were survivals of historically undeveloped corvée, employed mainly in the landlord's garden steading or house, and so on, rather than on his fields.

In India, there were many such phenomena, but they characterised only the strength and power of the landlord, who not only took all or almost all the surplus product from the peasant in the form of produce or money rent, but also exploited peasant labour in its physical form.

Labour service rent, i.e., corvée, did not develop in India to the same extent as it had been developed in the countries of Europe. On this basis, some researchers try to deny the existence of feudalism in India altogether, ignoring even such obvious processes of feudalisation in precolonial India which Marx pointed out in his works.

Yet, the absence in India's historical development of labour service rent, i.e., corvée, as a factor determining the agrarian system, underlines specific historical features to which Lenin drew particular attention.

Finally, the question of the possibility of capitalism developing in a Prussian way should not be considered in isolation from the development of industry. The Prussian course of capitalist development, as one form of bourgeois adaptation of landlord farming, is carried out "wholly in the interests of the landlords and at the price of the utter ruin of the peasant masses, their forcible ejection from the countryside, the eviction, starvation, and the extermination of the flower of the peasant youth with the help of jails, exile, shooting, and torture."[45] The failure of the Prussian development course in India was also a result of the extremely slow development of industry, which was unable to absorb the ruined peasant and artisan masses, who were exerting a tremendous pressure on the land and swelling the already unprecedented agricultural population surplus.

Only very small numbers of Indian peasants emigrated to other countries, so this could in no way provide a major channel for syphoning off the population that was surplus under the given agrarian system. The slow industrial development like that of the productive forces, was, however, a result of the rule of British imperialism.

Lenin pointed out that the Prussian course "is the kind of 'operation' in which it is extremely easy to break one's neck".[46] This is particularly true of India where, in both town and countryside, the unprecedented economic crisis and the mass expropriation and ruin meant that enormous quantities of socially explosive matter were accumulating.

The impossibility of any reformist solution to the agrarian question, given India's concrete historical specifics, can be demonstrated scientifically, but its absolute impossibility as a development prospect can only be proved by the class struggle. It is the class struggle that decides which class will solve the agrarian question and how.

The economic opportunities for carrying through agrarian reforms were infinitely fewer in India than in Russia, as already demonstrated, the reasons for this being not only all the historical-economic specifics of India's development, but also the historical stage of development of world capitalism between the world wars. The existence of the USSR, which exerted a tremendous revolutionary influence on the national liberation movement in the colonies, the accelerated decay of imperialism, especially British, the world economic crisis that hit to the colonies hardest of all and speeded up the advancing degradation of Indian agriculture: all these political and economic factors could not but play a decisive role with respect to the economic and political opportunities for applying the Prussian bourgeois method for solving the agrarian problem in the colonies in general, and in India in particular.

In addition to all these factors, the reformist solution to the agrarian question, imposed from above, failed because the development of capitalist relations in Indian agriculture and the disintegration of the peasantry into hostile classes of peasant bourgeoisie and peasant proletariat were hampered historically by the incomparably deeper-running domination of feudal survivals (supported by imperialism) than in Russia.

This aspect of the matter should not be forgotten, for it is the best proof that the system of social relations in the Indian countryside was economically unready for the imperialist attempts to solve the agrarian question from above, at the expense of the peasantry and in favour of the rich peasants and landlords, to be an even partial success.

The attempts to speed up the crystallisation of a rich peasantry in India and the conversion of semi-feudal landlords into capitalist entrepreneurs undoubtedly testified that the British imperialists understood the need to expand their class support in the countryside. British imperialism was inexorable in breaking down the Indian peasant commune, but it could not be so determined at a completely different stage in the development of world capitalism, when it was a matter of breaking down the agrarian system from above and thereby evicting tens of millions of peasants from the production process for the benefit of a small number of landlords. British imperialism could not pursue its reformist policy on the land question "come what may". The imperialist politicians understood what this would lead to and that it would be "extremely easy to break one's neck".

In one way or another, however, the task of changing India's agrarian system was becoming more and more pressing, as the British imperialists recognised. The struggle between the classes had to decide how this task was to be fulfilled.

Chapter Four

Agrarian Relations in Bengal, an Area of Large Landed Property

Bengal was the most densely populated province of British India: according to the 1931 census, it had a population of 50,100,000 to an area of 82,277 sq miles, with feudal principalities with a population of 972,290, occupying 5,434 sq miles or relatively less than in other Indian provinces. The population density of 646 people per sq mile was the highest in India and higher even than that of Holland, England, and Germany, and second only to Belgium (654). Successive famines in the 19th and 20th centuries claimed a toll of millions of lives. The peasant movement in Bengal, distinguished by its tenacity and radicalism, was the most massive in the country.

The typical feature of the Bengali countryside of the 1930s was the supremacy of large feudal landlordism, the traditional buttress of British capital in India. This buttress was shaped with the introduction of the system of permanently settled zamindary estates in the 18th century, viewed by Karl Marx as an aristocratic "agrarian revolution" that expropriated the immediate producer's inherited right to his land, destroyed communal tenure and the related village crafts, and converted the essentially subsistence farming into commodity farming. Marx described the introduction of the permanent zamindary system as a caricature of English landlordism: this "upper-crust agrarian revolution" carried out by the British made the Bengali zamindar a nominally large landlord, on the one hand, and a middleman between the colonial monopoly established by British capital and the ryot (payer of taxes and levies), on the other—the vehicle, therefore, of British imperialism's agrarian policy.

Given the supremacy of the feudal landlord in the Bengali

countryside, the historically shaped insignificant percentage of landlord farming could not meet the demand in raw materials and food created by the industrial development of the metropolitan country and the growth of the world market (even by statute labour or on a junker-style basis). Other ways had to be found to meet this demand by adapting the holdings of small cultivators to this aim. Hence the extremely contradictory and variable land tenure policy. Hence the systematic governmental interference in the production relations prevailing between the zamindar and the peasant. Hence also the different types of tenure, expressive of the varying degree of adaptation of the Bengali rural producer to working for the market.

British imperialism and its feudalist understructure in the countryside encountered an ever rising discontent of the continually plundered mass of peasants which often snowballed into riots and insurrections. Dividing this mass, therefore, and raising tenancy partitions within it became, to a certain extent, a basic political motivation of the land tenancy legislation. British capital also resorted to such legislation whenever the claims of the Bengali zamindars to the surplus product of the peasants grew to excess compared with the share given over to the imperialist regime, and, besides, when this threatened to precipitate an outburst of peasant revolt. This was so in 1859, 1885 and 1928, when the basic tenancy acts were passed.

In Bengal, 87.3 per cent of the total assessed area (59,628 sq miles or 38,161,920 acres) was held by permanently settled zamindary estates. The zamindar holding averaged 409.4 acres, with the average for the Presidency division rising to 795 acres, for Burdwan to 604.8, and Rajshahi to 1,627.9. Landlord estates functioning under the zamindary system totalled 98,209. Naturally, average figures tend to obfuscate the overall picture of large-scale landlord holdings. Baden-Powell estimated that, at the end of the 19th century, 10,000 landlord estates of from 5,000 to 20,000 acres occupied 10 million acres, while 500 estates, of over 20,000 acres each, occupied 12.5 million or roughly half the land taxed under the permanent settlement zamindary system. An Indian source tells us that "the largest estates are few in number (about 600), the middle-sized estates are many, while the small-sized estates are legion". The same source informs us that zamindary estate No.

203 in the district of Faridpur is 133,957 acres, of the Selimabad and Chandradwip zamindars of the Backerganj district are 199,010 and 127,922 acres respectively. "Some of the estates lying in the Mymensingh and Rajshahi districts," it amplifies, "are also immense in size."[1]

In Jessore, nearly 98 per cent of the land belonged to permanently settled zamindary estates, with the holdings averaging 577 acres. In the same district, 1,021 estates were so small that the tax they paid was a mere 10 rupees and even less. In Faridpur, 2,523 estates were of less than 50 acres and only 756 of from 50 to 100 acres. Thus, some 600 estates belonging to permanently settled zamindars who were the leviathans of feudal landlordism in Bengal and who determined the land regulations in the province, had behind them a considerable number of middle-sized and a multitude of small-sized zamindary estates. This was the result of a dual process witnessed in the province, with the bulk of the land in the decisive areas concentrated in the hands of a relatively small but numerically stable landlord elite (600 out of 93,000), on the one hand, and the urban middle classes, the lesser gentry, moneylenders and merchants seeking to gain a grip on land as zamindary holders of permanently settled estates, no matter how small, on the other.

It is also quite clear that the ruin of middle, and notably of small, landlords was a concomitant of the ongoing concentration of land in the hands of the small but influential feudal elite. Hence the fairly sharp contradictions that prevailed within the class of landlords scrambling for monopoly on landownership and thereby for a share of the lucre squeezed out of the peasants and sticking to the hands of zamindars. And this despite the essentially similar class role of all the sections of landlords in relation to the toiling peasantry. These contradictions were made still more complicated by the fact that the scramble for the peasants' surplus product—especially during the world crisis of 1929-1933—was joined not only by large, middle and small landlords, but was also witnessed within large, middle, and partly also small, estates, and saw the zamindar pitted against a highly numerous group of rent-collecting middlemen. It would be a mistake to exaggerate the role of these contradictions within the landlord class of the

1930s, but, all the same, they must be taken into account in the context of the labouring peasants' class struggle as a factor that eroded landlord unity.

The second set of contradictions closely connected with the above was that between the Bengali zamindars and the Anglo-Indian government. The annual tax paid by the former amounted to 29,112,591 rupees. In 1793, when the Permanent Settlement of the Land Revenue Act went into force, this stood for nearly 90 per cent of the rent collected by zamindars from the peasants, whereas in 1925/26 this percentage declined to 25. In the 125 years of the zamindary system government revenue fell short by an estimated nearly 4,000 million rupees. We may recall Lord Curzon's attempts as Viceroy of India to abolish the system under which the government received a fixed share of the surplus product exacted from the peasants, because it prevented British imperialism from appropriating the proportion of the rent to which it thought itself entitled. This contradiction prevailed in the 1930s, and the British imperialists were quietly engaged in preparing an artful solution: the land of large, and mainly middle and small, landlords expropriated for defaulted taxes was turned over to new landlords, but this time under a system of temporarily settled zamindary estates.

In the course of time, landownership based on temporary settlement took shape in the main divisions of Bengal. Its proportion was fairly large. It accounted for 5.8 per cent of the land, that is, 3,978 sq miles or 2,574,920 acres. The average acreage of the 4,202 estates functioning under this fiscal system, namely 605.8 acres, and rising to 1,610 acres in the Presidency division while to 172.2 in Burdwan, exceeded that of permanently settled zamindary estates.

The growth of this system was also due to certain changes in the territorial boundaries of Bengal—the incorporation of the province of Chittagong and of some districts of Assam and of the United Provinces. But what we are concerned with here is only the emergence and development of this type of landed property in Bengal proper. In pursuance of its manipulations aimed at reducing the share claimed by permanently settled zamindars in the peasants' surplus product, the Anglo-Indian government set the temporarily against the permanently settled zamindars, and fell back on estates directly owned by the state, that is, on the feudalistic ryotwari system, remnants of which were still extant on a relatively large scale in Bengal. Here are a few pertinent facts and figures.

The *khass,* which were estates managed directly by the state and the revenue from which went to the exchequer, occupied 6.9 per cent of the land in the province, that is, 4,674 sq miles or 2,991,360 acres. Their average acreage of 1,115 acres was greater than that of other forms of feudal and semi-feudal landed property, rising to 5,185 acres in Rajshahi, 1,965 in Chittagong, 997 in the Presidency division, and 997 in Burdwan. In Dacca, the average size of the 1,029 government estates (out of the 2,682 in the province as a whole) was 34.4 acres.

Nalini Mohay Pal, whom we cited earlier, noted that out of the total khass estates, 201 had from 3,000 to 71,000 acres, while the acreage of most of the remaining ones ranged from 10 to 100 acres. The proportion of government estates in individual districts and divisions of Bengal may be illustrated by the following figures: in Midnapur 97 per cent of the land was held by 170 such estates averaging 3,030 acres, while another 359 small government estates averaging 33 acres held the remaining 3 per cent of the land. In Rajshahi, nine out of the total 198 khass estates averaged 70,644 acres, in Darjeeling 16 such estates averaged 17,460 acres, in Chittagong six (out of 371) averaged 71,573. As we see, therefore, the notion of Bengali feudal landed property having been confined to just the permanently settled zamindary estates is no more accurate, than that which overlooks the existence of the highly numerous middle, and notably small, zamindary estates.

Certainly, these facts do not wholly cover the question of the size and forms of land holdings in Bengal any more than the question of the share of each of the above-named systems. They refer to them chiefly in the light of the fiscal (tax) relations that had shaped historically between diverse sections of landlords and the Anglo-Indian government.

Large-scale landed property in Bengal, as in the rest of India, should be distinguished from large-scale landlord farming. By and large, the latter—be it statute labour or junker-type farming—did not, in fact, exist as a determining factor in Bengal's agrarian system any more than it did in that of India as

8—801

a whole. To be sure, remnants of historically underdeveloped statute labour in the form of road-building, carting, irrigation and other works, which even in the past did not constitute any direct foundation of agricultural production, occurred frequently enough on Bengal's feudal estates, as an additional means of exploiting the labouring peasants. It is a fact, nonetheless, that Bengali zamindars and intermediate rent-collectors of all types did not practise farming of their own on any significant scale, and, as a rule, leased out the land for what were, as a rule, exorbitant and oppressive rents. Accordingly, there was no division of land into areas tilled for the landlord and peasant parcels. Lenin's observation that "the monopoly of landownership based on property rights and the monopoly of the land economy are two entirely different things, not only logically, but historically"[2] is an essential guideline in our examination of the intrinsic economic structure and economic evolution of the Bengali landed estate, and is also largely significant in any study of the structure of Bengali rich peasant farming. Fittingly, indeed, the rich peasant has, suiting his nature, received the appellation of "ryoti landlord" (peasant landlord) in the works of local economists: he bought rights of perpetual tenure from ruined toiling peasants and thereupon exploited them as a kind of landlord within the peasantry in parallel with the exploitation practised by the zamindar.

In the setting of relatively developed commodity and cash cropping, their British-backed monopoly rights to property in land and water enabled Bengali zamindars to appropriate the surplus product of the immediate producer on so great a scale that, as Indian sources confirm, they lacked a serious incentive to organise their own, large-scale farming. Similarly, the colonial monopoly of British capital objectively hindered the passage to junker-type farming on any in the least extensive scale. The development of commodity and money relations in agriculture and the inclusion of land in commodity circulation could not by themselves radically alter the intrinsic economic structure of the Bengali estate. This, indeed, was the foundation for the emergence and spectacular growth of the primary capitalist accumulation of merchant and usury capital, which was fused with the accumulation of money by the landlord class as such. The conversion of land into a commodity that could be alienated by an ordinary transaction, though it did undermine the elitist nature of landlordism, could not by itself spur any extensive penetration of capitalism into agriculture through landlord farming. Quite the contrary. With capital used above all by merchants and moneylenders, prosperous peasants, urban industrial capitalists and the bourgeois intelligentsia to extract rents as an interest on investments in land rather than in farming, the conversion of land into a commodity resulted in its concentration in the hands of a relatively few feudal-type magnates, on the one hand, and in the fragmentation of the title to property, on the other. This, in turn, fostered fragmentation and sale of private semi-feudal rights to land and rights to the extra-economic exploitation of peasants.

Such, we hold, was the greatest of all the contradictions in the framework of the colonial monopoly of British capital that led to the absence of any monopoly on large-scale landlord farming in the setting of a landlord monopoly on landed property.

The Bengali form of landlordism had a specific feature: the existence and growth of a vast stratum of parasitic rent-collectors. The fragmentation of private feudal titles to land and their purchase by the propertied classes to secure a constant source of unearned income was witnessed throughout India, but in no other province did it assume such gigantic proportions as in Bengal, which, no doubt, is to be traced, in addition to the above-mentioned reasons, to the fiscal (tax) aspect of feudal landlordism, the system of permanently settled zamindary estates.

British land laws in Bengal provided for four categories other than that of the zamindar, who was regarded as the nominal owner of the land: the landlord, perpetual tenant, subtenant, and tenant without rights. The three basic tenancy acts (those of 1859, 1885, and 1928) endeavoured to fix the respective places of these categories in the general system of Bengali landownership and tenancy. In British legislation, the middleman rent-receiver was a person who had acquired title to land from a landowner or some other proprietor for the purpose of collecting rent or leasing land.

Exercise of the title to rent-collecting assumed two forms: that of joint ownership of the estate by a group of landlords each of whom received a share of the rent proportionate to the "capital" he had "invested" in the estate (here there were no middlemen between the immediate producer and the landlord, the former dealing with a simple, collective landlord), and that of a whole pyramid of intermediate rent-collectors, each successive one being at a lower tier of the pyramid corresponding to the share he received from the rent exacted from the peasant. However diverse the formal legal terms and the levels of non-cultivating tenants, there was no difference between them in the essential class context.

It should be borne in mind, however, that the specific conditions of the class stratification of the Bengali peasantry, compounded with the imperialist policy of land tenure and with commodity and money relations, resulted in the fact that among the peasants, too, and notably (but not exclusively) among the rich peasants, there developed a peculiar form of parasitic rent exaction from the most indigent and oppressed Bengali peasants. Bengali rich peasants (let alone moneylenders and merchants) were connected by a series of subtle links—and, in practice, on a massive scale—with parasitic rent collection, taking root thereby in the system of landlord property and landownership.

Feudal corrosion also affected those relations within the peasant class that had at first sprung from property inequalities and, thereupon, from the class differentiation of its various sections. Itself a product of the systematic inhibition of a truly capitalist development of agricultural forces of production, this system of parasitic rent collection had a formidable negative effect on the economic evolution of Bengal's agrarian system, on its agriculture, by strongly impeding the class differentiation of the peasantry and dooming the bulk of the peasant households to ruin and degradation.

It was in West Bengal that this system of middlemen assumed the greatest proportions. According to Pal, their number in just the one Backerganj district rose to nearly half a million, with the pyramid (excluding the zamindar) usually consisting of eight, often twelve, and occasionally twenty grades on any feudal zamindary estate.[3] Out of the 14 most widespread types of intermediate holders, the following are the most relevant:

1. The *etmander*—the zamindar's authorised rent-collector. He paid the landlord a share of the rent fixed beforehand and was allowed to keep "all revenue in excess of this sum". The etmander was generally a prosperous cultivator who in due course became a professional rent-collector.

2. The *ejaradar*—a prosperous peasant who leased fisheries from the zamindar and sublet them to lower-grade rent-collectors. As a result, a whole hierarchy of parasitic rent-collectors came to the fore, usually from among the prosperous peasants, to whom the immediate producers utilising a river or pond, that is, the fishermen, paid a "fish-rent" (a rent in kind) whose size depended on the number of boats and fishermen or the number and type of fishing nets.

3. The *mandal*—usually a prosperous peasant commonly known as "abadkar". He paid the zamindar a contracted rental for the use of waste land or forest. He developed most of the land, partly by the labour of the members of his family and partly by that of peasants under his influence, and founded a village on it which he gave his name. Here he was mandal or village elder. From time to time, the zamindar and mandal revised the terms of their transaction, but the former never interfered in the relations that the latter maintained with his subtenants. In the beginning, to induce peasants to cultivate the waste land, the mandal took no more rent from them than was necessary to cover his commitments to the zamindar. In time, however, he turned into the fiercest of exploiters. By the 1930s, in effect, the mandal had developed from a prosperous peasant into a professional collector of rent, though in many localities this process had not yet run out its course. According to K. B. Saha, for example, the mandal in Ramgarh was still a ryot, though he was already deriving a profit from the fellow ryots. As a rule, the villages that sprang up on waste lands or in forests were inhabited by peasants of the Santal, Bhumij, Mahato, and other tribes, over whose internal and external relations the mandal gradually seized complete control. It may be interesting to note that in the Silda, Bagri and Bhanjabhum districts mandali rights were purchased by a specially founded protocapitalist enterprise, the Midnapur Zamindari Company. This mandali system, also known as howla and jimba, was widespread throughout Bengal.

We have examined just these three forms of intermediate landownership that relate chiefly to the prosperous (kulak) element among the peasantry, because the economic structure of the Bengali rich peasant's household is of no small significance. In the absence of large enough opportunities for the development of capitalist enterprise run by rich peasants in the Bengali countryside, the wealthier exploiting strata of the peasantry became fused with the system of intermediate rent collection, distorting along colonial lines the course of the peasants' class differentiation common in independent countries because of the development of commodity farming and capitalism. This conclusion is confirmed by the fact that, in substance, an analogous process of the rich peasant's inclusion in the system of extra-economic feudal and semi-feudal plunder of the peasantry was reflected not only in the fragmentation and purchase of private feudal property rights but also in the purchase of the peasants' rights of so-called perpetual tenure. As a result, the mass of cultivators was reduced to the status of subtenants or tenants without rights of the new holder of the permanent title from among rich peasants and moneylenders, who thereby became "ryoti landlords".

It was not always possible to ascertain whether the tenant was a rent-collector or a peasant. Such appellations as, say *jot, jimba* and *patni* stood for either landlord or peasant depending on the locality. Throughout Bengal, for example, a *patnidar* was a rent-collecting estate owner, whereas in Noakhali district zamindars had for a long time permitted common peasants to buy *patni* for a certain share of the rent. In the Feni division nearly all the actual producers possessed patni rights. A system of mixed intermediate land tenure was widespread in Jessore and Backerganj, with the result that members of different classes had intertwining interests in each parcel of land. Besides, we often find that one and the same person could be an intermediate tenure-holder with one set of rights on one parcel of land and a different set on another—sometimes a peasant with perpetual tenure and sometimes even a second-degree subtenant receiving his appropriate share of the rent in all cases.

This historically long process of fragmentation of property rights to rent collection, which encompasses purchase of the tenancy rights of ruined peasants, resulted in an exceedingly close social fusion of rural monetary and merchant capital with feudal landlordism and peasant perpetual tenure as the basic form of exploiting the toiling peasantry, an exceedingly close social fusion of the prosperous section of the peasantry with the feudal and semi-feudal system of parasitic rent collection, and through it also with the class of landlords. In this regard, the Bengali toiling peasantry could not fail to set itself the aim of tearing down this whole exclusive system of feudal and semi-feudal exploitation. Those Indian economists who maintain that nearly 90 per cent of Bengali peasants enjoyed the rights of perpetual and life tenure are, indeed, in deep error.

Let us now go over to the forms and the true content of peasant tenure. It is needless either to set forth or analyse British tenancy acts in Bengal, and not because they failed to play a substantive role, but because their formal aspects are, in general, well enough known. We are concerned with showing the true relationship between the immediate cultivator and the proprietor of the conditions of production, whatever form this relationship may have taken. To begin with, a few illustrations of the conventional nature of the so-called forms of tenancy in Bengal as compared with the truly prevailing economic relations. Under the 1885 Tenancy Act, peasants in Bengal were classified under the following heads:

1. Peasants with the right of tenure, holding land either at a rent fixed in perpetuity or at a rate of rent fixed in perpetuity (perpetual tenant).
2. Peasants with the right of occupancy, inheritance and alienation of their rights, but without a fixed rent rate or fixed rental (occupancy tenant).
3. Peasants with no right of occupancy (temporary tenant).
4. Peasant subtenants or under-ryots.
5. Peasant tenants without rights.

In fact, however, all these categories of tenants established by law could not create even a relative stability in the actual tenancy relations. In Backerganj, for example, a large number of bargadar share-croppers, who had formal rights of tenure, that is, rights of perpetual tenure, were in fact reduced to the status of tenant without rights. In Faridpur, there was a formal division of peasants into those with and without rights of occupancy, but in fact there was no such distinction between them, with all peasants considered tenants at the lord's will, though they did, in many cases, hold the land for a few or more years in succession.

In Backerganj, the vast majority of subtenants, excluding those who paid rent in kind, had a recorded right of perpetual tenure. In many cases, a peasant listed in the cadastre as a perpetual tenant, was in fact a subtenant or under-ryot.

It is quite certain, therefore, that the real situation of some sections of the toiling peasantry did not conform with their recorded rights and legally established place in the Bengali system of tenancy. The actual position of the bulk of the peasants was usually much lower than provided for by their formal rights of tenure.

At the same time, however, the process of class differentiation also operated oppositely, with some sections of tenants rising above the relatively low place they occupied in the tenant hierarchy. Their status hung over them only as a survival which limited their economic initiative. People neither understood nor accepted the distinctions between tenant and subtenant established by law. Often enough, subtenants were far from rightless and, indeed, enjoyed many of the privileges of a peasant with full rights. Large sections of subtenants, who had "made their way in life", gained the right of inheritance and of alienating land. They did so contrary to the law by expropriating this right from ruined perpetual tenants. This was an expression of the peculiar process in which capitalism penetrated the countryside, and of the class differentiation of the peasantry. There was no rigid line of demarcation between a peasant who had the right of occupancy and the subtenant, because one function passed into the other in an unnoticeably subtle way.

In sum, the forms of tenancy relations or of attaching certain rights to one or another type of tenancy were not, in Bengal, a mirror-reflection of the actually prevailing relations of production. The state of affairs was far more complicated. K. B. Saha, a prominent student of the Bengali agrarian system, arrived at the following conclusion upon summing up his study of peasant tenure: "As a result of the gradual process of land being transferred from *bona fide* cultivators to moneylenders and other non-agricultural classes, a considerable number of the former in almost all the districts of the province has been reduced to the position of under-raiyats."[4] He amplified that the ryot is not always the actual cultivator, sometimes others work his land and pay him a rental. Gradually, there indeed emerged a group of "ryot landlords" who were little different from zamindars as concerned participation in the process of farming. They were, in fact, ordinary landlords, and as "ryot landlords" confined themselves only to lending seed to their bargadar share-croppers.

However different the forms of expropriating the peasants' rights of tenure used by the prosperous peasant and rural moneylender, they may all be summed up as follows: in the cadastre, a lot may be registered as belonging to a perpetual tenant, but that perpetual tenant has already been reduced to the state of a share-cropper without rights, while his right of perpetual tenure has been appropriated by a moneylender or a rich peasant. Saha observed that "in recent times, there has been a growing tendency on the part of moneylenders to purchase the holdings of raiyats when the latter fail to repay their debts. These lands, after they are thus purchased, are, as a rule, given to the former tenants on the *barga* system."[5]

It follows that the extreme diversity and the intertwining of various forms of tenure contrary to the true content of the economic relations between those who cultivated the land and those who owned it—whether zamindars, non-cultivating tenants, moneylenders, or rich peasants—were nothing but a product of a peculiar development of commodity farming and capitalism, and, indeed, a peculiar type of class stratification of the peasantry. At the top, this development of commodity and money relations expressed itself, along with other forms, in a concentration of land in the hands of feudal magnates, whereas at the bottom it led to a concentration of land and of the peasants' rights of tenure in the hands of an exploiting prosperous and moneylending peasant elite which, considering the slowing down of capitalist development, inevitably became contiguous with the feudal rulers of the countryside. The economic thrust behind the appropriation of the tenancy rights of peasants and the latter's reduction in fact to the state of share-croppers without rights amounted to a formally legal entrenchment of the right of peasant exploiters to a share of the cultivator's surplus product and a legalisation of methods of exploitation under cover of various juridical forms of peasant tenancy.

Now, let us turn to the actual relations of production and their forms as the framework for the farming carried on by the bulk of Bengali peasants. But let us make clear at once that the available factual material is insufficient for any exhaustive study. Whatever the rights of tenure of poor and middle peasants may have been, a considerable number of them were share-croppers in fact. Most such share-croppers had their own livestock, implements and labour power, but had no land. A smaller portion had nothing or next to nothing save their labour power. In the former case, the share-cropper is of the precapitalist type, and in the latter, we see a "direct transition to capitalism".[6] And slow transition from the former type to the latter was the prevailing trend of the economic evolution. The former type was still predominant, still widespread, but the movement was distinctly directed towards the latter. Though this movement was accompanied by appalling pauperisation, the economic trend, however slow, was capitalist in type. The average Bengali peasant had his own implements, his own seed and livestock, but had no land. The merging of his labour power and implements with the land monopolised by the feudal classes was put into effect through various forms of share-cropping.

What were these forms?

1. The *utbandi* system (in Nadia, Murshidabad, Jessore). Here, the share-cropper was a tenant without rights. The size of his parcel was inconstant. The rate of rent was established each year and, as a rule, at the will of the landlord. At the end of the farming season, the share-cropper could renounce part or all of his parcel. Similarly, after harvesting, the landlord could evict him. The rent depended either on the fertility of the soil or the size of the harvest, but the landlord had the final say in the matter. Land worked under this system was usually poor or inconvenient. In Nadia and Jessore, there were six or seven variations of this system. As a rule, rent was paid in kind and amounted to from one-third to two-thirds of the harvest. This system enabled the landlord to improve inconvenient and poor land with the share-croppers' labour, whereupon the latter was evicted shortly before the time when the utbandi share-cropper became entitled to claim the right of

perpetual tenure. This system enabled landlords to appropriate the mediaeval equivalent of the differential rent by evicting the lot of share-croppers who had improved the land and leasing it to another lot on far more onerous terms for the latter. This manner of boosting accumulation was practised by landed proprietors all over Bengal.

2. The *sanja* system (rice-producing areas in West Bengal). Here, share-croppers were chiefly subtenants. Frequently, the system also encompassed peasants possessing life or perpetual tenure. The sanja share-cropper was often a peasant whose land had been taken over by default by a usurer landlord. This explains the spread of this share-cropping system among perpetual tenants. "When the possession of the holding has thus been secured," says K. B. Saha, "it is given back to the former occupant on the basis of a produce rent."[7] Under this system, the share-cropper paid a strictly fixed share of the harvest as rent. Local researchers noted that compared with cash rent, under this system the rent, mostly in kind, was "exorbitantly high": usually one-third to two-thirds of the harvest, and sometimes even higher. Its spread in West Bengal may be traced to natural calamities and frequent crop failures. With a strictly fixed rent irrespective of output, the landlord always received his share no matter how poor the harvest.

The economic thrust of this type of share-cropping was that it assured the dominant classes appropriation of the cultivator's surplus product in kind during rice crop failures when the price of rice was high, yielding a high profit in a setting of sharply fluctuating prices. This type of share-cropping was also practised in East Bengal (in jute-producing areas) where its role as an instrument of exploiting a favourable market was, probably, no less significant.

3. The *barga* system (jute- and rice-producing areas in East Bengal) of share-cropping was widespread in nearly the entire province. In West Bengal it was known as *ghagchasi*. The landowner usually claimed one-third of the harvest, and as much as half the harvest if, as occurred on rare occasions, the producer was loaned seed and fertiliser.

K. B. Saha and a few other scholars note that the barga rent was exceedingly high compared with the cash rent. Available material shows that most barga share-croppers were ruined perpetual tenants. Under the 1928 Tenancy Amendment Act, a bargadar could acquire rights of perpetual occupancy only with the consent of the landlord and through the court upon expiry of a 12-year tenure as share-cropper. In effect, a bargadar had no rights. He could be evicted upon bringing in the harvest, with the land being let to another share-cropper. The landlord's fear that the bargadar who had been working his land for a number of years might stake out claims to it usually caused mass evictions and re-letting of the land to a new lot of share-croppers. Frequently, peasants with rights of perpetual tenure had holdings that were too small to feed their family and rented barga land. Thereby, they became dual tenants.

Saha wrote: "When the bargadar is an honest and efficient tenant, he is allowed to cultivate the same land for a number of years"[8], thus gradually acquiring the right of perpetual tenure. As a result, his legal status was brought into line with the true nature of his farm. It may also be taken as an established fact that this form of share-cropping predominated on estates belonging to landlords, rich peasants and moneylenders given over mainly to the production of food crops and vegetables.

This type of share-cropping served a two-fold economic purpose: payment of chiefly a rent in kind ensured the forcible spread in East Bengal of jute as a commodity crop and helped to maintain it at the desired level; at the same time, it gave landlords an opportunity to exploit the market to best advantage by requiring cash rent when this was more profitable and capitalising the rent in kind in the event of a crisis.

4. The *duna* system of share-cropping was mainly employed on state-managed estates, the *khasmahal*. Its distinctive feature was that share-croppers were usually loaned seed. This was done to attract the most indigent peasants to working state lands and forests. So-called forest settlements sprang up on this basis, whose inhabitants engaged in farming, on the one hand, and provided the state with timber, on the other. This system was applied mostly on government estates that had once belonged to zamindars expropriated for defaulting taxes. Tax collector James Peddie, a witness before the Royal Commission on Agriculture, referred to this system as follows: "In the Government *khasmahal* area . . . the *duna* system prevails. If I take

10 maunds of paddy in July, in December, repay 20 maunds. If it is not paid, then I am liable to pay 30 maunds in March, and if not paid then 37.5 maunds in July. If I still fail to pay, a mortgage is executed, the consideration money being 37.5 maunds converted into cash at the market rate and interest will be charged at 37.5 per cent on that. The result of this iniquitous system has meant that whole villages of people have lost all their lands, even their homestead lands."[9]

Those were the main types of share-cropping imposed on poor and medium sections of the peasantry. No matter how they differed in form and terms of rental, they were in economic content an oppressive, mainly precapitalist type of share-cropping. The upper section of the middle peasantry sought to escape the abuses of the landlord and the forcible crop rotation that went with the rent in kind by paying a cash rent. This gave it a certain amount of economic independence and created albeit barely perceptible elements of the métayer system, a transitional type of share-cropping. But for the bulk of the peasantry, share-cropping retained all its elements of oppression and extortion. N. M. Pal admitted that "the bulk of the people have a semi-serf like position".[10]

Some sources reveal that in a few districts of Bengal increasing numbers of serfs and slaves, called *chakran* and *golam,* were exploited on the landed estates of landlords, moneylenders and rich peasants. Lacking conclusive material on this score, we can only register the one-time growth of this factor.

Speaking of the size and the forms of rent, we proceed from the fact that rent in kind was predominant all over Bengal. Payment of rent in products, Pal writes, was practised throughout Bengal and was usual for the *jot* and *patni,* that is, the highest section of peasants holding rights of perpetual tenure. All the more must this be true of the share-croppers without rights, who made up a considerable mass of the peasantry.

Peasants who had not yet in fact lost rights of perpetual tenure or were on the road to prosperous farming, paid a more or less stable rent, whereas the bulk of the peasants (who were share-croppers without rights) lacked even palliative means of restricting landlord abuses.

We need not here examine that aspect of British tenancy legislation in Bengal which governed any possible increase or reduction of rent. All scholars point out that these regulations were not observed in practice, and that a tenant's application to a court of law usually led to results that were contrary to the desired ones because, to quote tax collector James Peddie, "it is so hard to obtain justice". Furthermore, in effect, there were no established rent rates and, as a rule, the rates could be changed at the will of the landlords. In some districts, there were about 15 different rent rates. The immediate producer, the virtually enslaved share-cropper who was the most widespread figure in any Bengali village, was compelled "to pay the rent which his landlord imposed when he let his land to the tenant" (Para. 42 of the 1885 Tenancy Act).

In many cases, the landlord set different rent rates for different strips of land let to one and the same share-cropper. Pal notes that rent rates could range from 1 to 10-12 rupees per acre for a subtenant, from 1.5 to 14 rupees for a perpetual tenant, and ran to infinity for the share-cropper.

It should be borne in mind that in Bengal permanently settled zamindars paid the government (on average for the province) a tax of something like 10 annas per acre, that is, about 20-25 per cent of the lowest, and about 3.5 per cent of the highest, rent extorted by them from the peasants. The figures cited by researchers concerning the rent exacted by landlords cannot be considered wholly authentic. They are greatly minimised and do not account for the entire sum extorted by rent-collectors at all levels right up to the zamindar. Besides, researchers systematically confused the tax and the rent, and vice versa, or, still more frequently, mechanically misapplied the notion of capitalist rental to the economic life of the oppressed share-cropper. While one group of researchers, chiefly British, maintained that the rent encompassed only a part—between one-third and one-half—of the producer's net output, another group, chiefly local, maintained that it embraced between one-third and one-half of the harvest, that is, of the gross output. No critical verification of this data can be made owing to insufficient records. It is safe to assume, however, that in the case of poor and middle share-croppers the rent, the landlord's levies, the usury interest and merchant profit combined, as a rule amounted to the entire surplus product of the immediate producer even in rich years and sometimes included part of his "wage", irrespective of his formal rights of tenure. It follows that for the share-croppers rent was still a "normal form of surplus product in general", that is, an oppressive, pre-capitalist rent.

* * *

Landlord cesses held a special place as an additional means of exploiting the mass of peasants. They were so great and so numerous that it was sometimes hard to say whether the rent was really the main source of the landlord's income. The number of various cesses reached a total of twenty. "It must not, however, be supposed," Pal writes, "that exactions of cesses are sporadic and particular but in fact they are chronic and almost universal phenomena... But although the tenants now fully understand that these exactions are illegal, they usually pay such demands without protest, in order to avoid the displeasure of the landlord and his amlas."[11]

As a rule, the burden of these cesses fell on the most impoverished and rightless groups of peasants. Prosperous peasants usually shifted the burden to their subtenants and share-croppers. The 1928 Act defined as legal only the following cesses: 1) the cess paid for the alienation of rights to land tenure; 2) the road cess and 3) the public work cess (canals, ponds). In practice, however, zamindars in many parts of Bengal extorted cesses over and above those established by law. The most oppressive levy was the cess exacted for the alienation of rights to land tenure, which aggravated the already predatory and usurious credits, etc. The same Act established that those who paid a rent in kind should pay the zamindar 20 per cent of the sum of the transaction involving alienation of perpetual or life tenure, while those who paid a cash rent could replace this cess by paying a sum equivalent to five years' rent. When exchanging holdings or their part the participants in the exchange were obliged to pay their landlords 5 per cent of the price of the exchanged land each or an eighteen-months' rent.

Now, let us go over to the condition of the peasantry and the state of peasant agriculture.

More than any other province in India, Bengal is exposed to the effects of the south-westerly monsoon. Average annual sedimentation is roughly 2,000 mm, out of which three-quarters fall to the May-August monsoon period. Territorially, however, the sedimentation is most nonuniformly distributed: 3,600 mm in Jalpaiguri district and up to 1,400 mm in Malda. Owing to floods caused by the Ganges and the Brahmaputra and their numerous tributaries, and the relatively high level of the subsoil water and the absence of efficient drainage, this nonuniform distribution of sedimentation, concentrated within a relatively short space of time, causes tremendous flooding and natural calamities in a number of divisions of the province, including swamping and salination of the soil. In areas of low sedimentation where irrigation works all but non-existent, and also in the foothills, there were systematic droughts, entailing loss of harvest and livestock, and followed by famine and epidemics. Naturally, the mass of the labouring peasantry was unable to combat these natural, but in their result socially conditioned, calamities by any organised and extensive protective measures. The state apparatus of British capital, on the other hand, had no stake in organising and effecting any large-scale irrigation and land improvement works, and did so only when and where this became unavoidable and profitable for finance capital.

The material of the Royal Commission on Agriculture enables us to determine that for at least two or three months each year the bulk of the labouring peasantry in Bengal dropped out of the process of production owing to the tremendous incidence of tropical malaria, which afflicted the population of whole districts, even divisions. Malaria epidemics, which were also socially conditioned factors in result and scale, were not combatted by any serious preventive or curative measures, not to speak of the fact that the wasted constitution of the labouring ryot, with the resulting low resistance, was badly susceptible to malaria and all sorts of other epidemics. It will not be amiss to note in this connection that in 1929 and 1930 the provincial government of Bengal, 75 per cent of its budget consisting of revenue from agriculture, chiefly from peasant farming, spent nearly 1.6 million rupees for irrigation works and drainage, 13 million for the maintenance of its governmental apparatus, 3.8 million for public health, 2.5 million for agriculture, 4.5 million rupees for salaries and pensions to retired British officials, and as much as 35 million rupees for the maintenance of prisons, the police and the judiciary. Naturally, productive outlays in the budget of the provincial government were the first to go down during the 1929-1933 crisis.

In this context, we must not overlook the so-called winter-time unemployment of Bengali peasants. The material of the Royal Commission and certain other sources show that even in the rice-producing areas, with rice being a most labour-intensive crop, the population was employed only for three or four months. It was almost entirely idle in the remaining nearly eight months. These three or four months of work in the rice-producing areas, however, were a period of extreme strain for all members of the peasant's family, owing to the specificity of the crop, its rapid vegetation period, and the tropical climate. Draught animals, which peasants usually sold after the working season was over and which they bought again at the beginning of the next season (thus stimulating profiteering and money-lending), were also badly overworked. The small size and low productivity of peasant households, which made it impossible to use the achievements of technology and agronomy in cultivating this labour-intensive crop, inevitably caused extreme overstrain of labour power. A peasant's working season in the country's rice-growing areas lasted three months with one rice harvest, from five to seven months with two harvests, and nearly eight months on mixed farms that cultivated both rice and jute.

Some general data on Bengali agriculture for 1931:[12] thirty-seven million or 77 per cent of the population in the province lived on agriculture; 30.5 million were cultivators, 4.3 million were debt slaves or farm labourers, and the rest were landlords and non-cultivating tenants. Cultivated land totalled some 24 million acres, out of which 1.2 million acres was irrigated. The irrigated area was divided as follows: government canals irrigated 20,700 acres; private canals 191,600; ponds 683,100; wells 31,800, and other sources 35,800 acres. In 1927/28, 4,159,000 acres yielded more than one harvest. Nearly 5,000,000 acres usually lay fallow. Despite the high population density, the colossal agrarian overpopulation, and the extraordinarily crowded parcels due to the prevalence of large-scale landlord estates, the exploitative role of the latter was so high that the impoverished peasant masses were unable to develop some 6.5 million acres of available uncultivated arable land. Useless land totalled 19.2 million acres, and the area under forests (a monopoly of landlords and imperialists) 4.6 million acres.

Bengal's main agricultural crops were rice, jute, rape and mustard seed, oil-bearing plants, sugar cane and tea. Areas under the chief agricultural crops made up the following percentages of India's total area under these crops:

Rice	25.9	Flax	3.3
Jute	86.3	Sesame	3.1
Tea	25.2	Maize	1.5
Oil-bearing		Barley	1.1
plants	11.5	Wheat	0.4
Sugar cane	8.1	Cotton	0.3

As we see, Bengali agriculture accounted for a large proportion of the agriculture of all India, especially as regards rice, tea, sugar cane and oil-bearing plants. Eighty-four per cent of the crop area in the province was given over to rice and about 13 per cent to jute. For jute, Bengal ranked first and, in effect, held a monopoly place, and this not only on the internal Indian market, but also in world agriculture.

Throughout the first quarter of the 20th century, jute production increased most rapidly, as illustrated by the harvest and export indexes below:

	Harvest index	*Export index*
1892—1897	100	100
1901—1906	129	127
1911—1915	154	127
1923—1924	160	182

Production and export of jute reached the highest level ever just after the First World War, whereupon it fell into a state of stagnation and then also a long crisis, which lasted until the mid-1930s. The considerable growth of jute production was systematically spurred by the world market and the expansion of the jute industry in Calcutta and Dundee (Scotland), whose demand for jute kept growing. To meet the demand, British finance capital, like the feudal merchant and usury elite of the

Bengali village, forced poor and middle peasants, chiefly by methods of extra-economic compulsion, the introduction of obligatory crops and obligatory crop rotation, and using the tenancy system, taxation, and their indebtedness to moneylenders, to take up cultivation of jute.

The Bengali peasantry did not have an absolutely one-crop agriculture either of rice or jute. Rice growing predominated in all parts of the province, combined to one extent or another with the cultivation of jute. This is borne out by the following figures (in per cent of the total value of the agricultural output in 1921):

	Rice	*Jute*
Midnapur	91	2
Bankura	90	1
Rajshahi	75	21
Backerganj	68	3
Noakhali	68	5
Jessore	66	10
Nadia	61	—
Faridpur	58	21
Mymensingh	57	31
Tippera	56	28
Dacca	44	29

Jute production was greatest in the following six districts: Mymensingh, Tippera, Dacca, Rangpur, Faridpur and Pabna.

None of the available material offers any clue to the magnitude of peasant land use in the context of rural class differentiation. Local statistics, and British statistics as well, was usually confined to mean figures for divisions and districts.

The average size of a perpetual tenant's holdings (in acres) was:[13]

Bankura	1.86	Dacca	1.52
Midnapur	1.29	Mymensingh	2.67
Jessore	1.78	Rajshahi	2.20
Backerganj	2.51	Noakhali	2.30
Tippera	1.90		

K. B. Saha maintained that, as a rule, cultivators paying a cash rent had larger holdings, and those paying rents in kind had smaller ones. He referred to figures submitted by tax-collectors to draw the conclusion that in Faridpur the average acreage of a cash-rent-paying peasant was 1.78, while peasants paying rent in kind held 0.63 acres. The respective figures for Backerganj were 2.54 and 1.48.

Ever increasing overlapping and fragmentation of peasant holdings were observed everywhere. In Dacca, share-croppers usually had no more than one-third to one-half acre, and plots of 0.04 to 0.20 acre were frequent in Murshidabad. In Faridpur, the size of a share-cropper's holding ranged from 1/160 to half an acre. Bourgeois economists traced the overlapping and remoteness of plots to the influence of Hindoo laws of inheritance and excessive population growth, which they claimed to be outstripping production growth and also the development of new land. Speaking of population growth, material published by the Royal Asiatic Society (March 1933) reveals the falsehood of the Malthusian notions nursed by bourgeois economists and politicians (Table 10).

Table 10

Population and Production Indices in India's Agriculture

	1900-1905	1910-1915	1920-1925	1926-1931
Population	100	107	108	120
Sown area				
Unweighted index	100	124	119	132
Weighted index	100	131	134	150
Production				
Unweighted index	100	129	125	127
Weighted index	100	134	137	141

In short, in the first 30-odd years of the 20th century, production in India grew at a faster rate than the population. Consequently, the reasons for the impoverishment of the village masses should legitimately be traced to the social system which conditioned the appropriation of the results of production by the exploiting classes in town and countryside jointly with imperialism.

According to N. M. Pal's estimates, an ordinary peasant family of four could maintain a more or less bearable existence only if it had 8 to 10 acres of land and an average annual income of 540 rupees, and this provided it owed nothing to the moneylender. The actual average peasant holding in Bengal, however, was 2.5 acres, the income 146 rupees per family, and the average debt 50 to 70 rupees.

Far more profoundly elaborated data on this issue was cited for Jessore to the Royal Commission on Agriculture by tax collector Momen, who also compared it to the data cited by Major Jack for Faridpur. Momen's data was obtained in a selective study of 50 villages totalling 1,643 families or 10,019 persons (Table 11).

Table 11

Selective Study of 50 Villages in Jessore*

	Per capita income, rupees	Per capita debt, rupees	Families, number	Families, %%	Compared with Faridpur, %%
In comfort	80	0	235	15	49
Below comfort	58	8	552	32	28
Above want (on edge of starvation)	50	12	555	33	18
Starving	35	30	331	20	4

* *RCAI*, Vol. IV, Evidence taken in Bengal, p. 323.

Momen drew the following conclusion: "The condition of the Jessore peasant is so miserable and his power of recoupment so small having no spare capital, he finds himself stranded whenever there is a failure of crops or whenever one out of two heads of cattle dies. He has to borrow at a high rate of interest, the average . . . being 25 per cent. And once in debt, he can never extricate himself, and finally becomes a landless labourer. The resistance of Bengali tillers is very low. The average annual income of an agriculturist in Bengal is about Rs. 200 for a family of four. If we take 30 per cent of the agriculturist population to be well off and in affluent circumstances, the income of the 70 per cent will be considerably less than the average given. The cost of food and clothing of a convict in jail is about Rs. 58 per year, so that the majority of the cultivators in Bengal have to maintain themselves and their families on much less than what the Government spends on the food and clothing alone of a prisoner."[14]

The extreme poverty of the bulk of peasant farms exploited by an array of large and small semi-feudal and semi-capitalist exploiters who were themselves subjected to systematic and increasing direct and indirect pressure of the imperialists, was reflected above all in the appallingly low technical structure of Bengali peasant farming. Saha estimates that the cost of the implements of an average peasant household was never more than 13-15 rupees. According to Momen's estimates, a sharecropper's property, including land and livestock, did not exceed 100 rupees—a sum that was usually insufficient to meet his debts when the moneylender wanted to foreclose. Hence the inherited bondslavery.

According to the Banking Enquiry Committee, in 1931 the Bengali peasants' debt to moneylenders was 1,000 million rupees. Later, owing to the increasing economic crisis, prices fell by about a half and the actual burden of the debt consequently doubled. This was admitted not only by local economists but also by officials of the Anglo-Indian government. Suffice it to say that the decline in the value of 1931 Bengali jute exports as compared with average in the preceding 10 years amounted to 57 per cent, that of rice exports to 54, and of tea to 38. The extraordinary spread of primitive predatory forms of capital in the Bengali countryside was stimulated by the traditional anti-industrial policy of the imperialists, which compelled native capital to go about its primary accumulation by feudal methods of exploiting the peasantry and to resort to feudal-landlord territorialisation of local financiers and industrial capitalists. At the same time, the predominance of small-scale parcel farming in a setting of large landed property created highly favourable conditions for merchant and usury capital which acted as the agent of British capital in the Bengali countryside.

How closely British finance capital in Bengal was fused with merchant's and usurer's capital may be illustrated by the following data. In the jute-producing areas, operating through a series of local and British middlemen, the Imperial Bank of India controlled something like a hundred moneylending offices with a circulating capital of nearly 100 million rupees. Formally organised along the lines of joint-stock societies, these lending offices really had no substantial share capital. Their basic joint-stock capital amounted to a mere 100,000 rupees, that is, to just 1/1,000 of the functioning circulating capital. The huge current capital of the lending offices, which operated on the security of the peasants' harvest and partly also on land mortgages (more precisely, on mortgages of patta land grants), consisted of the deposits of landlords, moneylenders, the bourgeois intelligentsia, and of loans from local and British banks. The purpose of these offices was exceedingly simple: by granting the immediate producer oppressive loans covered by the harvest, they were able to buy up jute and rice at low monopoly prices irrespective of the cost of peasant production. To say nothing of the profit they made on price differences and market speculation, their usurious monetary and credit transactions yielded the joint owners of moneylending offices a staggering profit. The average annual interest on deposits stood at 24 per cent, while loans to the immediate producers were granted at a 112-per cent annual interest.

Naturally, Bengal had no fixed interest. Various rates of interest existed in different districts and also varied for members of different classes and social groups of peasants. The lowest interest ranged from 10 to 37.5 per cent and the highest from 37.5 to 300 per cent per annum. Short-term loans were usually granted at 1 anna per 1 rupee monthly, that is, at 75 per cent per annum. In the absence of laws similar to the Punjabi law forbidding transfer of land to non-agricultural castes, Bengali moneylenders did not, as a rule, require regular payment of interest. They preferred interest to accumulate, so as to extort compound interest and, in the long run, to foreclose on the peasant's property. But seizure of these rights did not necessarily lead to the tenant's eviction from the land he tilled. "Here again profit is so easily made without his taking the trouble to farm,"

Faridpur tax-collector Burrows testified, "that he adopts the easy course of admitting the late ryot as his *adhidar*."[15]

As a result, the reduction of the perpetual tenant to the state of a share-cropper without rights was accompanied by the conversion of the moneylender into a rent-collector, into one more intermediate landlord. The nature of usury debt was parasitic throughout. "Agricultural indebtedness in Bengal," Saha wrote, "is mostly the outcome of loans not for production, but for consumption."[16] Saha refrained from saying that these loans were concluded not for peasant consumption but for consumption by the dominant classes, raising their incomes in the form of rent, interest, payment of old debts, cost of court litigations, landlord cesses, and the like. Hence, by the way, the growing importance of the so-called freezing of usury capital. Tax-collector James Peddie observed: "Cultivators... are a prey to anyone who has a little money to lend ... There are a number of men I know who now rank as zamindars who twenty or thirty years ago were nobodies."[17]

And here is how K. B. Saha refers to the methods of Bengali moneylenders: "The *mahajan* is not really anxious for the realisation of the loan, so long as he thinks that the borrower has enough assets. When the period of the bond which is executed at the time of taking the loan is about to expire, he takes another bond for the original sum borrowed together with all the interest that is accumulated. In this way, the debt goes on increasing, and successive bonds are executed until the *mahajan* thinks that it is no longer safe to continue the policy. He then institutes a suit for the realisation of the loan, and brings the holding of the borrower to sale in execution of the Court's decree. Often he himself purchases it and makes a settlement with the former occupant either on a fixed produce rent, or on the barga system. In this manner, the financing of the agriculturists by the village moneylender often reduces them from the position of occupancy raiyats to that of mere bargadars."[18]

Bengal had a highly ramified network of merchant's capital, which was closely related to usurer's capital and landlordism. Village middlemen (beopari, aratdars, dalals, arthia, etc.) were financed by urban traders and local banks against bonds covered by export crops. The juridically established right of foreclosing on mortgaged peasant harvests was an effective means of covering bonds issued by small village middlemen for credits which they received from large traders and firms. Large urban trading firms engaged chiefly in financing the carting of export crops from remote areas to the seaports. As a rule, they had a fairly large network of purchasing agencies and branches all over the province connected with village traders. These urban trading firms were, in turn, financed by large local banks and British export companies that controlled India's foreign trade.

A conspicuous part in purchasing jute from small village traders and its delivery to British firms was played by Indian packing and pressing firms, which took over the bulk of the jute harvest. A roughly similar monopoly on the purchase of the rice harvest from small village traders was held by rice milling and scouring firms. According to the exceedingly modest estimates of local economists, the hierarchy of distribution agencies, consisting of eight links on the rice market and of up to 12 on the jute-market, seized from 30 to 50 per cent of the ultimate market price, while the share of the immediate producer almost never exceeded 50 per cent. The price of commodities produced by Bengali share-croppers, depressed by the crisis and imperialism's monetary policy, increasingly included an inflated proportion of the rent, interest and merchant profit. This is why Momen did not exaggerate when he said that the actual cultivator did not benefit from any increase in the price of his produce. Conversely, however, the bulk of any drop in prices fell on the shoulders of the labouring ryot. He received nothing or next to nothing at times of high prices for raw materials and foods, but paid heavily for any price decline. This had an especially disastrous effect at the time of the 1929-1933 worldwide economic crisis.

Unlike some of the other provinces, more backward also in industrial terms, Bengal, being a world supplier of jute, jute products, rice and tea, had a ramified system of overland and river transport. Its railways added up to some 3,500 miles, navigable river lines and canals to 2,000 miles, and hard-surface roads linking the main markets dealing in raw materials and manufactured goods to 3,500 miles. Naturally, being a monopoly of British finance capital, this ramified transport system was a powerful instrument for exploiting the labouring peasantry. Material of the Royal Commission shows how profitable these means of communication had been for British finance capital and how great was the exploitation of the immediate producer they engendered by extortionate shipping and railway rates imposed on him in addition to the plunder practised by his feudal overlords, moneylenders and merchants.

Bengal had a fairly large capitalist cottage-type artisan industry: first of all weaving (more than 200,000 hand looms), silk reeling, silk weaving, pottery and copper casting. Directly or indirectly, the mass of Bengali artisans was subordinated to British finance or local industrial capital through a network of merchant's and usurer's capital which acted as its agent. The meagre surviving remnants of the former crafts worked partly for the local urban market, to reach which they could never bypass the sinister figure of the non-cultivating tenant and moneylender.

Artisans were pitilessly exploited by merchant's and usurer's capital. As a rule, craftsmen received no wages, not even the minimum required for their sustenance, and were, in addition, downtrodden and rightless. And though some witnesses called before the Royal Commission on Agriculture tried to portray the state of the Bengali artisan in rosy colours and called the attention of the Commission to various improvements in artisan production, all their proposals boiled down to nothing but bureaucratic and police projects whose ultimate purpose it was to intensify even more the semi-feudal, semi-capitalist exploitation of artisans and craftsmen. Bengali economists noted that wholesale seizure by merchants and moneylenders of the sphere of crediting, supplying raw materials to, and marketing the production of artisans was a patent fact. Some crafts, especially cotton weaving, silk reeling and silk weaving, had fallen under the control of the mahajan, who no longer confined himself to the sphere of exchange and went on to seize control over production, becoming an industrial capitalist and reducing craftsmen to labourers receiving a day wage or piece rates known as *bani.* Saha notes that the distinctive feature of the period in question was that the mahajan was increasingly becoming a businessman.

Nearly all local students of Bengal's land system observed

that each link in the landlord chain was able, thanks to its monopoly position in relation to the immediate producer, to systematically use the so-called rights of seigniory. Saha writes, for example: "According to established law and custom the zamindar or tax-collector is at the same time the judge; this gives him the right to use power and to sit in judgement over his subjects like a feudal lord. And though the semi-sovereign power of the zamindar was curtailed by the British administration, fiscal power has remained part of the zamindar's prerogatives... The zamindary regime is based chiefly on a parasitical consumption of the wealth produced by the working people. Wealth is distributed on the basis of domination and subjugation or according to the principle of power and custom ...The ryot is not only a tenant but also a subject of the zamindar. The zamindar maintains his power in the eyes of his tenants, and this helps to maintain discipline within the estate; for this reason tenants are forbidden to apply to a court of law without the zamindary permission."[19]

Daniel Hamilton, a liberal reformist and a foe of the zamindary permanent settlement system, wrote the following of the Bengali peasant's position before the law: "It is no use talking of independence while the people are not independent of the mahajan, and it is no use talking of Dominion Status, while the Status of the mass is the status of the serf."[20] It will not be amiss to note that this indignant but truthful description of the condition of the zamindar's subjects elicited an outraged reaction among feudal magnates. Speaking before the Legislative Council of Bengal, one of them said: "The British government will be well-advised to beware of agrarian socialism. In Bengal the permanent settlement has proved to be a lasting barrier between the State and Bolshevism. Permanent settlement is the guarantee against Leninism."

In this connection, we would do well to look into the question of caste oppression in Bengal. Certainly, the impact and importance of caste distinctions were great, especially in the rural communities, and this not only among Hindoo but also among Muslim peasants. Caste distinctions also affected the working class. And they existed in the midst of the dominant class, inasmuch as its ranks had been penetrated by local capitalists and landlords. Still, the market economy and the development of capitalism had a levelling effect, breaking down caste partitions, altering the economic substance of the caste system and the caste-imposed inheritance of trade or craft. The 1921 census showed that frequently large sections of a caste in Bengal crossed the border lines set by the caste system in their way of life, economic nature, and occupation (Table 12).[21]

Table 12

Occupations Per Thousand Workers

Caste	Caste occupations	Non-caste occupations	
		Agriculture	Other occupations
Kumbhakar	691	211	98
Barui	553	297	150
Dhoba	505	344	151
Napit	485	343	172
Jugi	435	354	211
Karmakar	397	289	314
Chamar and Muchi	284	304	412
Goala	250	460	290
Baidya	190	377	433
Bhuimali	204	405	391
Brahman	188	401	411

Saha records the fact that the erosion of castes in Bengal had gone a long way. Among selected castes, inherited caste occupations were engaged in by only 38 per cent, while 34 per cent went into agriculture and 28 per cent into other occupations. But though the caste system was in a state of erosion, the struggle against caste oppression and for the abolition of castes was a most serious objective of the revolutionary peasant movement, and likewise a crucial demand in the agrarian programme of the democratic forces.

We would do well to scrutinise the population movement in connection with the general trend of Bengal's economic evolution. This is doubly important because the specific demographic changes in India are often invoked as an argument in favour of anti-Marxist "agrarianist" principles being prevalent in the economic evolution of the colonial countryside, with India portrayed as a country that is allegedly turning more and more agrarian.

Table 13

Population Movement in Bengal

	Population size, mlns	Growth of population %%	Employed in agriculture %%	Employed in industry %%
1872	34.6	—	52.8	47.2
1881	37.0	+6.7	53.8	46.2
1891	39.8	+7.5	63.2	36.8
1901	42.8	+7.7	75.5	24.5
1911	46.3	+8.0	75.4	24.6
1921	47.5	+2.8	77.3	22.7

Let us see how matters stood in Bengal. For all of half a century, the peculiar economic development of the province saw the population employed in agriculture growing more rapidly than the urban population in both physical and relative terms (Table 13). Certainly, this was due above all to the ruin of crafts and of the middle-sized towns of craftsmen and traders of the old Moghul Bengal under the impact of colonial-capitalist penetration. This trend changed for the first time in Bengal's history in 1921-1931, when, given an overall population growth of 7.3 per cent (very low, being half that of Britain and one-quarter that of the USSR), the urban population increased by 15.6 and the rural by 6.7 per cent.

The emergence of large industries in medium-sized and small-sized towns in India, and notably in Bengal, essentially reflected the movement of the economy along capitalist lines, and this in a country that served Britain as an agrarian and raw-material appendage. As colony of British imperialism, India's road to capitalist development was exceedingly long and slow. The growth of the agrarian population was a reflection of a peculiar development of capitalism rather than of an absence of capitalist development. By taking the increasing agrarian overpopulation as a sign of the country's "agrarianisation" and by thereby mistakenly inferring that India was turning into an exclusively agricultural country rather than the other way round—form an agrarian land into an agrarian-industrial one (despite the survival and even consolidation of its colonial dependence)—the devotees of the "agrarianisation" theory fell prey to a narodnik (populist) type of error.

Since in Bengal we see a province where feudal survivals and classic absentee landlordism were more deeply rooted than elsewhere, the place of wage labour in agriculture is of special interest. Yet, the data on this score are meagre. According to figures cited by Saha from the 1921 census, Bengal had something like 2 million farm labourers. This did not include labourers employed on plantations in the north and north-east of the province, nor the many salaried servants of the feudal lords.

The vast majority of wage labourers were seasonal. Farm labourers, Saha notes, were "mainly local people", landless peasants or peasants with too little land to feed them, whose subsistence depended on sporadic sale of their labour power. Out of every hundred peasants in Faridpur, Saha observes, 35 grew all their own food, 40 bought food since they preferred growing jute to rice, while 25 sold their labour power to make a living. These figures, Saha adds, are typical of the entire province. But who hired labour power?

Nearly every Bengali landlord, and this also goes for the inferior landlord, set aside some land for his own use, cultivating food crops and vegetables for personal consumption. This land was worked partly by hired labourers and partly by share-croppers of a type transitional to capitalism. Though most of the land held by moneylenders was usually worked by barga or sanja share-croppers, part of it, especially the household land, was cultivated by wage labour.[22] There is no information about Bengali rich peasants also employing wage labour. But it is safe to assume from the material of the Royal Commission that rich peasants, especially in rice-producing and suburban zones, maintained a larger wage force than landlords and moneylenders. Among ordinary peasants, Saha points out, regular use of wage labour was made only by those who held relatively large holdings, and also by those who had no able-bodied adults in the family to cultivate their parcel. At harvest time, however, many of those who could afford it, evidently rich peasants above all, resorted to wage labour.

All sources note that there was fairly large annual migration of manpower within the province. And there is no reason to ascribe this migration in all cases to the greater pressure of feudal survivals and low earnings in some areas. Since nearly all the land in the province was monopolised by semi-feudal landlords and since working conditions on rice and jute farms were relatively the same, it is evident that these motivations played no more than a secondary role and were fully applicable only in the case of suburban farms, vegetable-growing, partly forestry and fishing, and chiefly village industries such as processing, scouring, pressing, packing and carting rice or jute.

The considerable migration of manpower within the boundaries of rice and jute growing was in many ways due to the order of the sowing and, still more, that of the harvesting. Thousands of peasants from Dacca, Faridpur and Mymensingh, which were mainly jute areas, migrated to Bankura to harvest the winter crop of rice. On the other hand, large bands of the most indigent members of the Santali and Barui tribes left Bankura each year to help with the harvest in Hooghly and Burdwan. In the east and south-east of Faridpur, rice harvesting in many of the villages was done by labourers from Nadia district. In many cases, they were peasants from other areas who had already brought in their own rice or jute and were free to sell their labour. Since their time of winter unemployment had come, they were eager for field work elsewhere, and did it for what were practically starvation wages.

We might only add that in the specific conditions of the exceedingly labour-intensive (manual) tropical agriculture, part of the middle peasants also used wage labour from time to time. It is quite certain, indeed, that peasants in the lower property brackets did employ wage labour, though it did not yet here determine the economic type of peasant farming. This is borne out by Bengali researchers, who show that in jute-growing areas ordinary peasants hired labourers fairly often to reap, ret and loosen the jute fibres, or to plant and harvest rice by hand. Saha makes clear that the middle peasant did not use wage labourers save for reaping or planting jute and for harvesting rice. To be sure, even in these cases the Bengali middle peasant would rather rely on neighbourly mutual assistance widespread among ryots of this status than go to the expense of hiring labourers. The considerable spread of neighbourly mutual assistance among poorer and middle peasants is recorded by all Bengali researchers.

Of certain interest from the point of view of the structure of the estates belonging to minor rent collectors who were formerly rich peasants is the testimony laid down by one of them before the Royal Commission on Agriculture of India, which follows in full. It merits our attention for more than one reason:

"The Chairman: Would you mind telling me how much land you yourself cultivate?

"I cultivate 50 acres.

"Is that one of the biggest holdings in the neighbourhood?

"It is not in one plot; it is scattered.

"In how many different plots?

"More than 100 plots.

"And you cultivate all the 100 plots?

"Yes, I do.

'Then you must be spending all your time in walking from plot to plot?

"I work from 5 in the morning till 10 at night.

"These 17 hours you spend in supervision?

"Yes.

"You do not sub-let any of your land?

"I do.

"How much do you sub-let?

"I do not sub-let on rent but on division of paddy.

"Half and half?

"Yes.

"I want to get from you your relations with the cultivators of your neighbourhood.

"I mix with them very freely.

"In what way do you mix with them?

"I give them advice; I work with them. If possible, I lend them my seeds.

"Do you lend money?

"Not much.

"Are the principal landholders of a circle ever called together to discuss matters of common interest?

"Never.

"For instance, men like you who hold about 50 acres of land or thereabouts?

"Never.

"We are kept in awe by the zamindars... The zamindars do very little; they take very little interest in village affairs; their case ends as soon as they get the rent; if they do not get the rent they charge four annas in the rupee as interest per month [300 per cent per annum—*R.U.*]"[23]

The above material relating to wage labour in the Bengali countryside is, of course, no more than illustrative. If usable at all, it is merely auxiliary evidence of the process of property and class differentiation.

In this connection, it may be useful to say a few words about the "new" elements in imperialism's agrarian policy in Bengal. "Ideas that resemble those of Tolstoy are preached in India these days," says a source, "but they are not anywhere close to the ideas of Marx. Consequently, we have a breathing space... Continued existence of the medieval land system in India is impossible. It is essential, therefore, that large-scale farming must be introduced in some parts of India."[24] Jevons, one of the pioneers of colonial junker-type farming in India, demanded in almost frenzied terms that landlords should be induced to engage in cultivation. If this turned out to be impossible, he said, they should be replaced with new and better landlords, and if these, too, failed, tenants should be helped to buy title to the land.

We cannot deny Jevons a certain amount of common sense. Unlike the Bengali zamindar who maintained before the Legislative Council that the zamindary system "is a guarantee against Leninism", he was perfectly well aware that it was a very poor guarantee and that it would be far better for this guarantee to be replaced, if only gradually and if only in some parts of India, by what he fancied to be a more dependable one—that of large-scale capitalist landlord farming. Jevons was in a frenzy because the feudalists could not be prevailed upon to turn to the land. But despite the "convincing" ring of Jevons' arguments, imperialism failed to secure any palpable changes in that direction. The class struggle that was mounting in the country denied any breathing-space to Jevons and to many other who needed it. In the circumstances, projects were brought to light to disguise the senility of imperialism and its allies in India. A witness called before the Royal Commission in Bengal suggested, for example, that a bill should be put before the Legislative Council obliging every landowner to spend at least four or five months a year on his own estate, because landlords with enough means deserted their villages to live in luxury in Calcutta for which they are to be censured.[25]

Frightened menials of imperialism eager to please their master suggested holding landlords on their feudal estates by force. But magnates of local industrial capital dreaded the rising peasant movement no less than the landlords who deserted to the towns. On a tour of Bengal, members of the Royal Commission had the following dialogue with a member of the Jute Manufacturers Association:

"Supposing some discovery were made which showed them [the peasants—*R. U.*] that they could grow better and more profitable crops than jute, that would affect your interests in which you have invested a huge sum of money?

"Yes, we should have to turn the key of the door and get out.

"Do you not think, therefore, it would be wise to ameliorate the conditions of the growers to a certain extent?

"No, I am afraid the jute mills will not consider that. Mills think that is a question for the consideration of Government.

"Then you are following a suicidal policy. Are you aware of the agrarian movement?

"Yes, we are now feeling it."[26]

Owing to the specificity of Bengali agriculture, the high population density, the colossal relative agrarian overpopulation, and the limited funds allotted for colonisation, and, moreover, in the absence of any effective palliative in the shape of internal or external migration of manpower, imperialism was here even afraid of combatting the fragmentation of land holdings, as it did in other provinces (Bombay, Punjab, and the Central Provinces). K. McLean, a student of the Bengali countryside, was asked by the Royal Commission if he thought the idea of consolidating land in Bengal hopeless or merely a question of time. He replied:

"About fragmentation of holdings I understand the difficulty is the existence of numerous sub-interests."

He was asked: "You might have a plot of land in which five people might have an interest?"

He replied: "Yes, about fifty."[27]

It is quite certain, in the light of this evidence, that imperialism's capacity for manouevre in its bid to shape a so-called new positive agrarian policy in Bengal was exceedingly narrow both from the purely economic angle and the social class, political angle. The experience of the 1930s offers enough material, indeed, for a reply to any question as to what economic manoeuvres could be expected on imperialism's part in suppressing the rising peasant movement.

In areas where the class struggle was the sharpest and which were seats of large-scale peasant actions, imperialism compounded a policy of outright or veiled police reprisals with a policy of temporary and partial tax reductions or determent of tax payments derived from landlords and rich peasants. In so doing, at especially acute junctions, the authorities required landlords and rich peasants to reduce accordingly the exorbitant rent they extorted from their tenants or at least to defer its payment.

In areas of the fiercest anti-manajan peasant movement (which tended to grow into an anti-landlord movement), the Anglo-Indian government, while loosening police terror, posed as an impartial, sometimes even anti-mahajan, arbiter who sought to establish peace and order between those who had lent money and those who had borrowed it. Various projects appeared concerning a moratorium on old usury debts, establishment of arbitration councils (partly set up in the United Provinces), the right to declare bankruptcy, and enforcement in other provinces of some variety of the Punjabi law on land alienation. These projects were made public at various meetings, in the press, and in some provincial legislative councils.

The crisis badly reduced the domestic market and prompted imperialists to seek recovery in a more rapid development of colonial junker-type farming and in assisting the kulak element. This on the one hand, but on the other the crisis caused extensive ferment among the peasant masses, which was beginning to cross the bounds of passive resistance. As a result, the crisis and the upturn of the peasant movement reduced the chances of any in the least far-reaching and effective colonial junker-type reform in India as a whole and also in individual provinces and districts. In its drive to carry out these reforms, imperialists had no choice but to confine themselves to partial "laboratory" experiments, and these in specially selected areas where the capitalist differentiation of the peasants was more advanced. The old policy of backing survivals of feudalism and of relying on their class bearers was still the only possible policy. At the same time, imperialists took advantage of every decline in the peasant movement and of every defeat of local peasant actions to carry forward initial, albeit cautious, moves to promote their so-called positive agrarian policy. No other approach, no other option was historically open to imperialism in its search for a way out of the crisis of the agrarian system.

Chapter Five

Indian Merchant's and Moneylender's Capital as an Agent of British Finance Capital

In 1931, in Calcutta, two general reports and more than a dozen provincial ones were published by the Indian Central Banking Enquiry Committee investigating the state of Indian finances, money circulation and agricultural and industrial credit.[1] The material of this Committee, like that of the Royal Commission on Agriculture in India and the Royal Commission on Labour, is of undoubted interest for everyone studying the Indian economy in order to develop a Marxist elaboration of problems that have not, as yet, been completely clarified, especially the problems of the agrarian system. We shall devote this chapter to analysing the Banking Committee's material relating mainly to the state of trade and money circulation in Indian agriculture.

The Banking Committee was forced to state the indisputable impoverishment and ruin of the Indian peasantry. Moreover, it did so using just average statistics—the usual method employed by bourgeois economists.

The Banking Committee assessed the total output of Indian agriculture at 12 billion rupees (in 1928 prices), added 20 per cent to this sum as the probable income from subsidiary occupations, ignored the increase in the population and the tremendous drop in the prices of colonial raw materials and foodstuffs during the world agrarian crisis, and excluded outlays on restoring means of production (but resorted to false anticipation of the "fixed capital" of the peasant economy). The Committee divided the resulting sum by the number of the agricultural population (including paupers and owners of big latifundia, the bonded tenant and rich moneylending peasant) and took the result—£3 (42 rupees) a year per capita—as the per capita income of the Indian peasant. Even calculated in this way, the impoverishment of the agricultural classes was indisputable.

If this question is considered from the angle of the class stratification of the countryside and incomes are grouped by class, the result is a picture of acute impoverishment of the rural masses and a rapid growth of money and landed property in the hands of the rich peasant, merchant-moneylender and feudal upper crust. The crisis did not reduce the property and class polarisation, but intensified it even further, as can be seen from the fact, established by the Banking Committee, that the mortgage indebtedness of the peasantry increased from 6 billion rupees in 1928 to 12 billion in 1931; the correlation between the surplus and necessary labour, in both money and especially in kind, thus changed in favour of the exploiting classes, i.e., the exploitation of the countryside by landlords and moneylenders increased. The size and share of rent paid to the landlord, interest on loans or merchants' profit in the peasant's annual product went up. The Banking Committee presented a pile of factual material illustrating the most merciless exploitation of the Indian countryside, in no way differing from the era of the primitive accumulation of capital, but it did not, of course, draw the right class conclusions from this, nor could it do so.

The Banking Committee, the Royal Commission on Agriculture, as well as Indian bourgeois economists wrote much about the fragmentation of peasant farming and the monstrous degree of strip-farming, about the deterioration in the conditions of production and the impossibility for the average-sized peasant family to eke out a living on a plot of 5-6 acres, scattered between 10 to 15 locations. All this is true, but a deliberate "blindness" was characteristic of all the "scholars" on these commissions. Tens of millions of peasants could not be forced to forget that their unprecedented land shortage meant an equally unprecedented land surplus in the hands of big landlords, a situation ardently protected by British imperialism. The total area sown in 1927/28 was about 220 million acres, i.e., roughly an acre per capita of the rural population or about 6 acres per family of five.

Yet, nor the Royal Commission on Agriculture, nor the Banking Committee, nor the Simon Committee, which arrived in India in 1932 in order to "present" it with a "constitution", stated that 19 landlords in Assam owned an average of 210,000 acres each, while 7 million peasants had 3 acres; that 125 landlords in Bengal owned 500,000 acres each and 37 million peasants—2.5 acres; that 300 landlords in Madras owned 16,000 acres each, while 30 million peasants—only 5 acres; that 20 landlords in Audh owned 65,000 acres each and 34 million peasans had plots that averaged 2.5 acres. There was no mention of this. Nor did the top officials of the endless commissions make any mention, of course, of the oppression exercised by the feudal latifundia, the sharp class polarity in the distribution of land and water, the monopolisation of the land by the landlords, merchants, and moneylenders, the retention and support of all this feudal and semi-feudal scum by British imperialism as its class support in the countryside.

The representatives of British imperialism in India often asserted that the investment of exported capital in irrigation facilities was doing a lot for India, liberating the country from chronic famine.

This is not to mention that, under British rule in India, enormous irrigation facilities fell into ruin and that India suffered many years of famine and epidemics that claimed a toll of at least 60 million lives; after the 150 years of British colonial rule, only 16 per cent of the cultivated land was irrigated by rivers, reservoirs and wells, while the remaining 84 per cent depended entirely on atmospheric precipitation.

Such were the "progressive" consequences of imperialist rule. But the profits of the foreign companies that turned the irrigation and water rent paid by the peasants into the most profitable and, essentially a monopoly source of income, were considerable, especially in the most arid parts of India which had also, thanks to the enforced specialisation of agriculture, become monoculture regions producing colonial raw materials and foodstuffs.

In the Punjab, for example, 441,165,897 rupees had been invested by 1930 in the irrigation system. There were 23,901 miles of canals and 13,164,999 acres were irrigated. This irrigation network, belonging entirely to British capital on a monopoly basis, "controlled" the harvest of various crops, mainly wheat, worth 500 million rupees. From 1887, the sum of water rent paid by the peasants in money or in kind, which formed the gross profits of British irrigation companies in the Punjab, reached 885 million rupees, i.e., double the cost of all the facilities. The companies' dividends reached 40-45 per cent. Even in the crisis years of 1929 to 1933 the shares paid 15-20 per cent. The tax revenues of the state treasury in the Punjab, the source for which was the labour of the Punjabi peasants, increased by 43.5 million rupees over this period.

The land monopoly, in combination with the monopoly of the water, the land rent in conjunction with the water rent, served to enrich a handful of parasitic exploiters who, by swallowing up the mass of the surplus product and a substantial part of the necessary product of the peasants,[2] were directly responsible for the impoverishment of millions of immediate producers, doomed to famine and extinction.

The most eminent Indian financiers and industrialists, making up the Banking Committee, understood, of course, that it was precisely the impoverishment of the masses in the Indian countryside, the extremely narrow home market, the rapacious exploitation of the peasantry by the unreasonably inflated lowest and worst forms of capital, and the tax burden of imperialism that fostered the development of modern capitalist credit, in relation to which British imperialism in India pursued the same pressurising policy as it did in relation to India's industrial development. While stating that the banks could not, given the universal impoverishment, ignorance and helplessness, advance any credit, the Commission timidly reminded imperialism of the desirability of measures to industrialise the country, resolutely demanding, at the same time, that junker and rich peasant farming be implanted from above through the eviction from the land of the "bankrupt" peasant tenant farmers. The bourgeois, landowning economists deliberately concealed the real reasons for the indebtedness of the population: the oppression of parcel farming by the serf-type latifundia, the tax burden imposed by imperialism, the need to pay back old debts, most of the peasants' lack of any livestock or implements—in a word, the extreme economic weakness and poverty of the small producer as a result of feudal-imperialist exploitation.

The archaic living customs, caste prejudice, the petty regulation of all aspects of life, undoubtedly agonizing for the peasant, the ruinous weddings and funerals, and so on are connected with the domination of feudal survivals in the consciousness and lives of the peasants, who had been thoroughly enserfed by the exploiting classes.

The data on peasant indebtedness are very relative, and it is difficult to establish its actual scale. The report made by the Banking Committee noted, for example, that the total sum of agricultural indebtedness in the Punjab increased from 900 million rupees in 1921 to 1,350 million rupees in 1929. The debt burden was, in fact, much heavier than can be guessed from the general increase in terms of rupees, for the prices of agricultural produce had fallen by about 50 per cent over this period.

From 1930 to the beginning of 1933, the prices of colonial raw materials and foodstuffs had fallen by another 40 per cent on average; i.e., the actual debt burden had increased and the share of the product taken away from the peasantry merely to cover the interest on his debts to moneylenders increased in direct proportion to the fall in prices and intensification of the crisis. The indebtedness curve was rising and that of money incomes from the output sold by the peasants was falling. The economic laws were such that, given the catastrophic drop in the peasants' money incomes, their debt burden grew even more.

The world economic crisis revealed with particular force that the weight of loan interest and indebtedness in all provinces of India was considerably greater than that of the tax burden. In Bombay, for instance, debts to moneylenders were 15 times greater than the amount of tax levied. The same was true of the Punjab and Bengal. Given the feudal nature of the taxes, which took a significant share of the peasants' output, indebtedness and the interest on loans were several times greater than the tax burden. Together they, therefore, formed an exceptionally strong force, compelling the peasantry to run their farms on a highly commercialised, monoculture basis, in spite of the persistent famine and the fact that the peasant was forced to act as both merchant and industrialist, though the conditions did not favour him producing his output as a commodity. Marx wrote that merchant's and moneylender's capital, when pre-eminent, represents a system of robbery, and this has been fully proved by the development of the economies of all colonies, especially India.

The Banking Committee could not but recognise that the main general reason for indebtedness was old indebtedness, resulting in new loans, chiefly as a result of high interest rates or the purchase of land at high competitive prices, or the leasing of the land for high rents.

The instability of the small, parcel farm, given the random movements of the market, unstable climate, constantly recurring epidemics among animals and people, and the extreme unreliability of the harvest—all these factors exacerbated the indebtedness for, given the lack of grain and forage stocks on the peasant farm, the impoverished peasant and even the middle peasant, who could hardly make ends meet, could do nothing but go on his knees to the moneylender. According to the Banking Committee's data, the percentage of the population not in debt stood at 9-38 per cent in Assam, 14-21 per cent in Bihar and Orissa, 13-70 per cent in the Central Provinces and 33-61 per cent in the United Provinces. There can be no doubt that these figures are exaggerated. In fact, simple checks show the percentages to be much lower. Indebtedness was particularly high in the regions of export monoculture, imposed by means of moneylender and merchant bondage, where the peasants' harvest of raw materials or foodstuffs became the property of the merchant or moneylender even before being harvested.

What was the outcome of the peasantry's high level of indebtedness? This is the Banking Committee's reply: "The indebtedness leads ultimately to the transfer of land from the agricultural class to the non-agricultural money-lender, leading to the creation of a landless proletariat with a reduced economic status. The result is said to be loss of agricultural efficiency, as the money-lender sublets at a rate which leaves the cultivator with a reduced incentive to raise a good crop."[3]

Mortgage indebtedness to moneylenders was one of the reasons of direct expropriation or of the protracted process of the ruin of the small, parcel farms, which ultimately led to the expropriation of the direct producer and his conversion from the peasant, who was a conditional landowner, into an unconditional bonded tenant, with no rights at all. The land now belonged to the moneylender, who took over part of the peasant's harvest. Once he became a landlord, the moneylender did not usually organise any capitalist farm on the land, but leased it to the ryots on the worse possible terms for them, i.e., narrower reproduction possibilities for the peasant farm. The parcel-holding peasant thus became a sort of debt slave. While retaining superficial personal independence, he worked for the moneylender, having to submit to his demands and orders.

Having expropriated the peasants' land, the moneylender did not, as a rule, invest his accumulated money capital in agricultural production. Without transforming production itself, he continued to engage in moneylending operations, while becoming, at the same time, a landlord with a mass of land at his disposal. A large, comparatively new stratum of Indian landlords emerged from among the moneylenders and merchants, especially in the southern regions of India. It can be stated with confidence that the overwhelming majority of the whole class of Indian landlords, whatever their social background, were, at the same time, moneylenders and merchants. The transfer of the peasant's land into the hands of the moneylender, i.e., the simultaneous conversion of the moneylender into a landowner and the peasant into a landless tenant, led to a sharp deterioration in the conditions of reproduction of the peasant holding, to the moneylender appropriating the peasant's surplus product not only in the form of interest, but also that of bonded rent.

In regions of industrial monoculture, the moneylender usually acted as the village merchant, too, maintaining links with the town market and sometimes British Purchasing firms. The Banking Committee's report stated that when moneylenders were also shopkeepers and commission agents, they often made it a condition that the agriculturists' produce had to be sold through them. This very seriously affected the liberty of action in marketing the produce and was undesirable when parties to the bargain were not matched. Even when the moneylender was not a trader, and did not want to buy the produce, he knew that if the debtor did not pay after selling his produce, it would not be possible for the latter to pay till after the next harvest. He had, therefore, to put pressure on the debtor immediately after the harvest, and the effect of this pressure was so great that the borrower was compelled to dispose of his harvest as quickly as he could. As every grower was equally pressed for cash and had to sell at the same time, the price obtained by the cultivator was naturally depressed in consequence.

The Banking Committee divided the peasants' indebtedness into two parts: the principal and current debts. Since the majority of indebted peasants were unable to cover even their current debts after the harvest, the unpaid part was added to the principal. This main sum hung like a weight round the neck of the direct producer: in most cases he was unable to remove it throughout his life. Debts outstanding when a peasant died were passed on to the next generation. On this basis, inherited debt slavery arose.

The Banking Committee did not establish the real number of moneylenders. Its information on this was greatly underestimated, and cannot, therefore, be trusted. The Committee grouped moneylenders as follows:

1. Professional moneylenders: town, village and itinerant.
2. Non-professional moneylenders: cultivators, rich peasants, commission agents, merchants and others (advocates, pensioners, cult priests).

The second group of moneylenders was growing extremely rapidly. This was because, on the one hand, a number of legislative acts had been passed by the Anglo-Indian government to limit somewhat the transfer of the peasants' land and means of production to professional moneylenders and, on the other hand, cultivators, merchants, rich peasants and so-called "professional men" were increasingly investing their capital in moneylending, which was being so profitable in India. The tremendous growth of indebtedness and the ruin of the peasantry were accompanied by an increase in the number of moneylenders. Once the land was transferred to the moneylenders, a large part of the peasant's money income followed it.

The concentration of landownership in the hands of moneylenders of all types and the conversion of the peasant into a bonded tenant led to a further concentration of the peasant's product in the hands of the exploiting upper crust of the village. The usurious monetary capital, as a transformed form of the appropriated surplus and part of the necessary product of the peasantry, was concentrated among a growing mass of moneylenders, who, together with the landlords, fulfilled one of the most important functions in the system of extra-economic coercion of the direct producer, in the system of means keeping India an agrarian-raw material appendage of Britain.

Let us consider the nature and methods employed by the different groups of Indian moneylenders.

I. Professional village moneylenders.[4]

1. "Loans are given on mutual trust without a document or even a witness. Loans are made on promissory notes when the amounts are large."

2. "Conditional sale-deeds are often taken and the oral arrangement is that the land would be re-transferred on the repayment of the debt."

3. "For current agricultural needs, the money-lender usually accepts personal security on the understanding, expressed or implied, that the produce is to be sold to or through him."

4. For short-term loans, the security is mortgage of crops, but "where the amount is large or the loan is for a long period, the security is the mortgage of land".

5. "The money-lender is not interested in the purpose for which the loan is taken."

6. "Interest is added at interests rates. This form of compound interest produces prodigious results in a short time."

7. "The village money-lender does shop-keeping and trading, in addition to money-lending, and he is also engaged in agriculture. His advances to the cultivator are both in cash and in kind."

8. For the purpose of insuring his income, "the money-lender resorts to various devices, such as taking bonds for larger amounts than are actually lent".

II. Itinerant moneylenders (pathans, kabuls, mahajans, rohillas, and gistwalas).[5]

1. Their moneylending operations embrace the poorest strata of the peasantry, agricultural labourers, poorly paid clerks and factory workers.

2. "The usual limits of advance are from Rs. 5 to Rs. 50. Promissory notes and signatures of thumb impressions in *khata* books are the most common form of acknowledgement obtained from debtors."

3. "In cases of default, the money-lender uses force and sel-

dom resorts to law courts. Actual cases of violence may not be many, but the methods employed are such as to keep the borrower in perpetual fear of being victimized."[6]

4. "Loans are also given under the instalment or *kist* system, the first instalment being in some cases deducted at the time the loan is advanced."

5. "In some cases the borrower is made to sign a promissory note stipulating that the loan shall be repaid in any of the several districts mentioned therein, so that if the borrower defaults, the moneylender can sue and obtain an uncontested decree in a distant place and then execute it at the place where the debtor resides."

6. "Almost all itinerant money-lenders sell goods, specially cloth, on credit, usually recovering the value in the next cold weather."

III. Non-professional moneylenders—landowners and agriculturists.[7]

1. The agriculturist moneylender is often more exacting than the professional moneylender. He usually lends seed secured against future crops, or cash against the security of land, and eagerly seizes the opportunity to pounce upon it.

2. "His main and sometimes his sole object is to get possession of the land of his debtors."

3. "He is said to be avaricious and exacting, and being to some extent in a stronger position than the professional moneylender, he recovers a large proportion of his dues."

4. "Money-lending to them is not always a mere investment; it often has ulterior motive. It is also common for landlords to finance their tenants . . . Landlords are the most dangerous creditors, as they acquire a double hold over the tenant borrower. If a tenant pays his rent, but not the interest on his debt, a landlord can sue him in a civil court. If the tenant pays the interest on his debt, but not his rent, the landlord can sue him in a revenue court. Worse, still, the landlord can, if he chooses, credit all payments to the debt and so keep the tenant in arrears with his rent, which puts the latter's crops in his power by distraint, and gives him the right to eject him if he pleases. . . Occupancy tenants have occasionally been compelled to surrender their rights to their landlords in liquidation of debts".

IV. Merchants and traders.[8]

1. "These sometimes lend money to the agriculturist on the understanding that his crops should be sold through them." This was the most widespread sort of moneylender.

2. Moneylenders who own factories for processing agricultural produce in some cases finance the agriculturist on condition that he sells his crop to the lender's factory or gets it processed there. These moneylenders usually have links with the commission agents of foreign purchasing firms.

3. The incomes from moneylending operations are combined with commercial profit. This dual, trade and moneylender, exploitation of the peasant also accounts for the high, dual income of the merchant moneylender.

Such are the characteristic groups of Indian moneylenders. Now let us consider the size and rate of interest.

Assam. Loans to peasants were advanced at a rate of 12 to 75 per cent interest per annum. Rice loans in kind were quite frequently given at 24 to 37.5 per cent a year. Loans to landlords and merchants brought in 12 per cent.

Bombay. Itinerant moneylenders, who were particularly numerous in this province, took from 75 to 360 per cent a year, in Sind—50 per cent, in cotton-growing regions (Khandesh, Konkan, the Deccan, the Karnatak)—from 12 to 24 per cent. In Gujarat, a cotton region, where rich peasant farming was comparatively well developed, the interest rate was from 9 to 15 per cent. Loans on security brought in 12 per cent or more.

Bengal. The lowest interest rates were from 10 to 37.5 per cent, the highest from 37.5 to 300 per cent (East and North Bengal). Loans on the security of land brought in 18.75 to 37.5 per cent. In jute and rice monoculture regions, the harvest was usually taken as security; if the interest was to be paid in kind, it was much higher than if paid in cash.

Bihar and Orissa. From 50 to 100 per cent interest was charged on seed loans for an eight-month period. Failure to pay on time led to compound interest being charged. The interest on money loans was from 25 to 37.5 per cent a year in Orissa and up to 18.75 per cent in Bihar.

Central Provinces and Berar. Loans on the security of the land cost from 9 to 15 per cent in the Central Provinces and from 12 to 18 per cent in Berar. Most of the landless peasant tenants paid 37.5 per cent a year. There was nearly always a stipulation that, in case of default in repayment on the fixed date, a higher or penal rate of interest would be charged. Seed (wheat and rice) loans brought in 25 to 50 per cent and even 100 per cent sometimes.

Madras. Loans on the first security of the land were usually charged at 12 per cent per annum. The average interest rate, depending on the security provided, varied from 12 to 48 per cent. Landlords and rich peasant moneylenders usually advanced foodstuffs and seed loans at 25-50 per cent for the season of 5-6 months.

The Punjab. The lowest rate charged by the Pathan was 75 per cent per annum, but if the security was not good, virtually any rate could be charged. Land was considered as first class security, on which 9 per cent was charged.

United Provinces. The village moneylenders charged from 18 to 37 per cent, itinerant ones—from 44 to 300 per cent. Seed loans usually brought in 25-50 per cent. The sale of cattle on two years' credit was carried out at a rate of 150 per cent per annum.

Such were the interest rates charged in the different parts of India. There was no uniform rate: an extremely high one was charged when a loan was advanced to an ordinary small poor or middle peasant, but a substantially lower one for a prosperous peasant. The landlord paid only a normal rate of loan interest. The class stratification of the countryside on the basis of the distribution of the land, means of production and money capital told on the character and scale of the interest rates charged. The laws of capitalist credit, its average rate of interest, conditioned by the average rate of capitalist profit, did not, of course, apply in Indian agriculture, since it applied to the peasant masses. Rent, which, for most of the peasants, was still a normal form of surplus product in general, rent, which was not limited by the average rate of profit, i.e., precapitalist rent, had a precapitalist rate of interest that corresponded to it in scale and character. Only then the scale and character of the rate of interest acquired a capitalist sense and significance when the rich peasants or rural capitalist landlords acted as moneylenders.

Indian monetary loan capital, based on semi-feudal production, functioned on behalf of British finance capital. In this respect, it fulfilled the role of one aspect of the general circuit of capital. In relation to the production basis in the Indian countryside, in relation to the masses of direct producers, it acted as an independent sort of capital, as the most rapacious, the worst and most primitive sort, which did not subordinate labour to itself directly or stand in opposition to the producer as industrial capital. Its relationship with production was only superficial.

The monopoly of imperialism and the semi-feudal landlords over the land and water—the object of labour and the primary conditions for production—was responsible for monopoly of market relations enjoyed by merchant's and moneylender's capital both within the village and beyond it. The Banking Committee had to admit that the moneylender was the only financial agent accessible to the cultivator and occupied a semi-monopoly position, so the interest rates he charged were naturally high.

Any consideration of Indian merchant's and moneylender's capital functioning on the semi-feudal basis of production must be carried out in the context that transformed it into an agent of British capital. The Banking Committee noted that the village moneylenders supplemented their capital by borrowing from moneylenders in the towns and even accepted deposits. Some town moneylenders, in turn, accepted deposits and sometimes borrowed money from local bankers. Big and small merchants did business with joint-stock banks.

The question of the link between Indian merchant's and moneylender's capital and British finance capital will be considered in detail below. Meanwhile, let us merely note one extremely important circumstance—the exceptional flexibility, manoeuvrability and mobility of merchant's and moneylender's capital.

The Banking Committee was forced to reject a multitude of different proposals made by provincial committees and individuals for the mandatory registration of moneylenders, the fixing of the interest rate, the abolition of compound interest, the application throughout the country of the rule of ancient and mediaeval India on damdopada, according to which interest cannot exceed the sum of the loan.

The material of the Banking Committee makes it possible to establish that the multiple legislative measures taken by British imperialism in an attempt to "normalise" somewhat the unbridled thirst for accumulation of merchant's and moneylender's capital, measures that were always hypocritical (in the official press they were put over as "laws to protect the peasants from moneylenders"), came down virtually to a redistribution of the shares of the peasants' produce (the Punjab), moreover, in favour of an increase in the share gained by imperialism itself, and over time revealed their true sense. The few secondary concessions made by imperialism to the peasantry in certain regions in order to avert open revolutionary actions lost any significance under the conditions of the world agrarian crisis.

The Royal Commission on Agriculture in India also declared that the law on moneylending had remained on paper. The same fate awaited the equally well-known act on assistance to the cultivators of the Deccan. As for the Punjab act on moneylending and on a ban on the transfer of the land to non-cultivating castes (1901), its adoption was dictated by a specific consideration—the need to "normalise" relations between the moneylender and the peasants in the region, who were the main source of recruits for the Anglo-Indian army.

The Royal Commission on Agriculture in India admitted that the agrarian legislation had failed to achieve its purpose.

During the sittings of the Royal Commission in the Punjab, the following interesting dialogue was held:

"Is the agricultural moneylender in any way better off than the old type of moneylender?

"No, worse off.

"Then there is no advantage in creating a new type of agricultural moneylender by artificial means, by legislation?

"There can be no law which will be effective, because if an attempt is made to regulate interest, the moneylenders will lend Rs. 100 and get a receipt in writing for Rs. 200, and accept a lower rate of interest. An Act to regulate interest was contemplated, and I think it is a good thing it was not passed."[9]

The laws passed by British imperialism in India in order to put partial restrictions on the loan operations of the professional moneylender brought a considerable increase in the number of landlord and rich peasant moneylenders. The Banking Committee wrote that the most important of the professional moneylenders was the landlord, who advanced loans to his own or other tenants, as well as the tenant with free cash, who lent money to other people in his village. The rich tenant moneylender was, in the pursuit of the land belonging to other peasants, the most merciless and exacting of the moneylenders. The Banking Committee had to state that the greater the limits imposed on the moneylender's rights, the worse the position of the debtor became.

The overwhelming majority of legislative experiments by British imperialism in India at state regulation, the setting or restriction of loan operations essentially made the situation of the direct producer even worse, nurtured the extreme resourcefulness of the moneylender, who skillfully got round all formal bureaucratic obstacles put in his way, and resulted in the terms of loan credit for the masses in the villages becoming harsher by the year. All objective bourgeois researchers into India's agriculture had to admit this.

What, then, were the proposals made by the Banking Committee?

1) To involve the moneylender in agricultural credit co-operative societies and include the means and experience of the moneylender in the co-operative movement. He could hold a particular post. His presence on executive committees of co-operative societies could be invaluable. The moneylender could be admitted to the co-operative society on the condition that he stopped advancing loans on a private basis to the members of the co-operative.

2) To create a special credit co-operative of moneylenders to advance credit not to individuals, but to peasant societies.

3) To transform local moneylenders into representatives of joint-stock banks in the localities. The Committee considered that, in time, the joint-stock banks could grant moneylenders such agent's functions as the acceptance of deposits, transfers and payments, but only once the moneylenders had gained sufficient strength and instilled confidence. With the further development of banking, the registered moneylender could, in the Committee's opinion, become a branch of the finance bank, which itself could come to an agreement with the registered

moneylender and become his financial companion, instead of organising a branch of its own.

4) To pass a special act allowing itinerant moneylenders considered harmful to society to be evicted.

What was the essence of these proposals? The Indian peasant masses were fleeced of everything. The degradation of agriculture, exacerbated by the economic crisis, gave rise to another phenomenon that, in the Banking Committee's opinion, consisted essentially in the capital of the village moneylender becoming increasingly frozen by the year.

There is some truth in this. The reverse of the unprecedented indebtedness of the peasantry, enormous numbers of whom were either ejected from the agricultural production process or deprived of the conditions for remaining an object of constant and methodical moneylender exploitation, was the extraordinarily "frozen" nature of moneylender's capital. The chicken had stopped laying golden eggs. Having worked hard to rob the peasantry, bringing the peasant masses to terrible poverty and transforming them into its non-paying debtors, merchant's and moneylender's capital itself got stuck deep in the quagmire of the countryside it had itself ruined. Throughout the period of British capital's domination in India, its agent, local merchant's and moneylender's capital, carried out the primitive accumulation of capital in the countryside.

Merchant's and moneylender's capital of the primitive accumulation type, in conjunction with the domination of feudal survivals, had a disastrous outcome. Not even the most submissive and quiet sheep can be shorn forever, without the wool being allowed time to grow back. The home market contracted and the small producer was ruined. The once fertile soil was exhausted. Harvests fell from one year to the next. The cattle degenerated everywhere. Famine was looming. Peasant rebellions broke out here and there, often at the same time as struggles by the urban workers. Nationalisation of the land did not seem a very distant prospect, according to one eminent landlord.

Such were the conditions under which the Royal Commission on Agriculture in India and the Banking Committee raised the question of a reformist solution to the agrarian problem from above, by implanting colonial junkers, and recommended the Anglo-Indian government also to pursue a policy of transforming the parasitic moneylender into an agrarian capitalist.

According to this policy, tens and hundreds of thousands of money capitalists, differing not in the size and management of agricultural production, but merely the amount of money in their possession, were to be encouraged to invest their capital in agriculture, to set up and run large-scale rich-peasant type farms on the land of the indebted and impoverished peasants, evicted from the land and transformed partly into agricultural labourers. Merchant and rich peasant moneylenders were allotted a responsible task in this junker policy of British imperialism, which had not yet got beyond individual attempts at a reformist clearing of the land of poor and middle peasants in order to set up large-scale capitalist estates. Numbering more than the class of landlords and being tied more closely to the peasant masses, the hundreds of thousands of merchants, rich peasants and moneylenders were to constitute one of the main supports for the attempts to implement British imperialism's "new" agrarian policy in India.

The Banking Committee's suggestions for setting up an even closer union between British banking capital in India and local merchant's and moneylender's capital, for turning the hundreds of thousands of moneylenders into the direct agents of British finance capital in the Indian countryside, were in full conformity with this policy.

The striving to involve accumulated capital in commerce and moneylending more broadly in the British banking network, having transformed the moneylenders into stock-holders of the multitude of British banks in India, to combine with the registered moneylender, to make use of the enormous accumulations of local money capitalists in the interests of British imperialism, the attempts to "rationalise" moneylending by setting up moneylending credit co-operatives and drawing the accumulation of merchant's and moneylender's capital into the village agricultural co-operative system, to provide the moneylenders with agent's functions, i.e., turn them into their legally sanctioned network—such was the essence of the proposals made by the Banking Committee for consolidating the power of British finance capital in the Indian countryside and establishing an even closer union between them and merchant's and moneylender's capital, in the face of the growing agrarian movement.

A distinguishing feature of Indian village moneylenders was the almost complete absence of large-scale or in any way mass operations on accepting deposits. This is understandable. Most of the rural population had no substantial savings, while the prosperous upper crust preferred to retain its links with agriculture and itself engage in moneylending, rather than depositing its money in the operations of a professional moneylender. This is particularly understandable since a number of legislative acts by British imperialism which raised certain formal obstacles to the concentration and transfer of peasant land into the hands of professional moneylenders, engendered a quite substantial stratum of moneylender agriculturists from among the rich peasant upper crust in the village.

The capitals of village moneylenders did not always belong to them completely. To some extent, they consisted of loans advanced by small urban Indian bankers, whose capital included deposits by bourgeois intelligentsia, petty urban bourgeois and professional people. The stratum of town bankers was quite numerous and ramified. In Bombay, (shroffs) for example, there were 20,000 of them. This enormous development of comparatively small-scale town banking was naturally connected directly with the overall economic development of the country, the extreme inflation of village merchant's and moneylender's capital, the slow development of industry, the absence of extensive ways for transforming merchant's and moneylender's capital into industrial capital—in a word, with the agrarian-raw material nature of India's economy as a colonial appendage of Britain.

This ramified network of town banks was connected, on the one hand, with the lower level of loan capital—the village moneylenders and, on the other, with the big Indian banks and, through them, the British banks or even directly with British capital. The role of the town bankers as middlemen between the millions of merchant moneylenders and Indian and British banking capital can hardly be exaggerated. It was significant both in the volume of their activities and the economic task they fulfilled. Being the middle link in the chain of loan capital, on orders from above they commanded its lowest links

—the village moneylender's and linked them with British finance capital operating in India. Its functions in this respect were just as intertwined, as interwoven and merged was the finance capital of the metropolis with the mediaeval merchant's and moneylender's capital in the colony.

The favourite security given to the town bankers by the village moneylenders was the peasants' harvest.[10] When the village moneylender took a loan from the town banker on the security of the harvest—rice, cotton, oil-bearing seeds, wheat, jute, and so on, an average 6-12 per cent annual interest was charged. It is enough to compare the interest rates charged on the village moneylenders by the town bankers and those charged on the direct producers by the former to find the motives for such a close combination of moneylending operations with commercial ones and especially the "indifference" of the village moneylender towards the peasant harvest.

The summit of the banking system of British finance capital in India was the Imperial Bank—the state issue bank. With an underwritten capital of over 100 million rupees, it brought its annual operations up to 2 thousand million rupees. This leviathan of British finance capital held the dominant positions in India's commodity-money circulation and was thus one of the strongest commanding heights of imperialism.

In connection with the attempts by British imperialism to pursue a junker-type agrarian policy, the Imperial Bank tried to come into even closer contact with the semi-feudal landlord and rich peasant and, through financial operations, to some extent to speed up their transition to a large-scale capitalist enterprise. Thus, the Banking Committee wrote that the Imperial Bank of India began, in the province of Bombay, to finance big landlords on their personal guarantees, with a warrant or on the security of commodities, and that it had 34 branches in the Punjab giving advances on agricultural output and striving to establish a link between local grain merchants and local producers of agricultural output.

In the jute monoculture regions of Bengal, the Imperial Bank of India controlled, through a number of intermediate, local and British links, the financial activities of about a thousand loan agencies with a circulating capital of roughly 100 million rupees. Being formally organised like joint-stock banks, these loan agencies had no substantial joint-stock loan capital. Their total realised joint-stock capital consisted of only 100,000 rupees. The circulating capital of the loan agencies operating on the security of the peasant harvest and partly their land consisted of deposits by landlords, moneylenders, and urban bourgeois intelligentsia, as well as loans from Indian and British banks. Big jute merchants—Anglo-Indian export firms, and the Calcutta jute manufacturers, maintained the closest business relations with the loan agencies, whose aim consisted in using moneylending and the advance of fettering loans to the jute producers to purchase their jute and rice at monopoly low prices.

The profitability of the financial operations of these agencies, to say nothing of the commercial profit they reaped at the expense of the direct producer, can be seen from the fact that the loan agencies accepted deposits and paid 24 per cent per annum interest on them, while they advanced loans to direct producers at 112 per cent a year. The tremendous difference between the interest on deposits and loans, which swallowed up a substantial share of the peasants' produce, also constituted a source of major profits for these loan agencies controlled by British capital.

The existence of a multitude of intermediary links in the realisation of the small producer's output speaks for itself. The commodity transfer network throughout the country was overloaded by a variety of middlemen, each of whom absorbed a certain share of the peasant harvest. A fierce, though silent, struggle over the size of the share of the peasant's produce to be appropriated always broke out between the intermediary elements when they fulfilled any function in the commodity transfer network of finance capital in the colony (functions that quite often formed the economic basis for the organisation of some merchant caste, guild, society or group, operating on monopoly or semi-monopoly terms). A characteristic feature of the intermediary elements was that the overwhelming majority of them were connected, to some degree, with semi-feudal landownership and semi-feudal exploitation of the peasantry.

The extremely high degree of territorialisation (land purchase) by the merchant, moneylending and comprador bourgeoisie is not open to doubt. Being merchants and money capitalists, on the one hand, and semi-feudal landlords, on the other, personifying both landlord landownership and merchant's and loan capital, they formed one of the most significant strata of the Indian landowning class. At the same time, they were, at the initial stages of India's industrial development, one source for the formation of an Indian industrial bourgeoisie.

The methods by which Indian moneylenders and merchants operated were quite diverse. Here are some of them:

"In the market in the morning the *adtya* gets, say, 100 clients who bring him 200 carts. He has thus 200 carts to dispose of and there are 5 or 10 big merchants willing to buy. Then he negotiates the rate with the purchaser or his agents. If the purchaser is not present in person (and the Ralli Company's agents are not always present in person) his agent or nominee is in the market. He sees the quality of the cotton and then quotes a certain rate, and if the agent of the cotton grower, *viz.*, the *adtya*, is not satisfied he says that this is not a proper rate, that quality is higher, the lint percentage larger, and so on, and he asks for a better price. Some sort of bargaining goes on and the rate is settled. What happens then is that they begin to weigh the cotton and part of the cotton is tipped out of the carts on the heap of the purchaser and then, when the cart is, say, half empty, the purchaser takes objection to the quality and says when he quoted his price it was for a better quality than the cotton turns out to be. He says he is not willing to pay the rate he quoted in the morning and that he wants a discount. Naturally the cart being half empty and the cotton thrown on the heap it is very difficult for the cotton grower to take it back again, so he is forced to abide by the wish of the purchaser, with the result that the cotton grower is not able to get a fair price for the time...

"...Generally there are 100, 150, or 200 of these brokers attached to a big cotton market such as Amraoti and Akola. No sooner does his cart get to the gates of the cotton market than 50, 60 or 100 of these brokers surround him; some catch hold of the nose-string of his bullock, some his turban and some his coat, and they pester him in order to get his agency.

"...The broker, who is generally mixed up with these sellers, goes and settles the rate secretly; he does it by some signs under a cloth taking up a handkerchief and moving his fingers."[11]

"From all provinces we received complaints of the disabilities under which the cultivator labours in selling his produce in markets as at present organised. It was stated that scales and weights and measures were manipulated against him, a practice which is often rendered easier by the absence of standardised weights and measures and of any system of regular inspection. Deductions which fall entirely on him but against which he has no effective means of protest are made in most markets for religious and charitable purposes and for other objects. Large 'samples' of his produce are taken for which he is not paid even when no sale is effected. Bargains between the agent who acts for him and the one who negotiates for the purchaser are made secretly under a cloth and he remains in ignorance of what is happening."[12]

There can be no doubt concerning the monopolistic position of the moneylender and merchant both in the market relations between town and village and in village market turnover, where the moneylender and merchant could, thanks to their money and commercial capital, control and virtually set prices. This is also evidenced by data from the testimony of the Director of Agriculture for the Madras province: "In the case of food grains, the bulk of the produce is sold to middlemen, merchants and moneylenders to whom the producer is indebted for cash advances for cultivation or family expenses... In the case of paddy, there is a large class of professional dealers who go about the villages and arrange to buy stocks and supply them to big merchants in towns. The dealers always approach the village *sowcar* who acts as subdealer and also as a petty merchant... The ryots in Bellary centre are for the most part under the thumb of the commission agents and middlemen to whom they are always indebted.

"...At Nandyal, most of the cotton is sold on forward contracts... The produce, in the case of food grains consumed locally, pass from the ryot to the middleman, who sells to the merchant. In the case of produce sent out of the district by road or rail, the channel of distribution is from the ryot to the moneylender or middleman, who sells to the commissioned agent on behalf of the exporter."[13]

Merchant's and moneylender's capital decided how much of the harvest was actually left for the peasant, the "subsistence minimum" of the indebted direct producer, once the landlord and tax-collector had taken two-thirds or at least a half of the total harvest.

The Royal Commission on Agriculture noted that the producer, when in need of a loan, as he always was, had no security to offer apart from his labour and his as yet unharvested crop, and as he was virtually insolvent and could starve before the harvest ripened, he had to pay as much for his debts as demanded by the man with the money.

The monopoly role of the moneylender, merchant and commission agent of export firms in setting the prices at which the producer sold his produce was recognised by the Royal Commission on Agriculture and the Banking Committee. Here is some of the information given on this:

"To the small cultivator there are three ways open to sell his surplus produce:—

"1) He can take them to the market *(hât)* and sell them either to the actual local consumer or to the petty trader who buys them for cash;

"2) He can take them to the village shopkeepers who are usually local people in the Surma Valley and generally Marwaris in the Assam Valley, and dispose them off either for cash or in settlement of accounts with them;

"3) He can wait till some local trader calls at his place and purchases the produce usually at a price very favourable to the trader.

"From the local traders or local shops the produce goes into the hands of *mahajans* in important trade centres or towns whence it is sent down to Calcutta for disposal. Usually the local shops have trading connections with the *mahajan* in the towns or trading centres or very often the village shops are branches of the *mahajans* in the town. Moreover, the Marwaris have established a network of trade connections by which even the petty shops in the remotest part of the country are connected with Calcutta firms through two or three intermediaries. Thus, the export and import business is well organised; however, the middlemen reap a large profit at the expense of the actual consumers and the cultivators."[14]

"The agriculturists are mostly compelled to sell their produce to the Banias (grain merchants) while the crops are standing green in the fields, at a rate fixed by the 'Shylocks' ... It is, therefore, the moneylenders who have the system of marketing and distribution in their hands after the crops are harvested. The grain trade is a very lucrative one, and the prices of foodstuffs and other agricultural produce rise enormously after the harvesting time and continue to rise up till the next crops, but the poor farmer has nothing to do with the profit and the rise of rates, and ... he is deprived of selling his crops even at the rate prevailing at the harvesting time."[15]

The monopoly of British imperialism on India's foreign trade merged with the monopoly of merchant's and moneylender's capital over the village and other markets. There was no price formation based on free competition on the Indian home market. Calculations made by one Indian economist show that the direct producers of fruit in the Bombay Presidency received only 11 per cent of the retail price, middlemen retained 71 per cent of it and 18 per cent was swallowed up by transport costs—the monopoly of imperialism.

The economic significance of this phenomenon common to all India requires no comment. The price at which the direct producer sold his produce bore no relation to the costs of production and, as a rule, even in pre-crisis times, was below costs for the producer. This was one of the sources of imperialism's colonial superprofits and the profits reaped by its supporters and allies—merchant's and moneylender's capital.

It is known that there were the army of debt slaves in India. According to the 1921 census, there were about 6 million of them, but their numbers had increased considerably by 1931. Now let us look at how this debt slavery took shape and the role played in this by moneylender's capital. During the work of the Royal Commission on Agriculture in Bombay, the following dialogue took place:

"I have just two questions to ask. Did you say ... that cultivators in debt who were unable to pay occasionally worked as labourers for the lender of the money?

"The backward tribes usually do; it is their sole method of obtaining credit, to agree to work off the debt by labour.

"So many days' labour, is that the term of repayment?

"Usually a Bhil gets into debt because he wants to get married. He borrows Rs. 80 from a *patel* and agrees to serve him for a year for that sum. He gets the cash in advance, and he is supposed to work for a year.

"If he does that he liquidates his debt altogether?

"Yes, but usually he wants some clothes or something and goes on borrowing from the *patel* so that eventually he stays for years working for him or is a *badmash* and bolts."[16]

The same source goes on: "In Bihar and Orissa, we were told of a system known as *kamiauti* . . . which is practically one of cultivation by serfs. *Kamias* are bound servants of their masters; in return for a loan received, they bind themselves to perform whatever menial services are required of them in lieu of the interest due on the loan. Landlords employing labour for the cultivation of their private land prefer to have a first call on the labourers they require, and hence the practice arose of binding the labourers by means of an advance, given conditionally upon their services remaining always at the call of the landlord for the purposes of agriculture. Such labourers get a daily wage in kind for those days on which they work for their creditor, and may work for anybody else when they are not required by him. In practice, the system leads to absolute degradation of the *kamias*. . . A *kamiauti* bond therefore involves a life sentence. . . Daily work is not guaranteed by the master, and no food is supplied when there is no work to be done.

"The result is that the master takes the *kamia*'s labour at a sweated wage for most of the year, but at a time when there is no agricultural work to be done and the *kamia* has least chance of getting any daily employment elsewhere, he is left to shift for himself as best he can. He is even free to get work wherever he can, but cannot leave his village for any time in search of it, for fear that he might abscond. . . The restriction of his movements renders the *kamia* nothing better than a slave. An absconding *kamia* is unable to find asylum in any part of the area where the system is prevalent. The sale and purchase of *kamias* is by no means uncommon in the north-west of the district. The price is the amount of the *kamia's* debt."[17]

Debt slavery in India was not, of course, confined to one

province. In Bombay, the debt slaves were called "dubla" or "koli", in Madras—"vetti", "padial", "esuid", "cherumi" or "pulia", in Orissa—"galaif", and in the United Provinces—"savan".

One of the favourite methods by which the moneylenders and merchants operated was monetary advances on the security of the harvest, i.e., a sort of loan contract on the peasant harvest. When advancing loans for current agricultural outlays, the moneylender was usually satisfied with the personal obligation of the peasant, which envisaged the sale of the harvest to the moneylender or through his intermediation. In many cases, the harvest itself was security but, when the loan was a substantial sum or long-term, the land itself was mortgaged. The sum of interest was also charged; usually if the creditor was a shopkeeper or a trader, there was a condition to sell the harvest to him at a set price or 5 per cent below it. If this was a poor peasant this condition was detrimental to him because actually he had to submit to any condition of the trader. A better-off peasant could decide on his own when to sell his output and as far as he knew something about the market, he had the opportunity to sell it profitably.

The first thing that draws the attention is the system of advances on the security of the harvest, which prevailed in certain parts of India and was closely connected with commerce. A common feature of this system was that not only was a high interest rate charged on the advances; the debtor was also obliged to sell his output below market price. In those parts of Bengal where the *dadan* system of advances prevailed, the cultivator could not sell his produce freely. Sometimes, from 21 to 75 per cent interest was charged on the loans, while the prices at which the cultivator was forced to sell his output were from 25 to 30 per cent lower than those on the market.

In Bombay, the peasants who cultivated sugar cane received advances on the security of the harvest, on the condition that the sugar syrup was sold through the moneylender. The sale of mangoes almost always took place before they were gathered, and sometimes even before the trees flowered. The same practice existed in relation to the sale of oranges on the market in Kurga.

In Bihar and Orissa, various types of advance on the security of the sugar cane harvest were widely practised. Under all these systems, the harvest had to be delivered to the moneylender. In Bihar and Orissa, when jute prices were low, the peasants borrowed small sums of money, in exchange for which the moneylender obtained the priority right to purchase their jute. The producers received less for their produce than they would have done on the market, if they were not in debt.

Consequently, while it still stood in the field the peasant harvest was no longer the peasant's property. In the sale of his produce on the market, the producer was totally dependent on the moneylender or merchant. The producer had no experience of the process of free sale. Non-equivalent exchange began within the village, when the peasant had virtually to sell his produce to the moneylending merchant at a price bearing no relation to that obtaining on the market or to production costs, since he was under contract to the moneylender, i.e., tied by the plunderous system of advances on the security of the harvest. The overwhelming majority of direct producers were isolated from the town and even the village market, to say nothing of the world market, where British firms held the predominant positions and exerted a decisive influence on the internal commodity transfer network. Between the direct producers and the market (both town and village) stood the powerful figure of the medieval moneylending merchant, connected with finance capital, subordinate to it and transformed into its traditional political and economic agency. Merchant's and moneylender's capital, monstrously inflated on the basis of the colonial oppression of the country, had the peasant masses under its command and brought the peasant economies to ruin and collapse. We have already presented considerable data on the links between local moneylender's capital and British banking capital. The picture was the same for merchant's capital, which operated in close unity with the finance capital of the metropolis.

All India's export trade was, in fact, controlled by four British firms. These monopolies possessed a quite substantial network of commission agents and held the controlling blocks of shares in the majority of local trading and banking associations, which were, in turn, connected with big merchants who controlled and subordinated the activities of the tens and hundreds of thousands of small village merchants. Let us see how this system operated in different provinces.

Assam. The small merchant middlemen (beopari) comprised the basis of a network for purchasing the peasant's produce. Some of them had their own capital, but the majority were financed by bigger beoparis and so-called aratdars. The village merchants and shopkeepers operated with their own capital and that of marwaris and other town traders, connected with the Indian banks, and, through them, with British banking capital. The support and agent of merchant's capital in the countryside was the prosperous stratum of peasants who bought up the peasants' harvest with money borrowed from marwaris.

Bombay. Here, there was a developed system by which itinerant traders bought up the peasants' harvest. Enormous numbers of these traders, and of village ones, used capital borrowed from the shroff town bankers.

Bengal. The village merchants, beoparis, aratdars, arthia and so on were financed by town traders and local banks under bills of exchange for export produce. Big town-based trading firms were engaged primarily in financing the transportation of agricultural export produce from remote parts of the country to the seaports. As a rule, they possessed a quite substantial network of purchasing agencies and branches, scattered throughout the province. In turn, the town trading firms were financed by big Indian banks and British export firms.

Bihar and Orissa. Village buyers were financed by the commission agents of export offices, which either had their own banks or received loans on the Calcutta money market. Big village and town grain traders sometimes borrowed capital from Indian joint-stock banks or the Imperial Bank of India.

Central Provinces. The village traders were financed mainly by commission agents, who themselves operated with capital borrowed from local banks on the security of the agricultural produce.

Madras. Commission agents, connected with village traders, operated with short-term loans from joint-stock banks and the Imperial Bank of India, which discounted bills and advanced loans on the security of agricultural produce.

The Punjab. The Imperial Bank advanced big sums on agricultural produce. Its advances constituted 75 per cent of the value of the grain and 70 per cent of that of the cotton. Almost all the Punjabi banks advanced loans on the security of agricultural produce: the Allahabad Bank, the Central Bank of India, the Punjab National Bank, and the People's Bank of North India.

It is quite obvious that, like moneylender's capital, Indian merchant's capital was subordinate to British finance capital. British banks and export firms were in full control of the commodity and money markets of the country, relying on big and small Indian banking capital.

The fate of Indian agriculture was ultimately in the hands of British finance capital. All the main market processes—price-formation, credit, the interest rates, the rate of profit, the geographical distribution of commodity flows, transportation, storage and insurance of agricultural produce—were decided by British finance capital, which was an omnipotent dictator over the direct producers in India. The only specific feature was that the direct producer came into contact on the village market not with British finance capital itself, but with its local merchant and moneylending agencies.

Various experts were appointed to the Banking Committee, including foreigners. Some of them produced quite interesting documents—the reports presented below.

A. P. MacDougall, a Banking Committee expert, tried to give, so to say, a "radical" formulation of the agrarian problem in India in his report. He diagnosed the situation as follows:[18]

1. "The economic position of the Indian cultivator is not healthy. He is deeply in debt."

2. "It has been stated that the soil of India is naturally poor. This is not correct. It has become poor... Countless generations of cultivators have reduced the natural fertility of Indian lands until this soil is now producing almost the minimum quantity per acre."[19]

3. "Land holding under zamindars who do nothing to improve the conditions of their tenant and little or nothing to improve the standard of cultivation is not a good system."

4. The chief evil was the extreme fragmentation of farming, caused, in MacDougall's opinion, by Indian inheritance laws.

5. The land was badly cultivated and the seed poor.

6. The peasants were ignorant and illiterate.

7. The market and financial conditions under which the output was sold were not favourable for production.

MacDougall's diagnosis, although it does include some correct points, is far from being truthful as a whole. The domination of imperialism and feudal landlords as the main and basic factors behind the situation was ignored in this diagnosis, so it went no further than proposing elementary agronomic measures. The most this consultant could do was to suggest an energetic policy of agricultural reforms, geared to increasing the size of land holdings, supporting the prosperous peasant stratum in the countryside, and raising the feudals' interest in agriculture. MacDougall was not happy that the implantation of junker and rich peasant farming had not been universally and resolutely carried out by the Anglo-Indian government, and that the government was confining itself to individual, gradual attempts in this respect. He even declared that the longer the delay in facing the need, the greater would be the danger of India having to face social convulsions which could endanger her whole future.

There can be no doubt, that in the context of the economic and political situation both within India and elsewhere, British imperialism was restricted in pursuing any serious measures to reform Indian agriculture and especially in the sphere of the agrarian system, though this in no way excluded the possibility of individual attempts in some regions, in a given favourable situation, attempts following, in general, the line of its intended junker reforms. Its room to manoeuvre in this was very limited, which explains why the proposals of the Royal Commission remained, on the whole, unfulfilled. The rate at which they were implemented even in the sphere of agriculture, which could not be reorganised without a change in the agrarian system itself, was very slow indeed. MacDougall pointed out that the implementation of the elementary agronomic measures recommended by the Royal Commission on Agriculture would, at the current speed, require many generations. This is why the work of the Banking Committee was of such negligible effectiveness.

Even in the most capitalised parts of India, the feudal

survivals were extremely strong. One of the Banking Committee experts made quite interesting calculations for the Punjab, a region of wheat monoculture. The price of land for the province as a whole exceeded the net annual income from farming 25-fold in 1928 and 273-fold in 1929. There were two reasons for this: the exceptionally high rents and the exceptionally low net income from the land received by the producer. The data on this for the Gujranwala district (which produced wheat and cotton) are as follows:

Average sale price per acre of land (1928)	402 rupees
Average mortgage price of land (1928)	174 rupees
Net income from the cultivated land (1929)	1 rupee 15 annas 7 pais
The same in Mianwali	8 annas
The same in Lyallpur	5 rupees 7 annas 4 pais

Thus, the direct producer who cultivated estate land had to relinquish his produce at a price that hardly allowed him to survive, thereby ensuring the landlord, over a certain period of time, primarily in the form of short-term rent, the receipt of the land price as capitalist anticipated semi-feudal rent; the peasant was left with a literally minute part of the income, which could in no way serve as the basis for any serious expanded reproduction on his holding. Such was the pressure of the feudal survivals even in this comparatively developed part of India. Under these conditions, both the high degree of marketability of peasant farming and its specialisation acquired a specific hue.

The decisive factor in this sort of colonial marketability and specialisation was the underdeveloped rather than developed nature of capitalism, and the impact of feudal and semi-feudal survivals on the bonded peasant economy. No credit reforms, let alone the colonial reforms of imperialism, could, of course, do anything to reduce the very deep crisis of the agrarian system. In the circumstances, there were absolutely no grounds for MacDougall's hopes.

What exactly did MacDougall see as the way out of the situation? On what basis did he propose reforming Indian farming? He had a very interesting plan for this. However strange it may seem, the only way out, in his opinion, was to reconcile the Indian peasants and moneylenders. His advice was: "When co-operative credit banks were established to provide capital to the agriculturist at less cost, it was taken for granted that the moneylender was an enemy who must be destroyed. It might have been better to have made an endeavour to use his wealth and experience inside the co-operative movement... The co-operative organization should not... refuse to consider the possibility of making use of his capital and experience. It may be that, if this combination of forces can be brought into being, we shall have an organization capable of overcoming all difficulties. We shall then have the organized strength of the cultivator on the one hand and on the other—the collective wealth, business experience and money sense of the bania... It has been too readily accepted that in making such an attempt moneylenders will prove to be the more powerful force of the two, that will kill the weaker. Is this fear justified?... We suggest that the leaders of co-operation should consider the possibility of welcoming the co-operation of the moneylender, not only in the country, but in the towns, on the following terms:—

"1) That he should become a member of his local society.

"2) That after joining his society no further loans shall be granted by him...

"4) He shall be allowed to fill any position to which he may be elected by the vote of the members...

"The moneylender is no mean force for the co-operative movement to fight."[20]

This was the advice given by a British official in India. MacDougall's economically ridiculous idea merely testified to the helplessness of British imperialism, to the fact that, in order to delay the revolutionary explosion, it attempted to make use of the recipes provided by such "experts".

Manu Subedar, a deputy chairman of the Federation of Indian Chambers of Commerce, owner of several estates and a big shareholder in Anglo-Indian commercial and industrial companies, an ideologist of the Indian liberal landlords and rich peasants, in parallel to the reports given by the majority of the officials to the Banking Committee, wrote his own report on behalf of the minority. This report contained a special programme for getting out of the crisis at the cost of ruining the Indian countryside.

Manu Subedar pointed to the impoverishment of the countryside, the growth of loan indebtedness, the fragmentation of farming, landlord absenteeism, the harsh conditions for the sale of the peasants' produce on the market—in a word, the multitude of ills afflicting the Indian countryside. In contrast to MacDougall, Manu Subedar believed that a decisive change was required in the agrarian system from above, the aim being to consolidate the position of the "actual cultivator", i.e., in essence, the rich peasant. Like the Anglo-Indian government, he supported a gradual, reformist eviction of the ruined tenants from the land, proposing that it be carried out with the support of the rich peasants and capitalist landlords, in their interests and to their benefit. India's desire and ability to solve this problem (the problem of increasing the size of landlord and rich peasant holdings by evicting the tenants) would, he believed, be a test of the might of the government and the population of the country. It is quite clear why Manu Subedar needed to see the interests of the rich peasants and landlords as coinciding with those of the nation as a whole. This was, so to say, a necessary precaution and a way of concealing the true class essence of his programme.

Manu Subedar was a politician; he did not propose educative measures to encourage the peasants to leave the land "voluntarily". He stated outright that the main thing required for solving the problem was strength, not just words. Moreover, Manu Subedar was surprised that in India, where the government had a reputation of being a strong government, it had proved incapable of taking decisive steps in this direction. Even if the peasants hampered such innovations and put a damper on the reformist ardour of imperialism, Manu Subedar was sure the Anglo-Indian government was fully aware that "the Indian cultivator is too ignorant to know that such reforms have been carried out in other countries, that they are intended for his good, and that he should acquiesce by co-operating without any fear of being treated unfairly".[21]

Manu Subedar expressed his dissatisfaction with the government quite strongly: "It is to the credit of the Minister of Agriculture in Bombay that a bill for the consolidation of holdings was introduced. It was, however, very surprising that in Bombay, which is the one province, in which the Government have, ever since the introduction of the reforms, consistently enjoyed a majority in the legislative council on all issues, on which they wanted it, this measure was thrown out!"[22]

Manu Subedar deliberately kept quiet about the fact that the Bombay bill "on small holdings" had been thrown out by the Legislative Council because of the force of the peasant movement and that the failure of the bill was one of the side effects of the peasant struggle. In one way or another, Manu Subedar was unhappy with the government's slowness and did not hesitate to blame officials and even landlords for this. The first thing he called on the government to do was to take its courage in its hands, be resolute, firm and consistent in implementing the rich peasant-landlord programme for bringing India's agrarian system out of crisis.

The next issue tackled by Manu Subedar was what to do with the tens of millions of evicted peasants resulting from his proposed programme. He saw the solution to this in their "transfer to new lands", i.e., colonisation and an increase in the "demand" for labour, as a result of which the "actual cultivator", i.e., the rich peasant, would be "the initiator of new jobs". In this respect, Manu Subedar obviously had nothing new to say. He was just repeating what the Royal Commission on Agriculture in India had suggested: the colonisation of new areas of the country. The Commission could not, however, conceal the evidence given by one of its witnesses to the effect that, at the current rate of colonisation, about a thousand years would be required to counteract the shortage of land in the central parts of India.

Of more interest in Manu Subedar's programme was the way he posed the question of landlords and rich peasants: "Where an agricultural policy is enunciated, through whom is the salvation of agriculture to come? Is it expected that the landlord will improve the lands, will increase production, and bring prosperity and should, therefore, be assisted in every possible way, or is it that the improvement of the land is to be secured through the improvement of the economic position of the tenant or actual cultivator?"[23]

Manu Subedar was for a compromise, a union of the Indian landlord and rich peasant. He was not against the continued existence of landed estates. His programme provided for their retention, but allotted them a secondary rather than primary role in the capitalist restructuring of the agrarian system. The person to implement this way out of the crisis he saw as the "strong Indian peasant", the colonial rich peasant, to whom the landlord should, in the interests of his own survival, render every assistance as his own ally.

He said that India would have to choose whether to change credit terms in favour of the landlord or the tenant. He was convinced that the way to improve agriculture was to strengthen the position of the actual cultivator, that this would encourage him to bend extra efforts and make improvements, and would make his rights to the land firm.

He went on that the presence of a strong and prosperous class was important for society, and government intervention would be necessary under such circumstances. He called for the welfare of the "cultivator" to be put first and for more attention to be focused by the government on the grounds for the cultivator to claim more tangible rights to the land than on the interests of the landlords.

He was convinced that changes in the laws should be made to the benefit of the "actual cultivator" and that limitations on the right of cultivators to dispose the land reduced their credit, so everything possible should be done to strengthen their right of ownership of the land they cultivated as well as their feeling of ownership and to encourage them to greater efforts and desire to increase production.

In Manu Subedar's view, the "actual cultivator" should enjoy stability of his position. Everything that hampered the growth of a rich peasant stratum was, therefore, to be removed from the path of its development.

While noting the collapse of the attempts at a co-operative unification of small peasant commodity producers for the purpose of organising the sale of agricultural produce, a collapse that was predetermined by the domination of finance capital in both India's internal and foreign trade, and stating that the countless multitudes of small village traders were also, to one degree or another, subordinate to the wishes of finance capital, Manu Subedar proposed that the sale of the rich peasants' output be organised by the formation of a pool, i.e., a price agreement. He pointed out that voluntary organisation of such agreements could not be expected in India. The initiative would have to come from above. He declared, not at all surprisingly, that the organisation of such a pool would be an "experiment in socialism".

The possibility of expropriation, at any moment, and unrestricted by landlord-feudal monopoly, of the land rented from the landlord, the free mortgaging of land, the development of capitalist relations in the countryside, government assistance and credit, and guarantees against the possibility of arbitrary actions on the part of landlords with respect to excessive rents and various extortions—all these were to be granted to the rich peasant stratum, the chief, in Manu Subedar's opinion, future support of imperialism in India, capable, in conjunction with the landlords, of countering an agrarian revolution. In order to avoid being accused of radicalism, Manu Subedar admitted that, although his programme might be considered as a prelude to a "general socialist policy", he did not support this idea. He stressed that his purpose was a timely and rational change in the feudal organisation of society. He did not suggest that the cultivator should be declared the unrestricted landowner and tax-payer, which would amount to an act of universal expropriation and would be a major infringement of the social order.

Manu Subedar recognised that the "actual cultivator" in India often did not enjoy rights to the land he worked, rights that were subject to sale and purchase and on the basis of which he could receive a loan.

Manu Subedar saw himself as the ideologist of the liberal rich peasant opposition to the feudal landlord, his aim being to speed up the capitalist transformation and avert peasant uprisings. His play with the word "socialism" did not, of course, deceive anyone concerning the true nature of his programme.

The economic essence of this programme was clear: a policy of redistributing the surplus agricultural product, received at the peasants' expense, in proportions more favourable to the rich peasants. It also meant ensuring broader and increasingly capitalist production on rich peasant farms, on the condition of a limitation, objectively necessary for the development of capitalism, of the share of the landlord in the surplus product of the peasantry.

Manu Subedar was not against the development of landlord capitalism. On the contrary, he was for developing it as much as possible, but simply did not really believe in the success of this development. He was too well aware of the parasitic essence of the Indian feudals to entertain any illusions concerning their ability to use their accumulations in any other way than to increase their latifundias and the numbers of their bonded tenants, or at best to expand landlord moneylending and trade. For this reason he stated that should intermediate owners invest really big or just significant sums of money out of their rent in land improvement it would be to their credit. In his words, the Banking Committee's reports said that landowners merely kept expanding their estates, using their free means for land purchases rather than for land improvement.

Manu Subedar favoured radical measures but proposed to work out and implement them in most careful way. He believed that doing so it would be possible both to do away with markedly negative phenomena and avert "a sudden, anti-social catastrophe".

Manu Subedar's proposals on this account concluded with the following panegyric of the Indian rich peasant stratum: "The economic position of the agriculturist has got to be strengthened by various measures, which would give him a surplus, that he can call his own. It is on the strength of such surplus that the cultivator would secure, by measures foreshadowed elsewhere in this report, the necessary credit to finance him both for long period and for current purposes. A definite agricultural policy and a general economic policy calculated to improve the position of the cultivator, would not be effective, unless his position against the landlord is made secure and is strengthened, wherever it is weak at present. The welfare of the community lies in securing the welfare of the actual cultivator."[24]

The Indian rich peasant stratum, the capitalist development of which was hampered, on the one hand, by the prevailing feudal survivals, and on the other hand, by the colonial development of the country, was unable to carry out a revolutionary, objectively bourgeois and internally consistent agrarian revolution. Being, therefore, a fundamental opponent of agrarian revolution, beginning to join here and there, under the impact of the mass peasant movement, a reactionary bloc, the rich peasants, at the same time, reserved for themselves a larger share in the exploitation of the countryside. They also called on imperialism to pursue a reformist policy to ensure themselves, the rich peasants, alongside the continued existence of landlord farming, the leading role in the economic development of the countryside.

By the 1930s, the Indian national industrial and merchant bourgeoisie had already territorialised, but the rich peasants, whose economic motives were basically the same, had still not managed to get out of the feudal Middle Ages enough to retain, even on the distant opproaches to an agrarian upheaven, the significance of a consistently revolutionary force (within the framework of the bourgeois-democratic stage of the agrarian revolution). Manu Subedar's programme was the first extensive document on this, testifying that the Indian rich peasantry was very weak as a revolutionary anti-feudal force.

The experience of the peasant movement during the 1920s and 1930s showed, however, the possibility of comparatively protracted conflicts between the rich peasant stratum in the countryside and the landlords and imperialism. Moreover, it might have been foretold that, in individual regions (Gujarat, the Punjab) in a specific historical situation, at a given stage of the peasant struggle, the rich peasants would participate in the peasant uprisings. The peasant movement in India had known such things happen in the past. At the same time, however, past experience (in Kishorganj, the United Provinces, Gujarat, the North-West Frontier Province) had shown that the rich peasants' participation in peasant uprisings, and sometimes their leading role, had been dictated mainly by a desire to take advantage of peasant dissatisfaction to their own ends, rather than to promote a consistent agrarian revolution.

The tactics in relation to the rich peasantry were, therefore, based on a differentiated approach, depending on the maturity of the peasant movement, the specific political and economic features of each centre of the peasant movement, its links with the working-class movement in the towns, the composition of its motive forces and the demands presented. It should, however, be remembered that the rich peasants could not play a consistent anti-feudal role.

Let us now consider other points of Manu Subedar's programme. He calculated that just the sum of the interest paid by the agricultural classes constituted at least a thousand million rupees. Interest was roughly treble the land tax.[25] Manu Subedar was convinced that the payment of rent reduced the standard of living of the cultivator, for rent was charged not on the net, but the gross income. Indian rent was not the surplus over and above the profit of the farming entrepreneur, nor was it limited by this. Together with loan interest, it absorbed the peasant's entire surplus product. His ideas on this were very vague, but he did suggest a limitation on landlord rent and the transfer of moneylending to capitalist credit lines. He believed that the resources of moneylenders should be strengthened and their operating conditions improved, and was in full agreement with the Banking Committee that a resolute capitalist reformation of Indian moneylending was needed.

Given the nature of agricultural credit in India, loans advanced by moneylenders to the producer resulted in the entire income of the producer going to his creditor, so not the peasant but his creditor reaped the peasant harvest. Manu Subedar was resolutely against this state of affairs. His views on this were set out as follows: "Trade flourishes on the labour of bankrupt people, for three-fourths of the people of India are unable to pay their debts. The country is run by a system of forced labour, the force being that of the moneylender . . . The secret of successful industry is to buy your finance cheap and sell your produce dear. The Indian buys his finance dear and sells his produce cheap. His creditor generally fixes the price of both.

" . . . It is the organisation of its capital that India wants more than its increase. There is plenty of capital in the country, but it is mainly in the wrong hands,—the hands of the non-producers. The greatest economic problem before India today is how to shift the control of capital from the hands of the non-producers to those of the producers of the country's wealth and until that problem is solved we shall look in vain for much progress."[26]

Cheap capitalist credit, high prices for agricultural goods, a limitation on loan bondage and the organisation of capital, the development of trade on the basis of a capitalist economy—such were the tasks, in Manu Subedar's opinion, to be tackled by the economic policy pursued by British imperialism in India. It is interesting that the recommendations made in the majority report of the Banking Committee included the point that the Committee considered it a misguided suggestion to eliminate the extremely widespread practice among moneylenders of charging compound interest. It put forward a variety of arguments to support the retention of this practice, taking as its point of departure, however strange this may seem, the supposed interests of the direct producers. Manu Subedar disagreed with the Banking Committee on this and declared resolutely that the charging of compound interest should be halted.

The essence of his argument was this: "Without being charged with undue pessimism, it appears to me that a silent revolution is going on, by which the independence of many agriculturists is being gradually sapped. The financial dependence of the agriculturists on other classes, whom they are unable to pay fully and to whom they, therefore, pay all that they can, must tend to reduce their standard of life and to destroy their motive for larger production.

"The process should, therefore, be to increase the number of agriculturists, who are free from debt and to put as many of them on the path towards such freedom as possible, so that when one set of agriculturists get ruined, there are at least equally competent agriculturists in the district, who would be willing to take up the land and cultivate it to its best capacity...

"It is desirable to increase that class... From the point of view of the community the passing of more land in the hands of capable and resourceful agriculturists would not be an evil."[27]

Manu Subedar considered the problem of the loan indebtedness of the peasantry from the point of view of the rich peasants. Ruin the peasants, but not all of them; hurry to create and strengthen a class of rural bourgeoisie; the more peasants take this road, the better and stronger will be the social support to counteract revolution in the country. Such was the true essence of Manu Subedar's anti-moneylender "radicalism", capable, perhaps, of temporarily satisfying part of the rich peasantry, but in no way of solving the problem of peasant indebtedness as a whole. His programme with respect to the financing of agriculture was, even on the condition that it would function for a given period of time within the framework of the existing agrarian structure, equally incapable of fundamentally resolving the tasks of the impending agrarian transformation.

One of the biggest contradictions of the Indian agrarian system was, on the one hand, the functioning and development of commodity-money relations on the basis of the feudal and semi-feudal mode of production and, on the other hand, the protracted existence and conservation of the feudal and semi-feudal mode of production given the unconditional predominance of commodity-money relations, used by the ruling classes of the feudal-imperialist regime. An inevitable result of this contradiction was the tremendous spread of the initial, primitive and rapacious forms of capital, only superficially related to the actual process and mode of production, not only not transforming it on a fundamentally new basis, but also conserving it to the extent that it decayed under the blows inflicted by the introduction of commodity-money relations by the capitalist colonialists.

This vital contradiction, which was expressed economically in a lack of free and extensive ways for commodity-money relations to develop into capitalist ones, constrained by the dominance of feudal survivals, could not be resolved in a reformist way at the expense of the majority of the peasants, given the maturing agrarian revolution. Manu Subedar tried to resolve this contradiction by inviting people with money to invest capital in production and farming, i.e., to use their capital productively.

Manu Subedar was still head and shoulders above his colleagues on the Banking Committee. His strong rich-peasant reckoning allowed him to be a much more realistic politician than the liberal bureaucratic schemers on the Committee, who recommended reconciling the peasant with the moneylender and drawing the latter into the Indian agricultural and credit co-operative movement. Manu Subedar had a short answer to these ridiculous and utopian schemes: "I have no hesitation in saying that it is not possible to replace the moneylender as a whole and the agriculturist moneylender in particular by the co-operative credit movement, by the Government themselves stepping into the field, by the machinery of ordinary banks, by commercial land mortgage banks, or by any means what soever."[28] He stated that the efforts were vain of those who hoped that the moneylenders, as a class, would put their money in co-operative societies; neither would the most conservative moneylenders join the co-operative societies, but only those who, without losing their rights, wanted to charge levies or use the cheap credit from the central co-operative banks for their own personal purposes, in a word, those moneylenders who would organise co-operative societies of their debtors and would manage them as long as it was profitable, and then leave them.

Even if the co-operative movement is developed and the moneylender drawn into it, nothing will come of this until the matter of the economic development of the countryside is given into the hands of the rich peasants and rural bourgeoisie. We are not asking for much. We need land and means of production from the ruined peasants. We need firm government support—a guarantee that no feudal or moneylender will be allowed to prevent us from reorganising the countryside in our own way, in order to avert a huge social catastrophe. Such were Manu Subedar's revelations. Although the historical pretensions of his class—the rich peasantry—in the sense of his suggested policy were no less illusory, given the growing crisis and revolutionary upsurge, than expectations of success from the proposals made by his feudal-imperialist opponents, these pretensions did rest on an economic force that existed objectively in India and was actually growing, though slowly,—the Indian rich peasantry.

By the 1930s, there were no reliable data on the numbers of the Indian rich peasants and their economic influence. The economic structure of the rich peasant economy itself and its share in the country's agriculture can be judged only from individual, scattered material.

It is quite obvious, however, that Manu Subedar was, from the angle of the tasks he allotted to the union of the rich peasant with the landlord, exaggerating the role and significance of the rich peasant farm in the country's economy, ignoring the most vulnerable and weak aspects of the rich peasantry with respect to their ability to implement his suggested programme and, finally, assumed that British imperialism, if it adopted his programme, would be a strict and resolute midwife to the rich peasant transformation of the countryside. Moreover, Manu Subedar was unjustifiably optimistic in his consideration (or rather, lack of it) of the class struggle that was developing on the basis of the world economic crisis and was exacerbating all the political and economic contradictions in the country.

His programme for a way out of the crisis of the agrarian system did reveal an undoubtedly clever and foresighted ideologist and politician, capable of considering the objective economic trends more realistically than his class allies and of pinpointing within modern Indian society the interests and strivings of a specific social group, of generalising them and linking them with the interests of British imperialism. It could not, however, be implemented. First, this programme ignored the 300-million toiling peasants who were beginning to struggle for their rights. Second, it abstracted from the world economic crisis that was shaking India's economy to its foundations. Finally, British imperialism was not capable of taking the risk, not only because of its narrowing room to manoeuvre in the face of the growing revolutionary crisis, but also because of the fundamental class unfeasibility for it of going over from the policy of historically conditioned and traditional reliance on the feudal and semi-feudal classes of rural India to one of relying on the rich peasantry, which was comparatively weak by Indian standards, essentially distorted in the socio-economic sense, and adjusted to landlord and merchant-moneylender bondage.

Chapter Six

The Specifics of Population Movements in India Under the Crisis of Colonial Capitalism

In 1931, the Anglo-Indian government carried out one of its regular all-India population censuses. The Anglo-Indian press of the time often referred to individual results of the census and published considerable material on the question of population movements. Among Marxists, this question also became a pressing one, for in the early 1930s some researchers put forward a specific conception of the agrarianisation of India. The impact exerted by colonial capitalism on population migrations had to be clarified.

In spite of the shortcomings of the Anglo-Indian statistics and the unscientific nature of many of the methods employed, the 1931 census was of extreme interest and provided material for revealing, on the one hand, the specifics of the development of India, incomparable with West European ones, and, on the other hand, the parasitic essence of the domination of British imperialism and its feudal support in the country.

Over the decade since the previous census (1921), India's capitalist development had proceeded apace. New, postwar trends in the colonial economy came down to a rapid growth of capitalism in the country, engendering a more or less numerous working class. The growth of capitalism in the colonies, which had gained momentum during the war and during the first period of postwar development, was noted in many research works. The Third Congress of the Communist International pointed to the vigorous development of capitalism, especially in India and China. The theses of the 6th plenary session of the Communist International's Executive Committee also noted the rapid industrialisation of India and the beginning industrialisation of the Orient, which resulted in new social foundations for the revolutionary struggle being created in the biggest countries of Asia—an industrial and agricultural proletariat, which was of growing significance in the liberation movement of the colonial peoples and in the revolutionary struggle. It should be taken into account, of course, that this development of capitalism was taking place under the conditions of the domination of feudal survivals and semi-feudal forms of bondage, supported by imperialism.

India's industrial development during the war and straight afterwards gave rise to new industrial centres and a certain growth of old ones with a comparatively concentrated industry and a concentrated big proletariat. This was also reflected in a change in the composition of the population. Data on population movements in the 1920s refuted the theory of decolonisation and, at the same time, testified to the invalidity of the theory of agrarianisation.

The mistake made by the supporters of the agrarianisation theory, who tried to derive the character and laws of India's economic development from those of population migration, rather than use the specific nature of the economy to explain that of the population movements, consisted in confusing the question of the relative and, undoubtedly, growing agricultural population surplus with that of the agrarianisation of the country's economic structure. The mistake made by the advocates of this theory was based on an incorrect identification of the growth of the agricultural population surplus with general agrarianisation of the economy and all its consequences, such as the blocking of economic development, its absolute stagnation, and so on.

The growing concentration of the population in the countryside over a historically long period of time was not, for India, an indication that it was becoming an increasingly agrarian country or that its economic evolution was leading with historical inevitability to this result. It was an objective reflection of the fact that, against the general background of development towards capitalism, India was, while the colonial monopoly of imperialism remained, its agrarian-raw material appendage, where feudal survivals prevailed and, consequently, a country where the laws discovered by Marx governing population movements in a country advancing freely towards capitalism could not but conflict strongly with the colonial-feudal monopoly. The supporters of the theory of agrarianisation forgot to make a specific analysis of each given historical situation—which is the basic law of dialectics.

Let us point out merely the main reasons for the growth of the agricultural population in conjunction with the growth of Indian industrial capitalism and the proletariat. The fact is that the ruin of local crafts, in which a huge number of peasants were engaged, took place much faster than the development of industry, and under the impact of three forces: imperialism, feudalism and local capitalism. Yet local and foreign industry could only absorb negligible numbers of the ruined urban and village craftsmen and peasant masses. In the same way, the industrial proletariat in Britain was growing faster, against the ruin of the urban and village craftsmen in the colony, than the industrial proletariat in the colony as a result of the investment of foreign capital. Local industry, based on exported capital, could not absorb the huge numbers of workers ejected from the production process to become paupers and compelled by the threat of starvation to engage in farming.

Let us consider population migration data for India.

Census year	Population
1881	253,896,330
1891	287,314,671
1901	294,400,000
1911	315,156,396
1921	318,942,480
1931	352,986,876

The absolute figures for the population increase, especially for the first few censuses, cannot be considered characteristic, since they include not only the net increment resulting from the excess of the birth rate over the death rate, but also the increase in the population due to the seizure and annexation by British imperialism of new territories to its Indian empire.

Taking 1891 as the point of departure, i.e., the time when British territorial seizures in India had mostly come to an end, the net population increase up to 1931 was 12.2 per cent, or an average of 4.8 per cent per annum (Table 14). From 1891 to 1901 and from 1911 to 1921 there were unprecedented epidemics

Table 14

Population Increase in India,
per cent

Year	India as a whole	British India	Net population increase*	Population increase in England and Wales
1881—1891	13.4	11.2	9.6	—
1891—1901	6.2	4.7	1.4	12.7
1901—1911	7.1	5.5	6.4	10.91
1911—1921	1.2	1.3	1.2	4.8
1921—1931	10.6	10.0	10.6	—
1881—1931	44.3	36.8	28.8	—

* Excluding population increase from territorial expansion.

resulting from famine. It is, therefore, natural that the main reason for the somewhat greater increase in the population from 1921 to 1931 compared with 1911 to 1921 was the absence of mass epidemics in the later decade. This did not mean that the toiling masses of India had ceased to suffer systematically from hunger. On the contrary, the degree of exploitation of the working masses in town and countryside, the extent to which the surplus and necessary product was taken away from them, had increased. The broad population's consumption had not risen. New huge numbers of middle peasants, petty urban bourgeois and so on now found themselves suffering from chronic hunger, to say nothing of the working class and poorest peasants, whose consumption level even before the crisis had been lower than that provided in the gaols of Bombay and Calcutta. Some regions of rural India suffered from famine and epidemics throughout the 1920s, the result being a substantial drop in the natural population increase there, and in some cases a significant excess of the death rate over the birth rate.

Statisticians and economists representing British imperialism and the local bourgeoisie spread the ridiculous idea of "too many mouths" and the "excessive multiplication" of people, and so on. A simple comparison of the data presented on the natural population increase in India and Britain refuted these

Malthusian fables and, at the same time, showed that, even during a relatively "favourable" period, without nationwide famine and epidemics, the natural population increase in India was from a quarter to half of that in Britain. Thus, on the Indian scale and from the point of view of the population's potential for natural growth, which could only be realised if the colonial-feudal regime were abolished, the natural population increase in India from 1921 to 1931 must, of course, be recognised as having been extremely negligible.

The specific character of the development of India and other colonial countries told particularly in that the growth of their productive forces proceeded with extreme difficulty, irregularly and artificially, and was confined to individual sectors of the economy. All this undoubtedly resulted in the pressure exerted by imperialism on the colonial and semi-colonial countries being reproduced each time at a higher level and engendered increasingly strong counteractions on the part of the socio-economic factors arising from imperialism itself.

The extemely low population growth of 12.2 per cent from 1891 to 1931 in India, or 4.8 per cent per decade, compared with 27.8 per cent over the thirty years for England and Wales, or an average of 9.3 per cent per decade, was a direct indication of the consequences of the dual oppression of the colonial toiling masses.

India's capitalist industrial development from 1921 to 1931 was reflected in migration primarily in that the percentage increase in the urban population exceeded the relative increase in the rural population for the first time. From 1921 to 1931, the rural population increased by 9.6 per cent, while the urban population by 19.8 per cent, with 10.6 per cent for the total population of the country. In 1921, the rural population made up 89.9 per cent of India's total population and in 1931—89 per cent. The urban population constituted 10.2 per cent in 1921 and 11 per cent in 1931. Thus, a 19.8 per cent increase in the urban population, and only an 0.8 per cent one relative to the total population, from 1921 to 1931, when the growth of capitalism was gaining comparative momentum—such were the insignificant rates of population reproduction in the colonial towns.

It should, however, be remembered that in Anglo-Indian

statistics a population centre with 5,000 people was considered a town. In India there were about 700 such "towns", of no industrial significance and really constituting just comparatively large villages. The inclusion of their inhabitants in the "urban population" naturally exaggerated the true size of the urban population, for there were 2.3 million such people according to the 1921 census, i.e., a fifth of the total urban population. A substantial proportion of these big "villages" were old commercial and craft centres that, at one time, had fulfilled the functions of towns—a concentration of administrative powers, the feudal court, trade and handicrafts. After the colonial seizures, these centres were reduced to ruins, with all those unable to live there escaping to the big towns or into the countryside. An enormous part of the population of the old Indian "towns" simply died out.

Let us look at the dynamics of the growth of the urban and rural population by provinces. The data in Table 15 are indicative in the following respects:

— The biggest relative urban population increase from 1921 to 1931 took place in those provinces where the development of industrial capitalist towns had been slowest until that decade: Bihar and Orissa, the Central Provinces, Berar, Madras, and the Punjab.

— The smallest relative urban population growth occurred in the provinces where the development of industrial capitalist towns had been greatest in previous decades: Bombay, Bengal, Assam, and the United Provinces.

This testifies that new provinces, economic regions and towns were being drawn into industrial capitalist development. Capitalism had made another step forward in involving previously almost purely agricultural regions in industrial development. Capitalism penetrated deep into the country, into new regions far from the seaports, and the rate of the relative increase there was higher than in the old centres of colonial industrial capitalism. The most advanced province in terms of industrial development—Bombay—revealed even an opposite trend, i.e., a relatively higher increment of the rural than the urban population. Even the capital of this province, the city of Bombay, showed a drop in the number of its inhabitants from 1,175 thousand in 1921 to 1,161 thousand in 1931.

Table 15

Some Data from the 1931 Census of the Population of India

Province	Population in 1921, thous.	Population in 1931, thous.	Increase in population in 1921-31, %	Increase in urban population in 1921-31, %	Increase in rural population in 1921-31, %	Average population density, people per sq mile
Ajmer-Merwara (territory of central subordination)	496	500	13.1	9.4	15.0	207
Assam	7,599	8,600	15.6*	15.8	15.2	157
Bengal	46,653	50,100	7.3**	15.6	6.7	646
Bihar and Orissa	34,000	37,600	10.8	20.3	10.4	454
Bombay	19,339	21,900	13.3	11.6	13.9	177
Burma	13,206	14,600	11.0	17.7	10.3	63
Central Provinces and Berar	13,909	15,500	11.5	20.5	10.5	155
Madras	42,322	46,700	10.4	20.4	9.1	329
Punjab	20,688	24,100	14.0	38.7	11.6	238
United Provinces	45,591	48,400	6.7**	12.9	5.9	456

* The relatively higher population increase in Assam was a result of the colonisation of certain free lands by people arriving mostly from Bihar, Orissa, Madras and partly from Bengal.

** The lowest growth population in Bengal and the United Provinces, compared with the other provinces, was undoubtedly directly connected with the domination there of big landlord farming and feudal latifundia. The degree of exploitation and oppression of small holdings was particularly high in these two provinces.

Bombay's position as India's biggest industrial centre, showing not only a relative drop in the urban population from 1921 to 1931, but also an absolute one, was undoubtedly characteristic, testifying that the further industrial capitalist development of this centre was in sharp contradiction to the imperialist monopoly. British imperialism was striving to stifle Bombay's further industrial development and put it in an unfavourable position in relation to the growing competition on the world market, on the one hand, and the very fierce competition from new centres of the textile industry that had grown up in the country, on the other. Whatever Indian bourgeois economists might say about the favourable influence of the anti-British economic boycott, which supposedly gave Bombay endless scope for industrial development, the fact cannot be hidden that this centre of local industrial capitalism fell into economic decline and had lost part of its former economic influence long before the beginning of the 1929-1933 crisis. New textile industry centres grew up in the country (Sholapur, Kanpur, Ahmadabad) to compete with Bombay.

The chief cities of the comparatively less developed provinces provided a substantial population increase, outstripping the population growth rate in the old industrial cities manyfold. In this respect, Lahore, Delhi, Bangalore and Madras came first. The old industrial cities revealed a slower urban population increase (Table 16).

Table 16

Growth Rate of Old and New Industrial Cities,*
per cent

	1911-1921	1921-1931
Calcutta and its surroundings	4.3	11.9
Bombay	20.0	—1.2
Madras	1.6	22.8
Hyderabad	—19.0	16.0
Delhi	30.7	47.0
Lahore	23.2	52.5
Rangoon	16.6	17.1
Ahmadabad	26.4	14.5
Bangalore	25.3	29.0
Nagpur	43.0	48.0
Sholapur	94.9	21.0

* *Census of India, 1931*, Vol. I, Part I, Delhi, 1933.

There can be no doubt that capitalism penetrated into the most remote parts of the country during the 1920s. In 1921, there were 23,236,099 people employed in all the branches of industry, on plantations, in transport, and in craft production; 2,681,125 of these were in factory industry as such. In 1931, the respective figures were 25,005,280 and about 3,250,000 people.

The trend towards a further penetration of capitalism into the heart of the country gave rise, in general, to an urban population increase in the feudal states—the princedoms of non-British India (Table 17); it was small by European standards but relatively high for India.

Table 17

Growth Rate of the Urban and Rural Populations in the Princedoms,*
per cent

	Total increment of population, 1921-31	Urban population increase	Rural population increase
Baroda	14.9	18.6	13.9
Bihar and Orissa	17.5	29.5	17.4
Bombay	15.5	24.3	14.3
Central India Agency	10.5	23.0	9.3
Central Province	20.1	55.9	19.3
Hyderabad	15.8	36.2	13.6
Cochin	23.1	62.3	17.2
Mysore	9.7	21.1	7.7
Travancore	27.2	36.4	26.2
Gwalior	10.3	28.2	8.7

* *Census of India, 1931.*

The reason for this lay in the striving of local capital to get round the imperialist monopoly of transport and freight and become established in a situation with less competition from foreign goods. National capitalism went into spheres where it was ensured a higher rate of profit and a higher rate of exploitation, but the growth of capitalism in the feudal princedoms was also accompanied by a rise in the proletariat's numbers, which began to become active even in the most backward provinces, steeped in feudalism. It was here that the economic and political strike movement was waged by the workers, a struggle that was developing alongside that in the old industrial centres. The tremendous historical significance of this cannot be exaggerated.

The relative growth of the urban population in India was not directly proportional to the growth of industrial capitalism, just as the rise in the rural population was not only a net population increment resulting from a rise in the birth rate over the death rate. Two aspects characterised the specific nature of the population increase arising from India's colonial status and the pressure of feudal survivals. First, the inflow of rural population due to the drop in the urban population in medium and small-sized towns, which had once played a substantial economic role in the country's life. Together with the net increment in the rural population, this process had not, in previous decades, been overlapped by the growth of the urban population in the big modern towns. Second, the outflow of population from the old towns into agriculture was relatively and absolutely higher than the growth of the population in the big new industrial centres.

It was during the 1920s that this situation began to change. The medium and small-sized towns were virtually deserted. The outflow of their working population into agriculture was accompanied by part of it settling in the countryside; to a significant extent, the population of these towns became paupers and died out. Overall, from 1921 to 1931, this process proceeded faster than in previous decades. This did not, however, contradict the fact that quite substantial numbers of craftsmen, exploited by merchant's and moneylender's capital, remained behind in these towns. The craftsman in the 1920s worked in a cottage capitalist industry and was oppressed and mercilessly exploited. The first half of the decade saw a comparative acceleration of the development of capitalism in the country, while the second half was characterised by the crisis of 1929-1933. Under the influence of these two factors, the ruin of the urban and village craftsman gathered momentum, and handicrafts in the remote and most distant parts of the country were further subordinated to merchant's and moneylender's capital, and through this to British finance capital. The development of industry and the growth of the urban population from 1921 to 1931 outstripped the tendency towards a drop in the ruined population of medium and small-sized towns and the departure of their inhabitants into the countryside.

The 1929-1933 crisis introduced a new feature into the population movement, the influx of part of the ruined peasantry into the towns. The Anglo-Indian press made much of this fact, seeing a certain "danger" in it. An enormous section of the impoverished and expropriated toiling peasants escaped from the village during the crisis and filled the big industrial and commercial towns, flooding the town labour market with very cheap labour—the labour of the coolie and the pauper. This resulted in a relatively greater increase in the urban population, and the census taken at the height of the crisis partly reflected this process, too. It was particularly evident in the towns of princedoms and in the comparatively less industrially developed provinces.

In the United Provinces, the growth rate of the population in the towns, which was almost double that of the total population, cannot be explained merely by the growth in the numbers employed in industry. The same thing occurred in the Punjab, the Central Provinces, Berar, Bihar and Orissa, Hyderabad, and elsewhere. It is quite obvious that, alongside the growth that took place in the first half of the 1920s in the numbers employed in the industrial capitalist enterprises of these provinces and princedoms, i.e., alongside the growth in the truly urban industrial proletariat, the small, medium-sized and big towns of these provinces were filled during the years of the crisis with huge numbers of newly-arrived paupers and coolies, who took part in the production process only intermittently. This fact, against the background of the growing class movement of the traditional industrial proletariat, was of considerable significance, since the coolies, too, were drawn into the anti-imperialist movement.

The population migration from 1921 to 1931 also showed the specific features of the development of capitalism in India in both town and countryside, confirming once more that, under the domination of the colonial monopoly of imperialism, merged with the feudal land monopoly of the landlord class in the countryside, and the prevalence of merchant's and moneylender's capital, subordinate to British finance capital, in the market relations between the village and the town, the capitalist development of the productive forces was taking place under tremendous difficulties, with painful consequences for the broad population, and raising the conflict between the productive forces and the relations of production to a still higher level. The decade under review exacerbated this conflict, giving it a sharper class expression, and engendered new forces opposing the colonial and capitalist development even in the most remote corners of the Indian feudal princedoms.

Economists and politicians of the Indian national bourgeoisie and British imperialism foresaw, to some extent, the impending intensification of the class struggle stemmed from the aggravation of this fundamental conflict. For instance, N. R. Sarkar, an eminent leader of the Bengali bourgeoisie, said that urgent measures were required to avoid a universal cataclysm, which would finally draw the whole country into the agrarian movement aroused by extreme despair. He warned that individual violent actions by the peasants here and there, accelerated by economic factors, might be seen as the first indications of an impending catastrophic transformation. The editor of the leading British magazine in India noted, in a special New Year supplement, that, for Indian industry and commerce, 1932 had been even worse than 1931, which itself had been considered a year of unexampled and universal economic disaster. Millions of peasants were, in his opinion, on the verge of dying out from famine.

All the objective economic data and the material of the 1931 census, which revealed the acute, both open and concealed processes taking place within the social struggle, the demographic and social changes, showed that the 1920s and the years of the Great Depression in India had seen an unprecedented increase in exploitation, proletarisation and pauperisation. British imperialism faced the ignoble prospect of losing its monopoly power in India.

Chapter Seven

The Influence of the World Economic Crisis (1929-1933) on the Indian Countryside

The First Period of the Crisis (1929-1930)

The world economic crisis that broke out in 1929 differed in many ways from the first postwar crisis that set in in 1921. In the period following the end of the First World War, some colonies experienced a quite rapid internal capitalist accumulation; in particular, in India a number of industries developed quickly. These were years of an artificial and ephemeral inflation of the production apparatus, as well as an unprecedented accumulation by the colonial bourgeoisie. This period saw a tremendous growth of the profits of textile manufacturers, big profits in the jute industry and a growth of profits in the heavy industries in India—coal, and iron and steel.

The 1929-1933 crisis, differing considerably from the first postwar one, seized the colonial world, too, in its vice. It was a truly universal crisis that spread to all the capitalist countries of Europe and America and their colonies. It is worth recalling what Engels wrote in the pre-imperialist era, the era of the first crises of industrial capitalism, to the effect that the crisis assumes truly tremendous proportions when it penetrates the tropics and seizes the colonies. Engels' thesis became particularly topical in the period of monopoly capitalism. The second specific of the 1929-1933 crisis was that it was the deepest ever, without any precedent in the previous history of capitalism in general or the history of the development of the colonial economies in particular. The third specific of the crisis was its unusually protracted nature.

At this time, Indian bourgeois economists often brought up the thesis that the crisis would become even more serious. This was stated openly by Sir George Schuster, Minister of Finance in the Anglo-Indian government, in a speech on the introduction of an "extraordinary" budget for 1931/32. The fourth specific of the crisis consisted in a catastrophic drop in the prices of all commodities, especially colonial agricultural raw materials. A drop in commodity prices had occurred during previous crises, too, but certainly not to this extent. This time, the price drops hit the colonial peasant particularly hard and made his position much worse than it had ever been. The basic and decisive specific of the crisis was that it broke out and developed on the basis of the general crisis of capitalism, against the background of the struggle between two systems.

Two more characteristic features of the crisis should be noted as having been of exceptional significance for India and similar countries. These were, above all, the uneven development of the crisis in general, and in the colonial countries in particular, and the very close interweaving of the industrial and agrarian crises. This was all reflected in the economic situation in India from 1929 to 1933.

In order to illustrate the whole depth of the crisis in India's agricultural economy, which had taken shape historically and inevitably under the conditions of the feudal-imperialist domination, we shall present data on the most developed regions of India—the Punjab, Bombay, and Bengal, which specialised primarily in the production of wheat, cotton and jute.

The Punjab. Peasant farming presented the following picture here:

Size of plot, acres	Percentage of peasant farms
less than 1	22.5
1—2.5	15.4
2.5—5	17.9
5—10	20.5

In some parts of the province, from 30 to 65 per cent of all peasant farms were less than an acre in area—such was the exceptional fragmentation of peasant farming. Eighty-three per cent of the peasant farms were in debt to moneylenders; two-thirds of the total income tax gathered in the province was paid by the peasants. On average, for the whole of India, there was one moneylender for every 328 peasants, but in the

Punjab there was one to every 100 peasants. This is why mortgage indebtedness of the Punjabi peasant was 12-fold greater than the annual sum of the land tax in the province (40 million rupees).

The hopes the peasants laid in credit co-operatives as a major instrument for eliminating peasant indebtedness were not fulfilled, apart from a negligible change in the mortgage indebtedness in certain regions. On average, the mortgage indebtedness throughout the Punjab even rose: from 172 rupees in 1925/26 to 174 rupees in 1928/29 per acre of mortgaged land. Moneylenders were actively penetrating credit societies and establishing their own influence there and also, particularly important, there was a further concentration of the peasants' land in the hands of moneylenders, who usually leased it out. It is not surprising that, under such conditions for the existence of peasant farms, Indian wheat was gradually ousted from the world market, since it could not compete with that from countries with large-scale capitalist farming, and suffered one blow after another even on the Indian market. True, there was a simultaneous increase in the domestic consumption of wheat.

Of major significance for clarifying the position in India's agriculture and the impact of the crisis was the question of the crop yield. It turns out that, over 30 years, i.e., from the beginning of the 20th century, the yield per acre of sown area had dropped from 635 to 482 kg. for rice, from 524 to 377 kg. for wheat and from 1,057 to 463 kg. for cotton.

A similar picture was observed in relation to a number of other commercial crops. The crisis of livestock-breeding, manifested in the mass plague and degeneration of cattle, and the rapid exhaustion of the soil were results of the extremely unfavourable socio-economic living and working conditions of the Indian peasant. Account should be taken of the physical exhaustion and dying out of the Indian peasantry itself; only then does the picture of degradation become totally clear.

Table 18 shows how small-scale peasant farming was totally incapable of providing even the first essentials for the peasant family.

The drop in the living conditions of the peasant masses was accompanied by the crystallisation of a rich peasant upper crust in the village, usually engaged in moneylending, in the leasing

Table 18

Distribution of Land Among Peasant Farms,
acres

Province	Area sufficient for the survival of one farm (family)	No. of acres required per 100 farms (families)	Actual number
Bengal	4	400	30.9
Bombay	12	1,200	221

of tools and land and, after the First World War, increasingly in capitalist farming. This can be seen clearly from an analysis of the economies of individual regions of the Punjab (Lyallpur, Amritsar, Hoshiarpur, and so on), the United Provinces, Bombay, and so on. Thus, although the class differentiation of the Indian peasantry took place quite slowly, it would be wrong to consider the peasantry as some homogeneous mass in the class sense. There is no doubt that the 1929-1933 crisis accelerated this process.

Wheat. Even during the first stage of the world economic crisis there was a substantial drop in the price of wheat. The price of a maund of wheat was 5 rupees 3 annas in 1925, 4 rupees 10 annas in 1926, 4 rupees 2 annas in 1927, 4 rupees 6 annas in 1928, 2 rupees 6 annas in 1929, and 1 rupee 13 annas in December 1930. Thus, although the overall tendency was for prices to fall over the whole six years, there was an exceptional drop in 1929 and 1930.

Taking the wheat price index for 1924-1926 as 100, the drop in the price of Indian wheat in 1930 appears as follows: 112 in January, 72 in March, 66 in May, 54 in July, and 46 in September. Hence, over the first nine months of 1930, prices dropped catastrophically and the Indian peasant did not even get back the value of his labour inputs from the sale of his wheat.

It should be noted that the drop in wheat prices in India took place considerably faster than in a number of other wheat-producing countries. According to data from the Federation of Indian Chambers of Commerce, by November 1930 wheat prices in India had fallen by 50 per cent (Karachi), in Chicago by 42 per cent and in Liverpool by 33 per cent. Even the *Times of India* could not but admit that Indian wheat had suffered a phenomenal drop in prices. The competitor countries that were ousting Indian wheat from the world market (Australia, Canada) also suffered a similar fate, but to a lesser degree (by October 1930): 42 per cent in Australia and 47 per cent in Canada, while the figure for India was 54 per cent.

It should, at the same time, be remembered that, in India, there were a million tonnes of wheat stocks and that the Indian peasants in the biggest wheat-producing regions still had a substantial portion of the harvest to get rid of, but could not do so profitably. Thus, a further drop in prices was not out of the question. On the contrary, under the impact of a number of factors, it became inevitable.

India changed from being a wheat exporter to a wheat importer. The reasons for this are obvious: the peasant farm, which was extremely backward in its technology, had enjoyed no customs protection and was oppressed by the system of colonial-feudal and moneylender exploitation, could not stand up to the competition from the big mechanised capitalist farming in Australia and Canada. At the same time, the demand for wheat within the country was growing. All this, plus the government's foreign currency policy, struck a blow against the Indian producers, whose output was ousted from the world market and could not compete with that of the other countries even on the home market. Data on wheat exports from India describe this process (tonnes):

Average per annum before World War I	1917/18	1927	1928	1929
1,300,000	1,500,000	305,937	115,422	14,204

In 1929, when the export of wheat dropped to an extremely low level, India was already importing 700,000 tonnes. It relinquished its position on the world and home market mainly to Australia. In 1925, Australia exported only 35,500 tonnes of wheat to India, in 1927/1928—68,910 tonnes and in 1928/29—529,459 tonnes, or fifteen times more than in 1925. Over five months in 1930/31, the import of Australian wheat to Calcutta and Bombay alone reached 70,000 tonnes. In this context, note should be made of the role played by the Anglo-Indian government, which on India's railways and waterways pursued a tariff policy that reduced the competitiveness of the Indian producer to the minimum. In fact, all outlays, including the delivery of Australian wheat to Indian ports, amounted to no more than 8 annas per maund, while it cost 1 rupee 3 annas 3 pais to deliver Punjabi wheat from Lyallpur to Houra (near Calcutta), i.e., transport costs accounted for 60 per cent of the overall wheat production costs in the Punjab. The delivery of Punjabi wheat to Bombay cost even more (by 7 pais). Even the cost of transporting a maund of Punjabi wheat to Karachi by railway and from there to Bombay by sea amounted to 15 annas 8 pais, or double that from Australia to the main ports of British India.

The chief evil, of course, lay in India's actual agrarian system and the colonial character of the country. Using the specific example of the Anglo-Indian government's tariff policy, however, it becomes quite clear that British imperialism in India played a parasitic role and that such "cultural values" as the Indian railways—monopolised by British imperialism—were essentially exploitative.

Even at that time there were politicians, such as the General Secretary of the Association of Punjabi zamindars, who made declarations to the effect that a major factor affecting the needs of the ryots was the actions of the Russian Bolsheviks, who dumped wheat on the world market, instead of selling it in the usual way; this, plus their manipulations on the Chicago wheat market, was supposedly the direct reason for the further price drops. The Bolsheviks' aim, they announced, was to create disturbance among the world's farmers, thereby promoting a world revolution.

The peasants, robbed by the monopolists, landlords and moneylenders, simply would not believe that their poverty was the fault of the Russian Bolsheviks. Economists from the *Bombay Chronicle* rightly wrote that too much Australian wheat was being imported into India.

Under the impact of the crisis that hit the Punjab and a number of other wheat regions in the United Provinces, where the peasants, not having any stocks, could not survive the loss of even a single harvest or a sharp drop in prices and could not pay off their debts to moneylenders and their land tax, the Anglo-Indian government was forced to cut somewhat the rate charged for transporting wheat by rail. Yet this gave the direct producers virtually nothing, for the subsidised freight tariff operated only until February 28, 1931, and only in the direction from the Punjab to Karachi (the North-West railway line). The Punjab-Calcutta rates remained unchanged. The same newspaper wrote that, while there was little hope of any softening of the crisis on India's wheat market by means of exports (though the government used exports as the argument for reducing the rates in the direction from the Punjab to the seaport of Karachi), the place where protection was most needed was Calcutta, which received Australian wheat exports at dumping prices year after year and remained unprotected. This is why, as soon as the government had reduced the railway freight rates on the North-West railway line, the Indian Chamber of Commerce demanded a cut on the Punjab-Calcutta line, leading to the region where Australian wheat dominated the market. The government refused to comply, however, for important reasons, above all the substantial budget deficit.

Bombay. Cotton. Data on the state of the cotton market also testified to the deep crisis of this commercial crop, which was of such importance to India.

Concerning the importance of the sale of cotton for the peasant farm, the *Bombay Chronicle* wrote that the peasant did not suffer as great losses from low prices for wheat, rice, and so on as from low ones for cotton. This was because the peasant retained a large proportion of food products for himself, while he sold all his cotton in order to pay the government land tax and purchase essentials, and since the prices of cotton were well below average costs, the producer was not left with enough money to pay the tax or satisfy his normal requirements. The peasant was on the verge of total ruin as a result of the extremely low cotton prices.

The following data are available on cotton prices. The price of a maund of cotton in 1923/24 was 16 rupees 8 annas, in 1924/25—13 rupees 5 annas, in 1925/26—10 rupees 2 annas, in 1926/27—7 rupees 14 annas, in 1927/28—10 rupees 3 annas, in 1928/29—10 rupees, and in November 1930—5 rupees 5 annas.

The most widespead sorts of cotton in India were "Bengal" and "Omra". A khandi (784 pounds) of cotton, including outlays on pressing and transportation, cost, under more or less normal conditions: 225 rupees for "Bengal" and 260 rupees for "Omra". The peasant sold his cotton at a maximum of only 140 rupees for "Bengal" and 170 rupees for "Omra", however. At these prices, the peasant did not even cover his production costs. The export of cotton through Karachi dropped by 6 per cent from September 1, 1929 to September 1, 1930 in physical terms, but by 38 per cent in value. It is easy to see the sort of consequences this protracted and sharp drop in prices had.

The export of raw cotton from India stood at (April-October) 358,029 thousand rupees' worth in 1928, 360,582 thousand in 1929, and 270,842 thousand in 1930. The export of raw cotton for 1930/31 revealed an extremely serious drop over the previous years.

On this basis, huge stocks of cotton accumulated, and these had a considerable effect on market processes. The stocks of cotton on the Bombay market alone reached 800,000 bales, before a substantial part of the new harvest had even come on to the market. A further drop in prices and overstocking were, therefore, inevitable. This was also promoted by the fact that the Indian cotton industry was using less Indian cotton. In September 1929, for instance, the industry required 164,640 bales of Indian cotton, but in September 1930—only 141,652 bales, a drop of 14 per cent over a single year.

Finally, the dumping of American cotton was of major significance. Given the very unfavourable conditions, the Indian peasants who wanted to sell their cotton faced the threat of a further drop in cotton prices, compounded by another factor that made their position even worse—the dumping of American cotton.

In this situation, the Indian Central Cotton Committee suggested that the government: 1) fix minimum cotton prices; 2) cut the rail freight rates for cotton; 3) advance a loan through the Imperial Bank on the security of cotton to 80 per cent of its market value.

Commenting on the government's reply and admitting that the biggest and most important cotton regions were experiencing prices that did not even cover costs, the *Times of India* wrote that the government had been quite right to reject the proposals of the Central Cotton Committee on fixing a minimum cotton price. This statement was followed by references to the unsuccessful attempts by the USA and Canada to set such a rate. This was the government's reply to the Committee's first and most important suggestion. The solution to the questions, it said, should be left to the objective laws and the inevitable coincidence of demand and supply, after which the necessary shift will allegedly take place. This was the unsophisticated "philosophy" behind the Anglo-Indian government's policy in relation to the cotton producers.

The government also resolutely refused to cut rail freight rates for cotton. The *Capital* magazine announced that the minimum cut in rail rates that would have any noticeable eflect on the prices of a khandi of cotton would cost the railways 4.5 million rupees. Meanwhile, the gross revenue of the railways for 1930 had dropped by 55 million rupees over 1929 and, according to H. A. Lalji (the chairman of the Indian Merchants' Chamber in Bombay), the net deficit in 1930 stood at about 80 million rupees.

As for the suggestion that the Imperial Bank advance a loan on the security of cotton, it was the only one to which the government agreed. The Imperial Bank of India agreed, at the government's request, to advance loans on cotton (in the country's cotton centres) at a reduced interest rate, i.e., 25 per cent instead of the usual 30 per cent. The Imperial Bank retained the right, however, to raise this interest rate if cotton prices rose at all significantly. This was the sum total of all the "assistance" given by the government to the cotton producers, "assistance" provided at obviously usurious interest rates, and clearly of no real value.

Bengal. J u t e. The production of jute probably suffered more from the crisis than the other agricultural crops. Suffice it to point out that the total income of such an enormous province as Bengal dropped by 400 million rupees in 1930/31 as a result of the fall in jute prices and the cut in raw jute exports, though this figure is only a rough and rather optimistic one provided by Indian economists. This 400 million rupees constituted almost 50 per cent of the province's total income. The significance of the jute crisis becomes obvious if one considers that half the Bengali peasantry grew jute. The drop in jute prices was so great that the peasant did not cover even half his costs. Moreover, the Anglo-Indian press published many examples of it being uneconomical for the peasant to even harvest the jute at such low market prices. It cost more to deliver the jute to the market than the jute itself cost. Since he was unable to sell his jute even at extremely low prices, the peasant often took it back home or sold it literally for peanuts.

According to calculations made by Indian economists, the cost of producing a maund of jute was about 6 rupees, while the market price in a number of regions (Dacca, Balurgat, Faridpur, and so on) was 2-2.5 rupees per maund against 16-18 rupees in 1926. On the London market, a tonne of jute cost £27.5 in January 1930 but only £15 in January 1931. According to the *Capital* magazine, the stocks of raw jute purchased were the equivalent of seven months' requirements for the whole jute industry within India, and 17 months' requirements outside the country, while enormous quantities of unsold jute remained with peasants.

It is not, therefore, surprising that the India press printed many cases of death from starvation among the peasants in the jute monoculture regions. Almost all the regions, villages and settlements in Bengal were reporting on the extreme impoverishment of the population. A number of newspapers told of deaths from starvation, suicides and the sale of children, of economic living conditions constantly deteriorating and reaching such a state when nothing could save the people but a radical change in the system of policy and management. In the autumn of 1930, the Indian press reported repeatedly on agrarian "banditry", on crowds of starving people coming from the villages and begging the local authorities for help—but in vain.

As for the export of raw jute from India, it underwent tremendous changes, mainly as a result of a cut in exports to North and South America and Europe. The value of the raw jute exported from India over the first seven months of three economic years was: 1928/29—153,324 thousand rupees, 1929/30—141,979 thousand rupees, and 1930/31—69,701 thousand rupees.

By the end of September 1930, the Indian bourgeois press had already raised the question of the serious crisis in Bengal. This was, of course, because the profits of the jute manufacturers and merchants, the rents of the Bengali landlords and the interest of the moneylenders were in danger, but not because there was the need to help the ryots (as the press tried to suggest). All the exploiting classes and their yes-men almost physically felt the breath of the impending agrarian revolution. Moreover, they well remembered the recent peasant uprising in Kishorganj, where the peasants resorted to violence against the landlords and moneylenders and for almost two weeks were in charge in the region; they finally gave up in the face of superior police and troop forces.

The question of the crisis had to be raised, since the profits of the jute manufacturers had dropped from 35 million rupees in the first half of 1929 to 17 million a year later, when many factories suffered substantial losses, when the peasantry, threatened by death from starvation or complete impoverishment, refused to pay their land rent and debts to moneylenders, and when the spirit of rebellion among the people was spreading extremely rapidly.

What exactly was the Indian bourgeoisie's and landlords' programme for aiding the jute producers? The industrial and commercial bourgeoisie demanded government intervention in the jute business, mainly by fixing prices, passing special laws to cut the production of raw jute and abolishing duties on jute exports, which stood at roughly 50 million rupees. The bourgeoisie tried to get the government o organise a broad campaign to cut the area sown under jute and make the peasants retain their stocks of jute.

The campaign for government intervention in the jute crisis became very strong at times, but never got out of hand. In essence all the Indian bourgeoisie's demands and plans concerning jute, which were the same as those suggested for cotton, wheat, etc., were resolutely rejected by the Anglo-Indian government which agreed only to work for a cut in the jute-sown area.

Speeches of the most eminent representatives of British imperialism in India—G. Schuster, Minister of Finances, and the Viceroy of India, Lord Irwin himself, make it quite clear why the government was against aid and intervention. At the annual meeting of the Chambers of Commerce of India in December 1930, Lord Irwin noted that none of the plans adopted by other countries had managed to avert a catastrophic drop in prices; that the government was convinced that any such attempts in India would be just as fruitless and that they would merely lead to a big financial burden which the treasury would have to transfer to the debtors. Plans of this type (i.e., price fixing and so on), he said, would be of some help in countering minor price fluctuations, but were not only helpless in the face of big movements of world prices, he believed, but might also have a detrimental effect, by hampering the operation of the usual economic forces that might affect prices.

As if sanctioning this policy of the Anglo-Indian government, the *Manchester Guardian Weekly* noted that the government of India had reasonably refused to intervene in the operation of economic forces by subsidising the producers or manipulating the market.

The unsuccessful attempts made by America, Canada, Egypt, Brazil and other countries to counter the development of the economic crisis were naturally of enormous significance in determining the economic policy selected by the Anglo-Indian government, but this was not the only thing. First, the government was totally unprepared for the very deep-running processes of degradation of agriculture which, although they were not new to India, became unprecedentedly acute, deep, and all-embracing during the world economic crisis. Second, government finances and a number of the commanding heights of British imperialism in India (the railways, banks, the budget, foreign trade, and so on) could not avoid the common fate of suffering sharp blows from the crisis. The political situation in the country did not allow new taxes to be introduced; tax revenues dropped and their collection in some regions was carried out literally by stick or machine gun. Thus, the economic position of the government was also shaken. Third, the class struggle in India, the intensification of all the political contradictions, the open rebellions in a number of regions—all these tied the Anglo-Indian government's hands, undermining its economic and political stability. All these factors taken together determined the government's negative attitude towards the projects repeatedly put forward by the bourgeoisie for softening the crisis and revealed more clearly than ever the government's almost total helplessness against the free play of the laws of the capitalist economy, exacerbated to the extreme by the entire complex of particular contradictions inherent in a colonial country.

As for the demands made by the Bengali landlords and moneylenders, they came down mainly to granting the landlords deferment of their land tax payments and advancing the loans, called takawi, usually on a quite small scale, to the village upper crust on more favourable terms than those of the moneylenders (6.5 per cent annum). The central government of India replied to all these plans and demands with references to its lack of competence in this sphere and suggestions that the provincial governments be approached instead. The Bengali government, in the person of Stanley Jackson, received a large number of delegations from various bourgeois-landlord meetings, as well as resolutions and memoranda, and decided to advance takawi to the peasants. The amount involved was ludicrous (about 100,000 rupees) and the loans were distributed in only one region of Bengal, so they obviously had no effect. Even the local bourgeoisie pointed out repeatedly in its press that the advancing of takawi to the peasants would not improve their situation, but have the reverse effect, for these sums would be almost automatically transferred to the pockets of the moneylenders as interest on debts and of the Bengali zamindars as rent, and so on. This is why the resolutions of all the conferences of landlords and moneylenders in Bengal, which usually gathered on the pretext of working out measures to help the producers, were so ardent in demanding takawi from the government, knowing full well that these sums, for which the peasants would have to pay, would immediately fall into their own hands.

A few words on the price scissors, the enormous gap between the prices of agricultural and industrial goods, which exacerbated during the crisis to the extreme and resulted in the purchasing power of the "peasant rupee" being roughly half that of the "industrial rupee". Even a superficial glance at the price indices for agricultural and industrial goods is totally convincing. At the meeting mentioned above, Lord Irwin declared that, during the depression, the prices of raw materials were falling faster than those of manufactured goods. This was, he believed, to be expected. Even so, it should be remembered that the widening price scissors speeded up the impoverishment of the peasantry, further contracted the home market and intensified the main disproportions in the Indian economy. In direct connection with the problem of the price scissors, Lord Irwin had to announce that, under such conditions, sooner or later certain branches of industry would have to close down or cut working time, and the numbers of the unenmployed would increase.

Thus:

—The crisis of Indian agriculture was general in the sense that no important branch of the economy was left unaffected.

—The crisis was accompanied by a protracted degradation of the agricultural sector of the economy, a degradation that developed historically under the conditions of colonial rule. Under the impact of the crisis, the degradation of Indian agriculture became more intensive, thereby exacerbating the class struggle in the countryside.

—The catastrophic fall in prices, the accumulation of enormous stocks of commodities and a sharp cut in production—these were the main features of the crisis.

—A high land rent, enormous indebtedness of the peasantry, high taxes, the oppression of the prevailing feudal and moneylending relations, the extreme fragmentation of the technically backward peasant holdings—all these factors accounted for the uncompetitiveness of the chief Indian farm products on the foreign and home markets against the output of countries with developed capitalist agricultural production.

—The imperialist government was helpless to overcome or even soften the crisis of agriculture in India.

—The combination of the agrarian crisis with the degradation of agriculture, and hence the further sharp contraction of the home market, were behind the interweaving of the industrial with the agrarian crisis and created the situation of the general crisis of India's entire national economy.

The Second Period of the Crisis (1931-1933)

As already mentioned, India's agriculture was going through a deep crisis, but this did not mean that it was completely at a standstill. What determined the crisis of Indian agriculture? First, the fact that there was an extremely protracted stagnation of the agrarian system, engendered by the domination of feudal survivals, which were supported by imperialism. Second, that the crisis embraced all components of the productive forces in the Indian countryside. The entire postwar economy of India was suffering deeply from crisis processes, which were manifested particularly sharply in the protracted crisis of the home market. Many Indian economists explained the crisis of the home market in terms of the lack of correspondence between the population growth and the availability of foodstuffs.

Indian industrial capital reached the peak of its development during the war and directly afterwards. After the sharp rise of this period, industry then went through an extremely strong and uneven crisis. From 1923/24, idling of productive capacity became the norm for all industry, both light and heavy. The colonial bourgeoisie then started to rationalise production, in an attempt to bring industry out of the crisis, mainly by reducing the working class' standard of living, increasing the share of the surplus value appropriated, raising the production rate by reducing the share of necessary working time, i. e. increasing relative surplus value through stepping up the degree of exploitation. Mass dismissals of workers began. In 1923/24, up to 65,000 people were dismissed from the textile mills of Bombay and Ahmadabad. The Calcutta jute manufacturers got rid of 70,000 workers and another 50,000 were dismissed from the railways. This process of capitalist rationalisation in the colonial manner was accompanied by a fierce class struggle in almost all branches of industry.

The colonial domination of British imperialism was the decisive reason for the extremely deep economic crisis in India, the protracted crisis of the agrarian system and the chronic contraction of the home market and, on this basis, for the crisis in industry. Year by year, the reproduction of the peasant economy was taking place on an increasingly narrow basis, which meant that the toiling peasantry was rapidly becoming impoverished, while industry was losing its home market. The intensified tax exploitation of the peasantry and the petty urban bourgeoisie, the striving to transfer at any cost the consequences of the crisis in Britain and its dominions on to the shoulders of the colonial peasantry, working class and petty urban bourgeoisie, the defence of the Indian bourgeoisie and landlords, the extremely harsh class terror (suffice it to recall the 1931 Viceroy's decrees introducing a state of siege in India)—all these factors made the development of the crisis in India particularly tense, protracted and catastrophic and roused even the most backward peasant masses to the struggle.

* * *

The economic crisis in India confirmed once more that the Marxists were right in opposing the theory of decolonisation. Which itself revealed just how distorted and wrong it was. Under the conditions of the crisis, non-equivalent exchange, the scissors between import and export prices, used with the intention of putting Britain's payments and trade balance in order, the transfer of the consequences of the crisis in the metropolis to the colony, to its toiling masses, and the intensification of the struggle for the home market within India itself—all this confirmed that the theory of decolonisation did not stand the test of time.

In the light of the economic crisis, the populistic theory shared by some Marxists—the theory of agrarianisation, i.e., India's evolution as an exclusively agricultural country, was also shown to be incorrect. In fact, such provinces as Bombay, Madras and Bengal had quite well developed machine industries, where the intertwining of the industrial and agrarian crises had a particularly great impact, and this made it obvious that the supporters of the agrarianisation theory simply could not come out with consistent arguments.

In just the same way, the fact that under the impact of the economic crisis and the intensification of the class struggle the waves of the working-class and peasant movement were occurring more concordant than before, and in a number of regions had even started to merge, could not be explained or understood on the basis of the agrarianisation theory.

The focus of Marxist research of the 1920s and 1930s was on the problem of impoverishment and pauperisation of the peasantry, the degradation of the agrarian system—in a word, on all the questions connected with the crisis of the agrarian system in India, but disproportionately little attention was paid to the class stratification in the countryside, particularly on the basis of the economic crisis. Too few facts and observations were available, and the country itself was firmly isolated by British rule from the progressive world.

Moreover, this was an organic and component part of the problem of the impoverishment and pauperisation of the peassantry and the agrarian question in general. The world economic crisis provided a major impetus to the stratification of the countryside and the polarisation of property relations there, strengthened even more the concentration of all values and land in the hands of the moneylenders, landlords, merchants and rich peasants and, at the same time, within the peasantry itself, produced a further class differentiation. This fact should deffinitely be noted.

* * *

Let us now consider questions of certain interest with respect to empirical data available in British sources.

The first question is how to explain the fact that, for a whole number of such commercial crops as cotton, wheat, rice and sugar, there was such a rapid drop in prices that they became even lower than costs. Let us take the price index for cereal crops: by March 1932, the prices had fallen to 66 points, if July 1914 prices are taken as 100; the prices of sugar had fallen to 147, while they had reached a peak of 407 at one time; the prices of tea fell from a peak of 206 to 59, and so on. Even so, there was virtually no cut in the sown area of these crops during 1931/32. On the contrary, in a number of regions there was a certain increase in the area sown to wheat, rice and sugar cane. Thus, the area under sugar cane in 1931/32 was 103 per cent of that in the previous year, and the output of sugar stood at 121 per cent. The area under rice constituted 102 per cent of that in the previous year and output also 102 per cent. The area sown to cotton was 99.0 per cent and output—78 per cent. The wheat area was 105 per cent compared with the previous year.

Why did the sown area of the crops not drop and, in certain cases, the harvest remain the same, while for other crops the drop in the sown area was disproportionately small compared with the impact of the crisis and the drop in prices, etc.? The fact is that the area under rice increased not in regions of rice monoculture, but chiefly in the jute-growing areas of Bengal. The wheat area increased not in the Punjab (a wheat region), but in the Central Provinces, the United Provinces, Madras, Bombay, and so on, i.e., areas of other monocultures, the output of which could not find a market in the world. The area under rice, wheat, cotton and sugar cane did, however, as the data show, drop sharply in the areas of their monoculture production.

In the regions of the monoculture production of output that could not be sold on the world market, the direct producer was forced to introduce other crops, mostly food products that would at least partly ensure him against hunger and death. This was the first reason restraining the drop in the sown area of individual crops, despite changes in its distribution which were changing the structure of agriculture itself.

The second reason was that the relations between credit and rent, the relations that had taken shape between the direct producer and the moneylender or landlord, were fixed, i.e., they were relatively constant relations that were realised primarily in kind; even if the direct producer reduced his sown area, for a specific, previously determined period of time he still had to pay the same rate (an essentially raised rate) for the land he rented and the water he used, the same (and essentially higher) interest to the moneylender. This meant increasing plunder of the peasantry, for the correlation between surplus and necessary labour changed in favour of the exploiting classes in kind, too.

The relatively constant nature of rent and credit, the increasing burden of them and the peasantry's desire in regions producing industrial raw materials to partially ensure themselves against ruin by growing food products determined the situation where, with a fairly rapid and sharp drop in prices on the world and Indian markets, there was no proportional drop in sown area for any of the major crops, and in some areas even an increase. This testified to the growing exploitation of the peasantry.

The world economic crisis was one of overproduction, and in the colonies this meant primarily overproduction of industrial raw material crops. This crisis presumed, at the same time, an underproduction of foodstuffs in a number of the biggest monoculture regions of India, which in fact meant death from starvation and ruin for the peasantry. The bourgeois press was full of announcements concerning the arrival in the towns of a number of provinces of huge crowds of people from the villages, asking for alms and gradually dying out.

The colonial peasant masses did not receive even half their production costs in return for their output. The wholesale price index on the Calcutta market (Table 19) shows this clearly enough. That on the Bombay market was substantially lower than on the Calcutta one. Thus, in Bombay in November 1931 the wholesale price index for cotton was 59, for cereals—74, for legumes—83, and for sugar—126.

Table 19

Wholesale Price Index on the Calcutta Market,
July 1914 = 100

	Grain	Legumes	Sugar	Tea	Oil-bearing crops	Jute	Cotton	Pelts & hides
Highest index after 1914	163	180	407	206	198	154	309	184
1929	125	152	162	140	155	95	146	113
November 1931	76	96	147	75	80	60	82	61
February 1932	72	95	150	62	84	51	106	55
March 1932	70	86	147	60	74	49	89	54

If the wholesale price index is recalculated to exclude the share taken by dealers, commission agents of firms, Indian comprador and the multitudes of middlemen standing between the direct producer of colonial raw materials and foodstuffs and the world or home market, i.e., if not the wholesale price index is taken but that of the real prices at which the direct producer sold his produce, there is a drop of at least another 30-40 per cent for all groups of commodities. This can be seen from Table 20, which is compiled from selected data on the effect of the crisis on peasant farms in the United Provinces.

Table 20

The Impact of the Crisis on Peasant Farming in the United Provinces

District	Average farm area, bighis	Outlays on cultivation and rent		Price of produce		Losses after sale of produce	
		Rupees	Annas	Rupees	Annas	Rupees	Annas
Allahabad	13	143	—	73	3	72	4
Rae Bareli	16	137	—	59	8	77	8
Sultanpur	7	73	—	30	—	43	3
Unao	6.7	58	—	36	—	22	—
Gorakhpur	4.7	24	5	12	3	12	2
Average for the five districts	9.48	87	1	42	3	45	6

A study was made of 251 settlements in the Kanpur district of the United Provinces. The average area turned out to be 372 bighis; the average income from the sale of produce in each village—1,015 rupees, while just the rent paid to the landlord amounted to an average of 1,129 rupees. Thus, the total sum the direct producer received for his output was not enough to cover even his rent.

It is not, therefore, surprising that the peasants of the United Provinces waged a resolute struggle against the landlords and tax-collectors, that the region was filled with punitive detachments of the Anglo-Indian government. Here, the direct reason for the peasantry's actions was total ruin and the prospect of death from starvation. The United Provinces were no exception in this respect. The situation in Burma was even worse, with a genuine war being waged between the peasants and the Anglo-Indian army. The picture was similar in East Bengal, where a state of siege was introduced. Extreme poverty reigned in Assam. The events in the United Provinces—the meetings of many thousands of peasants, their violent actions against moneylenders and landlords, the burning of debt books and documents, the resistance put up to punitive detachments and the non-payment of rents almost everywhere—all showed that the peasantry was gradually rising to the struggle.

The crisis had a particularly serious effect on the regions of monoculture, including Bengal—the world supplier of jute, and Madras—the world supplier of oil-bearing crops. In 1931/32, the jute harvest for the agricultural season fell by 50 per cent, from 11 million to 5.5 million bales, while the area sown to it dropped from 3,492,300 acres in 1930/31 to 1,613,700 acres in 1931/32. In spite of the tremendous drop in the sown area and output, stocks of jute were constantly rising. On September 30, 1930, there were 5,485 thousand bales stored at the Calcutta factories, but a year later there were already 5,935 trousand, while the stocks at bazaars, warehouses and pressing works increased from 350,000 to 550,000 bales over the same period. The area sown to oil-bearing crops dropped from 4,828 thousand acres in 1930/31 to 3,803 thousand acres in 1931/32.

In Bengal, the monopoly supplier of jute, the transition continued from the cultivation of raw jute to that of rice and sugar, which was an extremely painful process for the peasants. This, of course, meant a tremendous strain on all the forces of the peasant economy. This process, as already noted, expressed the peasants' striving in the monoculture regions to at least partially ensure themselves by growing food products against ruin and death, given that the price of raw jute did not even provide them with a miserable existence. Here are some data describing this process. In Burma, a monoculture rice region, the area under rice dropped by 2.5 per cent and the harvest by 13 per cent, while in Bengal, a monoculture jute region, the area under rice increased by 22 per cent and the harvest by 4 per cent in 1931/32. The crop pattern was changing. This reflected, in certain sense, a tendency for the peasant farm to become more subsistence-based, as a result of the enforced commercialisation and deepening of the economic crisis. Such a process naturally had a limited impact and was manifested only in the outlines of a trend. The monoculture agricultural regions—Burma, Bengal, the Central Provinces and Berar, Madras and the United Provinces—thus became the centre of a more developed peasant movement that sometimes acquired the nature of peasant rebellions.

The financial position of the Anglo-Indian government can be described in one word—bankruptcy.

This was directly related to the Indian peasantry, since the government tried to save itself from financial collapse by levying new direct and indirect taxes on the peasants. Under the Anglo-Indian government's budget for 1930/31, a surplus of 860,000 rupees was anticipated. In fact there was a deficit of 135.6 million rupees. Under the 1931/32 budget, there was to be a surplus of 100 thousand rupees, while in fact, for only six months of that economic year, there was a deficit of 19.5 million rupees. To cover its budget deficits, the Anglo-Indian government resorted to new direct and indirect taxation. From March 1930 to September 1931, tax revenues went up by 420 million rupees. In the final account it was the direct producer who paid them. This could not but lead to greater impoverishment of the peasantry, urban petty bourgeoisie and the working class, to an even further deepening of the crisis and a contraction of the home market. The plunderous nature of the colonial apparatus became absolutely clear precisely during the period of the crisis (Table 21).

Outlays on maintaining and reproducing the colonial monopoly of British imperialism in India were rising at the expense of the increasing impoverishment of the broad population. Let us compare this with the general impoverishment of the peasant masses. The gross value of all India's agricultural produce at 1928 prices was 12 billion rupees. Taking this as the basis and adding 20 per cent for incomes received from subsidiary occupations, but leaving aside the population growth over the last ten years and the drop in prices since 1928, the income per producer works out as no more than 42 rupees a year, or just over £3.

Table 21

Chief Expenditure Items of the Anglo-Indian Government's Budget, million rupees

	1913/14	1931/32	Percentage increase
Military outlays	298.5	534.0	79
Loan interest (non-productive loans)	19.4	95.5	405
Outlays on civil administration	48.2	121.3	153

Thus, at one extreme, the exploiting classes were getting richer, while at the other, the colonial producer was becoming more and more impoverished. The polarisation of class forces was more sharply revealed than ever before, reflecting the private and primarily non-economic appropriation by imperialism and the classes supporting it of the results of the labour of the hundreds of millions of direct producers.

The peasantry's indebtedness to moneylenders became extremely burdensome during the crisis. This problem was discussed more and more frequently and persistently in the economic and political press, but, of course, the bourgeois economists could suggest no solution apart from the development of credit co-operation. They did not even consider a solution to this problem based on fundamental agrarian transformations. In fact, the concern shown by Indian economists over the peasantry's loan indebtedness was a result of the unprecedented contraction of the home market, even for such local industry products as cotton fabrics. Sales were maintained only because the leaders of the national bourgeoisie managed to draw hundreds of thousands of their followers into the movement for a boycott, directed primarily against the purchase of cotton fabrics from Lancashire. In spite of the mass boycott of British-made fabrics and the drop in the purchasing power of the Indian peasantry, the Indian textile manufacturers could not saturate the local market with enough cotton fabrics to replace those from Lancashire. Under the impact of the crisis, the cotton fabric market contracted. The consumption balance of cotton fabrics in the country provides sufficient evidence of this (Table 22).

Table 22

The Consumption Balance of Cotton Fabrics, million yards

	1913/14	1929/30	1930/31
Indian production	1,164	2,419	2,561
Imports	3,197	1,919	890
Exports	151	155	115
Balance	4,210	4,183	3,336

The per capita consumption of fabrics in 1930/31 fell to 9.49 yards against 12.04 yards in 1929/30. In 1931/32, the consumption of fabrics was, the Indian economists suggest, considerably lower than in 1918/19, i.e., the period of the lowest consumption in the postwar era.

The stronger the colonial-feudal and moneylender oppression of the peasants became, the more the home market contracted, the deeper the industrial crisis became and the closer the interaction between the agrarian and industrial crises.

The conclusions drawn by progressive Indian economists came down to the following: the economic position in India was becoming systematically worse; no turn had yet begun; trade, finance and industry were in recession; the Indian manufacturer's worst enemy was not the foreign producer, but the Indian moneylender; the Indian manufacturer and moneylender could not both flourish—moneylending undermines fundamentally the purchasing power of the broad population; as a result of the agrarian crisis there would be an increase of 1.5-2 billion rupees in peasant indebtedness, which had already reached 8 billion rupees.

The following example demonstrates the extent to which the existing price level increased the actual burden of loan interest charged the producers. In 1928/29, jute was sold at a price of about 11 rupees a maund, but in 1930/31—at only 5 rupees 8 annas. Since, in the previous year, loan interest debts averaged 66 rupees, the producer had to sell 6 maunds of jute to cover this interest, but in 1930/31, in order to contribute the same sum, he had to sell 12 maunds of jute, because of the drop in prices. It is not surprising that, under such circumstances, the peasant population's demand for industrial goods fell off markedly.

As a consequence of the 50 per cent drop in prices, the peasants' indebtedness in the Punjab doubled. The increase of the total debt here from 900 million rupees in 1921 to 1,350 million in 1929 meant, in real terms, a debt of 2,700 million rupees in 1930/31.

Material published by the Banking Committee put the loan debt at 9 billion rupees. For the chief provinces of India, it was distributed as follows (million rupees):

Assam	220	United Provinces	1,240
Bihar and Orissa	1,550	Punjab	1,350
Bengal	1,000	Madras	1,500

The *Capital* magazine published these data and added that, as a consequence of the 50 per cent drop in prices, indebtedness had doubled.

The extraordinary aggressiveness and exploitative unruliness of the Indian moneylender were fully revealed under the crisis conditions. On the one hand, as a result of the crisis, millions of peasants were evicted from the production process and by their extinction testified to the deep stagnation of the entire Indian social structure; on the other hand, even greater monetary wealth and larger tracts of land were concentrated in the hands of a few tens of thousands of moneylenders. The crisis led to a further absolute impoverishment of the peasant masses and enrichment of the upper echelons in the countryside.

The crisis showed that the development of commodity-money relations in the colonial countries, the involvement of the peasant economy in market turnover, the imperialist commercialisation of agriculture, and monopolisation of foreign trade were manifested in the adaptation of the scattered internal colonial trade to the requirements of export and use of the natural riches of the colonies by the imperialist monopolies, rather than in the development of a national home market.

The high commercialisation of the monoculture peasant economy was in practice a concealed expression of the relations of domination and subordination under the conditions of feudal-imperialist domination. The market price paid for the peasants' output concealed and blurred the bonded pre-capitalist methods of exploitation in the countryside, the excessive exploitation of the colonial producer. A superficial glance might give the impression that the colonial peasant economy was a truly free petty commodity economy. The removal, in the form of private feudal-imperialist appropriation, not only of the peasant's surplus product, but also a substantial part of his necessary product, the removal of the natural riches of the colonial countries by the imperialist monopolies, took place through exchange, but the relations of exchange between the metropolis and the colony, between the colonial producer of the raw material and the export monopoly firm concealed not equality of commodity producers, but the domination of finance capital over the small peasant economy, oppressed by feudal-moneylender exploitation. The continuation of this exploitation was a very important precondition for the possibility of removing the surplus product on a non-economic basis. The market form of removal of the peasants' output took place superficially according to the well-known formula: C—M—C (commodity—money—commodity), but the essence of the process was as follows:

1) The transformation of C into M was mainly carried out not by the direct producer, but by the buyer-up, moneylender or trader—the tentacles of finance capital in the colony. The colonial peasant masses, i.e., the producers, were not linked directly with the market.

2) The value of C did not correspond to that of M. The value of M was substantially below that of C. This difference between these two values was swallowed up by a host of agents of finance capital in the colony: banias, sahukars, mahajans, zamindars, dalals, beoparis, and so on. The gap in values became extraordinarily wide during the world crisis, and the value of

M received by the direct producer was often only 15-30 per cent of the true value of the C produced by him.

3) It is absolutely clear that M, as a transformed form of C, reduced by the feudal-colonial monopoly, could not reflect the purchasing power of the peasant economy corresponding to the true value of C. Hence the contraction of the home market and the impoverishment of the peasant masses.

4) The non-equivalent value of C received by the direct producer, expressed in the value of M, had to cover taxes, rent, loan interest, the superprofits of monopoly export-import firms, importers' bonuses from the artificially high exchange rate of the colonial currency, the incomes of the comprador bourgeoisie, and so on. It is not surprising, therefore, that the magnitude of the necessary and surplus product included in the value of M was derived from the feudal-imperialist pressure on the direct producer. It was not the amount of surplus product accumulated that limited pre-capitalist rent, loan interest, taxes, etc., but the size of these categories themselves, which also determined the amount of the necessary product remaining with the producer. That is why, usually, even simple reproduction became either very difficult or impossible in the colonies for the toiling peasants' economy. Even comparatively negligible changes in the market situation in the world told catastrophically and with unprecedented rapidity and strength on the position of the colonial producer.

5) When the magnitude of the value of M did not cover a half or even a third of the peasant's farming outlays, he could not pay his taxes, rent or interest, the result being the mass expropriation of the colonial peasantry. This process assumed the most acute forms and a massive scale. The imperialist and national bourgeoisie attempted to transfer the consequences of the crisis to the shoulders of the colonial producer. In practice, this was manifested primarily in a growing difference between the values of M and C. To reduce the value of colonial raw material meant to make exchange more non-equivalent in favour of the exploiting classes.

The feudal-imperialist domination in the colony removed any possibility of free development of the petty commodity peasant economy, of a broad transfer of this economy on to the lines of truly free capitalist development. For a long period of time, the capitalist development of agriculture took place in distorted forms, in spite of the colonial-feudal regime. In Volume III of *Capital,* Marx wrote: "This development takes place only where the capitalist mode of production has a limited development and does not unfold all of its peculiarities, because this rests precisely upon the fact that agriculture is no longer, or not yet, subject to the capitalist mode of production, but rather to one handed down from extinct forms of society. The disadvantages of the capitalist mode of production, with its dependence of the producer upon the money-price of his product, coincide here therefore with the disadvantages occasioned by the imperfect development of the capitalist mode of production. The peasant turns merchant and industrialist without the conditions enabling him to produce his products as commodities."[1]

In another place in the same volume of *Capital* Marx noted: "No matter what the basis on which products are produced, which are thrown into circulation as commodities—whether the basis of the primitive community, of slave production, of small peasant and petty bourgeois, or the capitalist basis, the character of products as commodities is not altered, and as commodities they must pass through the process of exchange and its attendant changes of form."[2]

It would be a mistake to assume that the economic relations characteristic of the form of C—M—C modified by feudal-imperialist domination covered the entire peasantry. The fact is that, in the Indian countryside, in spite of the stifling colonial-feudal monopoly, a stratum of rich peasant farming was taking shape (in the 1930s, not without the assistance of imperialism), though this process was a slow one and painful for the main rural masses. It is natural that the relations of the simple commodity economy according to the formula C—M—C were not characteristic of this type of economy. The production relations that inevitably arise from production according to the M—C—M formula, even though it takes place not in pure form, but in complex connections and links with production on the basis of feudal-moneylender bondage, are still relations revealing tendencies of a capitalist mode of production. A lack of understanding of this is no more than a sort of neopopulism on a colonial basis. That is why it would be wrong to assume that market, commodity-money relations were no more than a fiction in the colonies.[3]

Although commodity-money relations in the colonies were not relations between equal and free commodity producers, they were far from fictitious. Under the domination of feudal survivals, commodity-money relations not only oppressed the Indian peasantry and brought it to mass pauperisation and extinction, but also, to a certain extent, split and differentiated it.

The abolition of the gold standard in Britain in September 1931 and, in Britain's wake, in a number of other countries, produced in India a temporary, very insignificant growth of export prices for certain types of colonial raw material (Table 23).

Table 23

Wholesale Price Index on the Calcutta Exchange
1914=100

Year, month	Grain	Sugar	Tea	Jute	Cotton	Oil-bearing crops
1931, September*	73	134	63	51	74	79
1931, October	77	150	68	62	79	88
1931, November	76	147	75	60	82	80
1932, February	72	150	62	51	106	84
1932, March	70	147	60	49	89	74

* Before the abolition of the gold standard.

This short-lived rise in prices was followed by a further fall. The stocks of colonial raw materials increased not only in the countries using them, but also in India itself; the warehouses were bursting at the seams. During 1932, the Indian newspapers were full of announcements of massive fires of raw material stores; this was one of the specific (in the colonial manner) forms of physical destruction of the overproduction of raw materials.

When the gold standard was abolished and the Anglo-Indian government was faced once more with the problem of the parity between the Indian rupee and the falling pound sterling, the national bourgeoisie in the National Congress declared that the government was linking the rupee to the pound, instead of leaving it alone, to find its own level in relation to gold. The Indian national bourgeoisie found it economically profitable to insist on a random, market adjustment of the value of the falling silver rupee to the value of gold (Table 24).

Table 24

Rupee Exchange Rate Against the Pound Sterling and Its Gold Content

	Rupee exchange rate against the pound	Real gold content of the rupee	Effect on cotton prices, %
If the rupee is linked to the pound sterling	18 pence	13.5 pence	+24
If the rupee is linked to gold only	22.5 pence	16.5 pence	—24

Following the abolition of the gold standard, the Anglo-Indian government passed special legislation to confirm the old correlation between the rupee and the pound, though the latter had been deprived of its gold backing and its value had fallen sharply. The rupee, which had previously been indirectly linked with gold, was now separated from it completely, and remained linked to the fluctuating pound. This engendered a further drop in the competitiveness of Indian raw materials on the world market. In turn, it raised the competitiveness of Australian, Canadian, South and East African, Egyptian, and American cotton and sugar, and Australian wheat on the Indian market.

Given the falling pound, the British importers received an additional bonus, for the rupee remained linked by a specific rate (artificially raised even higher) to the pound. This did much to paralyse the effect of India's raised customs tariffs, in some cases reducing their impact to nil. How did these currency machinations tell on the Indian peasantry? Here is an example. An Indian trader sells a certain amount of cotton in Liverpool, receiving 20 shillings for it, but on his return to Bombay the banks pay him at the current exchange rate (1 shilling 6 pence for a rupee), so he gets a total of 13 rupees 5 annas for his 20 shillings. If the rupee exchange rate were lower (1 shilling 4 pence), he would receive 15 rupees for his 20 shillings. Arriving in his village, he finds that the existing policy has deprived him of 1 rupee 10 annas from every 20 shillings of the value of the output he sold in Liverpool.

Now let us consider an opposite case. An Englishman imports a certain quantity of goods from Birmingham into India and sells them in Lahore for 15 rupees; arriving back in London with these 15 rupees in his pocket, he receives at the current exchange rate (1 shilling 6 pence per rupee) 270 pence, i.e., £1 2s. 6p.; at an exchange rate of 1 shilling 4 pence for a rupee he would get only 240 pence, i.e., £1. Thus, the rupee exchange rate gives the importer an additional 2 shillings 6 pence for every 20 shillings worth of goods sent to India.

When the value of the pound dropped, the extra bonus received by the British importer at the expense of the direct producer of Indian raw materials went up. This gave rise to an even greater contraction of the masses' purchasing power, above all that of the peasantry, and this naturally led to a further narrowing of the home market and inevitably affected local industry, which was already utilising only half its productive capacity. The interaction between the agrarian and industrial crises within the colonial economy became even more intensive. British imperialism used its currency policy to block the penetration of Indian raw materials on to the world market, thereby achieving a drop in its price on India's home market. This was nothing but a specific way of transferring the consequences of the economic crisis in Britain and the dominions on to the shoulders of the Indian peasant—the bonded sharecropper.

In addition to the dramatic drop in exports of Indian raw materials (Table 25), there was a step up in the dumping of raw materials on the Indian market. Cotton imports from East Africa, the British cotton plantations in Uganda and Tanganyika, increased from 26.2 million rupees in 1929/30 to 47.7 million rupees in 1931/32. A roughly similar situation was observed with respect to the import into India of Australian wheat, Malayan sugar, and so on. This agrarian country, which itself produced cotton, jute, sugar and rice, was importing more and more foreign agricultural commodities; dumping, under the protection of the feudal-imperialist monopoly, progressed.

Table 25

Raw Material Exports from India,
thousand rupees

	1929/30	1930/31	1931/32
Pelts and hides	67,395	30,914	183,450
Oil-bearing crops	245,505	167,676	129,833
Cotton	582,867	421,400	220,884
Jute	258,450	120,694	105,824

The situation in the country was becoming more and more strained. A political crisis was brewing. The Gandhi movement of non-co-operation with the British authorities was becoming increasingly massive and threatening in character. Talk began about the need for a compromise between the opposing sides—the Indian national bourgeoisie and the British government.

The situation became even more serious after the collapse of yet another round table conference, when India found itself in the vice of a state of siege almost everywhere; it had been introduced by the Viceroy's decrees in Burma, the United Provinces, the North-West Frontier Province, Kashmir, and so on. Vallabhai Patel, one of the most eminent members of the National Congress, who exercised considerable influence over the peasantry, spoke to the peasants in Gujarat to the effect that, within six months or a year, either the country's administration would have to be transferred into the hands of the National Congress or an even fiercer struggle would break out. So those whose land had been confiscated and sold by the government and had not yet had it returned should not be worried.

The peasants of the United Provinces, Burma, Berar, Madras, Bengal, and Kashmir were burning the homes of landlords and moneylenders, refusing to pay their taxes and rent, and throwing out representatives of the authorities from their meetings. The growing threat of an agrarian revolution was realised by the ruling classes. The crisis, which exacerbated the ruin of the country's economy and the impoverishment of the peasant masses to an unprecedented degree, provided a major impetus to the growth of the agrarian movement, too. Enormous peasant reserves began to take the path of direct confrontation, seeking a revolutionary way out of the crisis.

The Indian people were striving, under great difficulties, in the course of a painful struggle against the feudal-imperialist camp, to get out of the crisis by setting out to struggle for independence, and achieved this soon after the end of the Second World War. The struggle in the 1930s was a precondition for the victory in 1947.

* * *

The economic crisis in India was part of the world crisis, and it embraced both industry and agriculture. It is particularly important, however, that it was proceeding in an agrarian country, where the agricultural sector of the economy was in a state of degradation, in a country where, for almost two hundred years, a regime of colonial oppression had reigned on the basis of a whole complex of feudal-serf survivals. The crisis greatly exacerbated the economic and political contradictions that were the "normal" state of affairs in a colonial country. The economic consequences of the crisis hit the Indian working class and peasantry with all their force.

The enormous political experience gained by the Indian working class during the time of the great strike movement and the period of open uprisings from 1928 to 1933, speeded up a redistribution of class forces as never before, given the acute economic disruption India was suffering.

Understanding this, on January 5, 1931, the London *Times* printed excerpts from a speech made by M. P. Isaac Foot, who openly expressed one point of the strategy employed by British imperialism in India: "The extremist elements in India could yet be defeated, but the defeat must come not from British machine guns, but from the responsible politicians among the Indians themselves . . . "

A mistake was being made here. The fact is that the ideas

of national liberation could not be considered as being merely potential in India. The liberation movement of the India people grew until it brought the British colonial rule to political crisis and, after some time, to collapse. The British colonialists had to leave India. This is precisely what Lenin foresaw a quarter of a century before it actually happened.

* * *

The 1932/33 economic year was marked by a further deepening of the crisis in all branches of agriculture and industry in India. The sharpest changes took place in the sphere of finances and foreign trade, following the abolition, in the autumn of 1931, of the gold standard of the pound sterling. The feedback from the financial and foreign trade crisis told with all its force on industry, and especially agriculture. The economic and political contradictions between the national bourgeoisie and the Anglo-Indian government gained in intensity; there was a substantial step-up in the struggle between the imperialist competitors for the Indian home market. The intensification of the crisis engendered a number of new processes that greatly affected the position of the toiling masses. It led to an acceleration of the impoverishment of the working people in town and countryside, to a rise in unemployment among the traditional industrial proletariat and a drop in the already starvation level existence of the population. The contraction of the home market continued. On this basis, a further narrowing occurred of the production apparatus of colonial industry. The profits of the industrial bourgeoisie dropped even lower. The weight of the colonial tribute rose both absolutely and relatively, as can be seen from the price movements over the four years of the crisis (Table 26).

Consideration of the data in Table 26 allows the following conclusions to be drawn:

1) Only sugar prices were higher than in 1914. The decisive factor in this respect was, of course, the prohibitive import duties at 160 per cent of the market price.

2) In terms of the drop in prices, pride of place belonged to cereals, legumes, tea, oil-bearing crops, raw jute, mustard, pelts and hides, and raw cotton.

Table 26

Commodity Price Movements in India Over the Four Years of the Crisis,
1914 = 100

	Grain	Legumes	Sugar	Tea	Oil-bearing crops	Mustard	Raw jute	Raw cotton	Pelts and hides	Average index for all goods	Cotton fabrics	Metals
Pre-crisis peak prices	163	180	407	206	198	161	154	309	184	201	325	301
Low point in 1929	119	141	151	101	140	103	81	128	102	134	158	124
in 1930	84	96	128	102	99	95	45	68	71	100	125	108
in 1931	73	81	126	63	78	64	43	71	51	96	118	105
in 1932	64	83	139	57	71	55	38	76	37	86	112	103
High point in 1929	133	171	167	165	175	114	108	161	130	145	163	130
in 1930	106	144	157	128	160	105	84	112	106	131	150	122
in 1931	85	108	150	114	90	75	62	97	84	100	130	112
in 1932	76	106	150	66	84	65	52	106	59	97	132	113
Limits of price fluctuations:												
1929	—14	—30	—16	—64	—35	—11	—27	—33	—28	—11	—10	— 6
1930	—22	—48	—29	—26	—61	—20	—39	—43	—35	—31	—25	—22
1931	—12	—27	—24	—31	—12	—11	—19	—26	—33	— 9	—12	— 7
1932	—12	—23	—11	— 9	—13	—10	—14	—30	—12	—11	—20	—10
Gap between pre-crisis peak and high point in 1932	—87	—74	—257	—140	—114	—96	—102	—203	—125	—104	—193	—188
Gap between high point in 1929 and high point in 1932	—57	—65	—17	—99	—91	—49	—56	—55	—71	—48	—31	—17
March 1933	61	81	127	70	69	53	38	68	54	83	112	92
September 1933	68	83	138	104	73	48	48	82	57	88	112	101

3) The drop in the prices of agricultural commodities over the four years of the crisis was several times greater than that of industrial goods. This unevenness of the drop in prices not only did not decrease in the last year of the crisis, it actually intensified.

4) In 1932, in spite of attempts to stabilise prices at a previously achieved level, there was a further drop in those of all goods, and especially of grain, legumes, and raw cotton.

5) The drop in the prices of colonial industrial raw materials, which began straight after the postwar boom (1919-1922), continued rapidly and unceasingly over all the four years of the crisis. Moreover, they fell as much in these four years as over the previous 7 or 8 years.

6) The drop in the prices of colonial foodstuffs was lower than that of industrial raw materials during the postwar boom years, but faster during the crisis.

7) Comparing the level and rate of fall of prices in India with those in other capitalist countries, the data show that India suffered from this process in its most acute form (Table 27).

Table 27

Price Index Movements in Several Capitalist Countries

	India, 1914	Japan, 1913*	Australia, 1913*	Canada, 1926	USA, 1926	Britain, 1914
1921	178	200	175	110	98	197
1929	141	167	166	96	97	137
1931 (August)	91	113	128	73	69	69
1932 (August)	91	118	130	67	65	100
Percentage fall from 1921 to 1932 inclusive	49.9	41.0	25.7	39.1	33.7	49.2
Percentage fall from 1929 to 1932 inclusive	37.0	31.4	20.8	30.3	32.0	26.0

* Year taken as 100.

The small and minute holdings of the Indian ryots, oppressed by imperialism and landlords, could not stand up to the substantial drop in prices. The dominating industrial-financial monopolies in the countries consuming colonial raw materials and foodstuffs and supplyng the markets of the colonial countries with industrial goods, systematically compensated for the drop in their profits by setting low monopoly prices for agricultural commodities on the one hand, and monopoly high prices for industrial ones on the other. The colonial state machinery and the economic policy pursued by the Anglo-Indian government did everything to promote the accomplishment and implementation of this plunderous policy of the monopolies.

For the four years of the crisis, the reduction in the total area sown in the country was accompanied by a fall in the area sown to industrial crops, which took place faster than that in the area under food crops (Table 28).

A more detailed analysis of regional data reveals that, given the rapid drop in the area under industrial crops, a fairly substantial redistribution of crops was taking place: cotton was being replaced by wheat, jute by rice, wheat by legumes, and so on. The tendency towards monoculture farming was countered by a tendency, intensified by the crisis, towards more subsistence farming and a redistribution of crops. In 1932, there was a further decline of peasant agriculture, which was manifested in an accelerated transition from the production of the best-quality and more labour-intensive industrial and food crops to the cultivation of low-quality and less labour-intensive ones (jovar, legumes, and so on).

One distinguishing feature worth mentioning was the more rapid drop in the yield compared with that in the sown area—a fact indicating the further degradation of Indian peasant farming.

The uneven drop in exports of Indian agricultural goods in physical and value terms was characteristic of all the crisis years, and in 1932 this process became even more marked (Table 29). Its economic significance lay primarily in an extreme intensification of the non-equivalent exchange between the colony and the world market, especially that of Britain.

There was a significant increase in the colonial exploitation of the Indian peasantry. According to data provided by In-

Table 28

Changes in Sown Area and Output of the Chief Crops During the Crisis

Year	Jute				Cotton				Wheat	
	Area		Output		Area		Output		Area	
	Thous. acres	%	Thous. bales	%	Thous. acres	%	Thous. bales	%	Thous. acres	%
1928/29	3,544	—	9,956	—	29,053	—	5,782	—	32,000	—
1929/30	3,317	—6.4	9,767	—1.9	25,922	—4.2	5,125	—11.3	31,654	—1.1
1930/31	3,492	+5.3	11,255	+15.2	23,500	—9.3	5,110	—0.3	32,181	—1.7
1931/32	1,862	—46.7	5,566	—50.5	23,522	+0.1	4,064	—20.5	33,745	+10.4
1932/33	1,899	+2.0	5,845	+5.0	22,558	—5.0	4,516	+8.9	32,293	—5.7
1932/33 over 1928/29	—	—46.4	—	—41.3	—	—22.4	—	—21.9	—	+0.9

Year	Wheat		Rice				Groundnuts			
	Output		Area		Output		Area		Output	
	Thous. tonnes	%	Thous. acres	%	Thous. tonnes	%	Thous. acres	%	Thous. tonnes	%
1928/29	8,507	—	83,000	—	32,138	—	6,351	—	3,211	—
1929/30	10,469	+23.1	80,000	—3.6	31,131	—3.1	5,748	—9.5	2,268	—16.9
1930/31	9,302	—11.1	81,900	+2.4	32,200	+3.2	6,579	+14.5	3,154	+18.2
1931/32	9,026	—3.0	84,260	+2.9	32,988	+6.0	5,489	—16.6	2,276	—27.8
1932/33	9,120	+0.9	82,026	—2.6	30,655	—7.0	6,952	+26.7	2,836	+24.6
1932/33 over 1928/29	—	+7.2	—	—1.2	—	—4.6	—	+9.5	—	— 11.7

Table 29

Changes in Indian Agricultural Exports

	Physical volume, thous. tonnes				Value, million rupees			
	Average for 1921 - 1930	1931	1932	1932 over average for 1921 - 1930, %	Average for 1921 - 1930	1931	1932	1932 over average for 1921-1930, %
Cotton	616	570	286	—54	690.9	320	160	—77
Jute	1,499	—	1,176	—22	728.4	—	314.9	—57
Tea, million pounds	346	343	368	+6	270.6	202	168.9	—38
Rice	2,067	2,090	2,067	0	369.8	161.0	171.6	—54
Groundnuts	448	—	472	+5	112.1	—	81.1	—28
Pelts and hides	70	—	42	—40	139.5	—	77.6	—44

dian bourgeois economists, the peasant's share in the price of the output he had himself produced was from only a fifth to a third of the market price of the mass of agricultural commodities sold.

The price scissors of export and import goods fluctuated, on average, from 25-35 index points in favour of imports from 1929 to 1932 (Table 30). On India's home market, the price

Table 30

The Price Scissors for Industrial (Import) and Agricultural (Export) Goods,
1914 = 100

Year, month	Export goods		Import goods	
	Price index	Percentage drop over September 1, 1929	Price index	Percentage drop over September 1, 1929
September 1929	227		167	
March 1931	139	39	144	14
September 1931	116	46.5	139	17
March 1932	124	43	154	8
July 1932	—	47	—	16

scissors for industrial and agricultural goods had reached 50 index points by the end of 1932, which was the record for the crisis years.

As a result of the crisis, debts and interest, merchant's profits, direct and indirect taxes increased substantially and embraced not only all the surplus product of the direct producer, but also at least half his necessary product. Even the previous miserable, chronically contracted reproduction of manpower, to say nothing of the means of production, became impossible for the peasant masses (Table 31). This universal ruin and impoverishment of the poor and middle peasantry could in no way be relieved by the partial and temporary cut in taxes and rents that was introduced in some Indian provinces. In the opinion

Table 31

Peasant Incomes in the Tanjore District of the Madras Province in 1924

1	2	3		4		5		6		7		8	
Class of land by natural fertility	Rice output per acre of irrigated land, kalams*	Price per kalam		Minus 15% for unfavourable conditions		Farming costs according to tax office		Balance of columns 3, 4 and 5		Land tax (rent)		Ryot's income	
		Rupees	Annas	Rupees	Annas	Rupees	Annas	Rupees	Annas	Rupees	Annas	Rupees	Annas
1	1,300	54	3	8	2	28	11	17	6	16	10	+0	12
2	1,150	47	15	7	3	27	—	13	12	14	4	+0	8
3	1,000	41	44	6	4	25	—	10	7	11	14	—1	7
4	900	37	8	5	10	23	11	8	3	10	11	—2	8
5	800	33	5	5	—	22	—	6	5	9	8	—3	3
6	700	29	3	4	6	20	5	4	8	8	5	—3	13
7	600	25	—	3	12	18	10	2	10	7	2	—4	8
8	550	22	15	3	7	7	—	2	8	5	15	—3	7
9	500	20	13	3	2	15	5	2	6	5	5	—2	15
10	450	18	12	2	13	13	10	2	5	4	12	—2	7
11	400	16	11	2	8	11	15	2	4	4	2	—1	14
12	350	14	9	2	3	10	4	2	2	3	9	—1	7

* Kalam = 28.6 kg.

of bourgeois economists, the cut in taxes was usually to the benefit of the exploiting upper crust in the countryside, who owned the land and, consequently, the peasants' harvest.

There was a further concentration of the peasants' land, water and means of production in the hands of moneylenders, merchants, rich peasants and partly the traditional landlords. Certain indirect data allow us to establish the formation of a new stratum of landlords from among the moneylenders and merchants, especially in the Punjab and the Deccan. In the same way, new strata of intermediate, semi-feudal rent-receivers appeared in the most diverse regions. As a result of the ruin of the toiling peasantry and of a certain drop in the price of land in a number of regions, the peasants' plots of land began to be concentrated, at a growing speed, in the hands of the village rich peasantry who definitely increased their landholdings as a result of the crisis and expanded their share in the village.

The crisis obviously speeded up the penetration of capitalist elements into certain branches of farming, particularly in the comparatively rapidly developed production of sugar cane in the United Provinces, Madras and partly on the moist soils of the Punjab and in Bengal. It was protected by prohibitive import duties. The area under sugar cane rose from 2,972 thousand acres in 1931/32 to 3,305 thousand in 1932/33, and the sugar output increased from 3,970 thousand to 4,651 thousand tonnes, respectively. In connection with this, over two to three years of the crisis, more than a dozen sugar refineries were opened. By promoting the expansion of sugar production in India, British imperialism was trying to relieve Britain of the need to import Dutch and Cuban sugar. This desire, arising from the policy of establishing a certain economic autarchy within the bounds of the British Empire, which intensified the international market competition and the struggle for sources of raw materials and foodstuffs, was clearly reflected in the so-called Ottawa Agreement between Britain and India.

Although, in the process of the capitalist penetration of the production of sugar cane in the countryside the chief figure was an insignificant stratum of junkers and rich peasants, the application of semi-feudal methods of exploitation of the peasantry by the landlords and rich peasants remained in full force and, as a rule, became even more intensive in this sphere of agriculture. Note should also be made of the policy pursued by the Anglo-Indian government, geared to creating, in the Sind, a major raw material base for the production of medium- and high-quality cotton for Lancashire, the aim being to liberate it from dependence on the USA. Plantations, big estates and sometimes rich peasant farms of a semi-feudal type—such were the class support of this policy. In order to supply these farms with cheap manpower, for two or three years during the crisis a major campaign was waged to resettle Punjabis, Belugi, Rajasthanis and other peoples into the regions of the Sind (Sukkur). The transformation of the Sind into an independent administrative unit should be viewed in this context.

In addition to individual, extremely timid attempts to impose colonial junker-type farming, attempts that were held back by the crisis and the class struggle waged by the peasant masses, it should be remembered that there was a policy, specific for the period of the crisis, of drawing the Indian moneylenders and merchants into agricultural credit and marketing co-operatives and into the banking system of British finance capital in India, as well as of transforming big Indian moneylenders and merchants into a legalised network of British banks. A closer economic union between British finance and local merchant's and moneylender's capital was created almost everywhere. This union had already been economically tested in the export of gold and its preliminary pumping out of the remote parts of the country. There were, of course, quite understandable political motives for this policy of British finance capital, motives that outweighed all others given the intensifying class struggle in the countryside, the strengthening of its support in the villages included.

One characteristic feature in the final years of the crisis was the freezing of merchant's and moneylender's capital. As a result of the fact that 80 per cent of the loans advanced by moneylenders were used for non-productive purposes, the enormous sum of such loans could not, given the contracted reproduction of the peasant economy, be reclaimed in money form, so it usually took the form of the removal of all or almost all the peasants' harvest by the creditor, the sale of the peasants' land and means of production by auction or the peasants' transformation into a debt slave. The Indian press in the most diverse parts of the country presented a multitude of facts revealing the particulary aggressive nature of the moneylenders. Precisely in this connection, the outstanding Indian bourgeois economists R. Mukerji and N. Sarkar came up with projects for creating "conciliation councils" in those regions where the peasants' indebtedness to moneylenders was greatest and the class struggle therefore most intense.

Under the crisis conditions, the extremely widespread practice of so-called punitive taxes, collective fines, collections for maintaining the small military-police units that roamed the country in order to "subdue rebellious villages" acquired particular significance. This practice was particularly widespread in Bengal, the United Provinces and partly in the North-West Frontier Province. The Indian press often reported the levying of collective fines and the sale of peasant property of whole villages to pay military-police and punitive taxes.

The last two years of the crisis were marked by a weakening of the economic positions and often bankruptcy of a substantial part of the intermediate semi-feudal rent-receivers, especially in Bengal. About 20,000 small holdings were auctioned off for non-payment of government taxes. Some of these were, of course, bought up by moneylenders and merchants, prosperous members of the bourgeois intelligentsia, and so on. It is characteristic, however, that about 3,000 holdings remained unsold. The intensified class struggle, according to police terminology "agrarian banditry," and non-payment of rent were evidently the decisive factor behind this phenomenon. The growing terrorist movement in Bengal was nourished largely by the ruin of small rent-receivers and the exceptional increase in unemployment among the petty-bourgeois and small landowning young people.

The years 1932 and 1933 were marked by a step-up in the sale of gold valuables, which began after the abolition of the gold standard of the pound sterling. The export of gold from India was, of course, a result of the exploitation of the labour of millions of workers and peasants and the "gold expression" of the surplus product appropriated by the dominating classes and imperialism. The actual mining of gold in India was on a negligible scale, so it could not constitute the true source of the gold exports. Gold was imported into India at one time as the colonial equivalent for the agricultural and industrial output exported. After hundreds of years of colonial plunder, the toiling peasantry and petty urban bourgeoisie were left with small treasures in the form of jewellery, coins, and so on. During the growing crisis, imperialism and the landlords robbed the peasant masses by expropriating not only the peasants' harvests, land and tools for the non-payment of rent, tax and interests, but also their insignificant treasures. Given the enormous overproduction of raw materials and colonial foodstuffs, which had lost their previous value on the home and world markets, the colonial tribute in kind underwent a partial change. The class meaning of the policy of the "free" export of gold, accompanied, what is more, by speculation, consisted in robbery of the Indian people, robbery exceeding that of the period when the East India Company held sway in the country.

The bankrupt landlords, intermediate rent-receivers, and rich peasantry, small and, partly, middle merchants and moneylenders often, of course, also sold gold to the government and indigenous bankers. In the towns, not only the ruined petty bourgeoisie and intellectuals were getting rid of their gold stocks, but also the multitudes of small and medium indigenous bankers, for the export of gold as an exchange operation brought in about 35 per cent profit, on the basis of the difference in the prices of gold on the home and world markets. The main source of the gold exports was, however, the ruined countryside. (In India, gold was bought up by the government and the British banks at a set price, fixed by the government for the home market.) This created a situation of speculation in gold and treasury securities on the markets of almost all the big trade and industrial centres in the country.

In 1932, the inflation of the rupee became a fact, though all the Indian press, as well as the official leaders of the Anglo-Indian government, did their best to conceal this. The policy of inflation did not, however, lead to the desired rise in the prices of colonial raw materials and foodstuffs on the home and world markets; nor did it improve the situation of the direct producer. George Schuster, Minister of Finance in the Anglo-Indian government, eventually had to admit this. The reason was the policy pursued by the government, especially in 1932, of blockading the home market from the world consumption centres on the basis of: 1) a monetary policy of an artificially inflated rupee exchange rate, which made Indian agricultural raw materials more expensive than those of the British dominions and other colonies; 2) a saturation of the home market with colonial raw materials and foodstuffs (so-called raw material inflation), which ensured the British monopolies high colonial profits from the purchase of Indian raw materials not only by Britain, but also by other imperialist countries; 3) the Ottawa Agreement, which formalised the tendency to transfer the consequences of the crisis in Britain and dominions to India.

Nalini Rajan Sarkar, chairman of the Bengal Chamber of Commerce and a supporter of the Swadeshi movement, wrote that it would be necessary to take rapid measures in order to avoid a universal disaster, which might finally draw the whole country into an agrarian revolution, engendered by extreme despair. The violent peasant actions, intensified by economic factors, he warned, should be considered as the first signs of an impending catastrophic upheaval.

Economists and politicians wrote in the Indian press suggesting various ways out of the crisis or means to relieve it somewhat. The members of the national industrial bourgeoisie planned a transition to economic revival by abolishing the Anglo-Indian government's monetary policy, and by introducing prohibitive customs duties on foreign goods, and believed that only the creation of a reserve bank and cheap credit were capable of saving industry and agriculture in India from final collapse—in other words, they put forward a variety of arguments for the need for serious changes in the Anglo-Indian government's economic policy. The official government economists, on the other hand, recommended other means for getting out of the crisis They said that, with the falling exports, the only way India could avoid a terrible commercial and financial catastrophe was to export a tremendous quantity of gold (which the Minister of Finance called the "key factor" which would have to be taken into consideration in an assessment of the economic situation in India). The only really effective means for avoiding a terrible catastrophe was, in their opinion, continued gold exports and, consequently, all other considerations had to be subordinated to this goal.

Robert Horne, one of the leading figures of British imperialism, together with a number of eminent British economists, proceeded from the assumption that the crisis could be overcome if prices were stabilised and that, in turn, this depended on effective demand, so he came up with a plan for introducing the free minting of silver. This, in his opinion, should lead to a remonetisation of the enormous stocks of silver in the East, which were absolutely inactive, and to a rise in the absolute level of effective demand in the countries of the East, above all India and China, as well as to a stimulation if not of a rise, then at least of a stabilisation of prices.

The question of the rise in the prices of silver and its remonetisation for the purpose of increasing the population's effective demand in India and other Eastern countries was linked by Indian economists with the London World Economic Conference. Some of them, expressing the desire of Indian finance, comprador and merchant-moneylender bourgeoisie, thoroughly welcomed the announcement made by Franklin Delano Roosevelt and James Ramsay MacDonald concerning the possibility of paying part of Europe's debts to the USA in silver. They foresaw the possibility of furious speculation and profits from the expropriation of the small silver hoards belonging to the working people in India. There can be no doubt that, if this plan were adopted, silver would be pumped out of India on an even more tremendous scale, the robbery of the toiling masses would increase unprecedentedly and the usual colonial tribute would be joined by a new form of it for the payment of debts to the metropolis at the cost of the Indian people.

* * *

The traditional contradictions between the requirements of the independent economic and political development of India and the colonial monopoly of imperialism intensified to the extreme during the crisis, while new, specifically crisis-engendered collisions occurred between the national bourgeoisie and imperialism. In spite of the weakening of its economic resources over the four years of the crisis, imperialism still possessed a certain politico-economic room for manoeuvre. It required the Indian national bourgeoisie to capitulate by recognising and approving the federative "constitution" and co-operating with it on this basis, and as a precondition for this co-operation, it demanded an end to the campaign for civil disobedience. The development of the anti-imperialist movement in India was characterised at that time (although there was a general tendency for the movement to grow, while the communist vanguard was weak in both town and countryside) by a certain unevenness. The working-class and peasant movement did not reach the level at which imperialism's room for manoeuvre would be exhausted, so imperialism agreed to make partial economic concessions to the national bourgeoisie, without weakening its decisive support in India.

* * *

During the crisis the bourgeois circles increasingly spread information to the effect that the British colonialists had substantially reduced taxes in some provinces or in the regions hit hardest by the crisis, but this was simply untrue. Official statistics on land and forest taxes by provinces show the true state of affairs and unmask the imperialist tax policy (Table 32).

In some provinces—in Burma in 1930/31 (the year of the uprising), in the United Provinces from 1930 to 1933, in the Punjab and in Bengal—partial and temporary cuts were made in the land tax, but these were not of any real economic significance. The political significance, however, of the partial tax cut in certain regions, in the centres of the peasant movement, was instrumental as a demagogic means for averting outbreaks of peasant indignation and as a means for splitting peasant masses that were already on the move. It is characteristic that, in Bombay, Madras, the Central Provinces, Bihar and Orissa, i.e., provinces where the peasant movement was so far only weakly developed, taxes were not cut (apart from a partial cut in the forest tax). On the contrary, the tax burden borne by the peasants in these provinces increased, so they learned a clear lesson: even partial and temporary concessions by imperialism cannot be achieved without a struggle.

The nominal sum of the land tax remained generally stable,

Table 32

Taxation During the Crisis,
million rupees

Year	Madras		Bombay		Bengal		United Provinces		Punjab		Burma		Bihar and Orissa		Central Provinces		Assam	
	Land	Forest	Land	Forest	Land	Forest	Land	Forest	Land	Forest	Land	Forest	Land	Forest	Land	Forest	Land	Forest
1928/29	52.4	6.1	48.4	7.3	32.6	3.1	60.4	6.1	27.7	3.5	54.0	1.6	17.3	10.9	21.9	5.4	11.7	3.7
1929/30	52.1	6.3	47.9	7.9	32.4	3.0	68.5	6.1	25.7	3.1	52.7	1.8	13.7	9.3	20.4	5.9	12.0	3.5
1930/31	48.8	5.2	47.4	5.2	30.8	2.3	64.7	4.9	26.9	2.3	28.2	1.4	18.0	8.11	21.8	5.1	11.5	2.2
1931/32	53.2	4.5	51.0	5.6	30.6	1.6	61.2	4.5	22.2	2.2	57.5	1.0	17.6	6.2	21.0	4.4	12.0	1.9
1932/33	75.7	4.9	48.6	5.7	31.0	1.5	57.0	4.5	22.9	2.0	44.9	0.8	17.8	6.4	25.3	4.2	11.4	1.7
1933/34	76.8	4.5	48.2	5.8	31.2	1.5	58.3	4.5	27.8	1.7	53.7	0.9	17.9	6.3	25.3	4.5	11.3	1.4

but there were minor fluctuations in both directions. Meanwhile, the real burden of the land tax, given the crisis and the drop in the prices of agricultural output, increased enormously (Table 33). The official press did not like writing about this, of course, but it was precisely this real burden of the tax on the Indian peasantry that reflected the plunderous essence of British imperialism.

Table 33

Value of Gross Product of Agriculture and the Share of the Land Tax in It

Province	Value of gross product in 1928/29, million rupees	Share of land tax, %	Value of gross product in 1931/32, million rupees	Share of land tax, %	Change in the product value, %
Madras	1,807.8	3	1,012.5	5	—44
Bombay	1,205.2	4	665.6	8	—24.8
Bengal	2,325.9	1.5	1,067.1	3.5	—54.1
United Provinces	1,405.2	4	922.1	6.5	—34.4
Punjab	767.8	3.5	374.9	6	—5.2
Burma	633.8	12	292.0	25	—53.9
Bihar and Orissa	1,351.7	1.2	710.5	2.5	—47.4
Central Provinces	687.7	3	324.2	6.5	—52.8
	10,185.1	3.2	5,368.9	6.2	—47.3

Considering that the land tax in India was paid mainly by landlords and constituted, on average, a third of the rent they charged the peasants, and subtracting from the value of the taxable product transport costs, i.e., roughly 10 per cent of the value, the cost of depreciation of the peasants' livestock and tools (under the simple reproduction of the peasant economy), the value of the necessary product, i.e., the peasants' minimum income, roughly 15 per cent of the value as the correction factor on the further, post-1931/32 fall in prices of agricultural goods, then the result gives the most realistic idea possible of the destructive force of the tax burden in relation to the peasant economy. Under these conditions, the real burden of the land tax relative to the peasants' money income increased, on average, 3- to 5-fold compared with the pre-crisis period. This is why the peasant movement was, during the crisis years, primarly an anti-tax movement in some regions, and on this issue the Indian National Congress was quite successful in influencing the peasant movement, taking it under its leadership and putting forward anti-tax slogans.

The Indian peasants paid taxes not only on the land, of which they were deprived, but also on industrial goods (excise and customs duties), as well as for irrigation, which served as an instrument for subordinating the peasant economy to imperialism and as a source of loan income for British capital (Table 34).

Table 34

Changes in Excise and Water Taxes,
million rupees

Province	1929/30		1930/31		1931/32		1932/33		1933/34	
	Excise	Water	Excise	Water	Excise	Water	Excise	Water	Excise	Water
Madras	59.2	18.8	52.4	18.6	42.5	19.1	42.7	—	44.8	7.9
Bombay	40.7	4.6	30.4	3.3	32.6	5.8	34.1	4.5	34.9	4.6
Bengal	22.6	—	18.0	—	15.6	—	13.9	—	13.9	—
United Provinces	13.0	12.7	11.2	10.9	10.8	9.7	11.8	12.0	13.0	11.8
Punjab	11.5	39.4	11.1	36.1	9.4	38.0	9.4	22.3	9.8	42.2
Burma	12.6	4.8	10.7	19.8	8.0	27.8	8.3	54.6	8.8	37.3
Bihar and Orissa	19.0	11.8	14.2	1.7	12.2	2.1	12.0	2.1	12.7	2.0
Central Provinces	12.4	—	8.6	3.2	6.5	—	5.5	—	5.7	—
Assam	6.6	—	5.8	—	5.2	—	4.1	—	3.7	—

The falling trend in the normal sum of the excise tax was obvious, but it was levied while the peasant masses were consuming only half as much as before, and the drop in consumption by far exceeded the partial cut in the excise tax. In fact, the peasant now paid about twice as much excise tax for every unit of industrial goods that he consumed. The total sum of excise, which was collected mostly from the peasantry, was equal to about half the land tax, so it could not be taken into account in the calculation of the tax robbery of the countryside during the crisis.

The imperialist incomes from irrigation also fell somewhat, but remained disproportionately high, and in some regions such as the Punjab, the United Provinces, and Burma, i.e., in the chief irrigated parts of the country, in 1933/34 they remained at a very high level, far above the pre-crisis one.

The means that were of growing significance in the overall system by which the colonialists made their onslaught on the Indian toiling masses included incomes from customs duties charged on Indian imports. These, again, fell most heavily on the mass consumers. Let us merely point out that, in 1929/30, when Indian imports reached a value of 2,400 million rupees, the Anglo-Indian government received customs revenues of 503 million rupees, i.e., about a fifth of the value of the imports; in 1932/33, however, with total imports valued at only 1,320 million rupees, it received customs revenues of 513 million rupees, or substantially over a third of the value of the imports. This seems paradoxical at first glance, but it provided the basis for a number of officials in the Anglo-Indian government to praise the "financial genius" of the colonial state and announce that India was the only country in the world where the government's revenues were, in spite of the crisis, at a very high level, unattainable for some countries.

Let us sum up concerning the internal plunder of the Indian peasantry by imperialism and the local dominating classes (Table 35).

Our calculations of rent are not exaggerated. The well-known Indian economist and capitalist Manu Subedar, who was the author of a pseudo-radical programme for agrarian reform, believed that the sum of land rent at the beginning of the crisis was a billion rupees.

In 1929/30, the Bengali landlords paid the Anglo-Indian government 32.4 million rupees in land tax out of the 280 million rupees they themselves received in rent, while in 1932/33 they paid 31 million rupees, i.e., a seventh part of the pre-crisis rent. Considering that in other provinces the tax was between a fifth and a half of the rent, the tax can be rounded to a third of the rent. This calculation probably underestimates rather than exaggerates the size of the rent, for it is

Table 35

The Share of the Colonialists and the Indian Dominating Classes in the Value of the Gross Agricultural Product,
million rupees

	1929/30	1932/33
Share of the colonisers		
Land tax (1928/29)	326.4	334.6
Forest tax	38.9	31.7
Water tax	102.1	135.5
Excise on commodities (20 per cent of the excise being accounted for by the towns)	197.6—39.5=158.1	141.8– 28.3=113.5
Customs duties (same percentage for the towns)	503—100=403	513—102=411
Total*	1,168.0—139.5= =1,028.5	1,156.6—130.3= =1.026.3
As a percentage of the value of the gross product of agriculture	11.5	20.5
Share of the landlords, moneylenders and merchants		
Rent (the land tax being taken as a third of the rent and the drop in rent as 30 per cent)	960	630
Interest (the mean annual rate being taken as 20 per cent of the total debt, which, in 1928/29, was 4 billion rupees and in 1931/32 was 9 billion rupees)	800	1,800
Merchant's profits (calculated as 5 per cent of the value of the output before the crisis and during the crisis)	50	50
Total	1,810	2,480

	1929/30	1932/33
As a percentage of the value of the gross product of agriculture	25	51
Aggregate share of imperialism and the dominating classes	2,978—139.5= =2,838.5	3,636.6—130.3= =3,506.3
The same, as a percentage	36.5	71.5

* Excluding fines on the villages, interest on government loans, currency bonuses, freight incomes, and so on.

known that, as a rule, the rent took half the peasants' harvest. We leave aside the water rent charged by the landlord as the monopolist of local irrigation sources.

As for the calculations of loan interest, we proceed from the fact that, before the crisis, the peasants paid an average of from 24 to 37.5 per cent on loans, and compound interest was paid on about a fifth of the total debt. We therefore get an average 20 per cent, obviously understated, interest rate.

Thus, although these calculations are based on official initial data, without a number of additional types of charge on the peasantry being taken into account, the results leave no doubt that, during the crisis, the Indian countryside was plundered to an unprecedented extent, by far exceeding the plunder carried out in India by the East India Company during the period of the primitive accumulation of capital. Hence it is understandable that there was famine and mass deaths in the Indian countryside, the peasants were extensively evicted from the land and the villages were filled with police and troops.

At the same time, the data indicate the growing parasitism of the local dominating classes and imperialism during the crisis, the result being that they jointly removed from the peasant about 60-75 per cent of the value of his output without any equivalent. Since the physical volume of agricultural produce remained comparatively stable, while prices fell by an average of 50 per cent, for each unit of feudal-imperialist payments the peasant had to hand over twice as much of his output, i.e., twice as much of his unpaid labour. This is evidenced, too, by the press, which stated that the ryots were handing over three times more jute to cover their debts than when the loans were advanced a few years previously.

In spite of the fact that the money accumulations of the feudal-imperialist masters of the Indian countryside fell somewhat during the crisis, nevertheless, the correlation between the surplus and necessary labour changed substantially in favour of the dominating classes. Thus, before the crisis, the usual splitting of the harvest under Indian conditions (i.e., of the gross product) between the peasant and the landlord took place on a half-and-half basis and the rate of feudal-imperialist exploitation of the peasant was not, as a rule, less than 100 per cent. Now, however, given the 50 per cent fall in prices, the landlord and the colonialist attempted to remove for themselves a share of the gross product that would ensure them their previous or almost their previous money incomes. This was the essence of the policy of transferring the consequences of the crisis on to the peasant masses in India and of the advance of British capital. This was only possible given a doubling of the exploiters' share taken from the gross product of the peasant by doubling the rate of exploitation.

This was not easy to achieve. The toiling peasant resisted with all his might. The struggle over the ratio of the surplus and necessary product—and, consequently, the struggle for land—was the economic pivot of the class struggle developing in the Indian countryside.

Instead of cutting prices to meet the drop in effective demand, the capitalist monopolies cut production, in an attempt to maintain monopoly high prices. The colonial direct producer, being the victim of the catastrophic fall in prices and the object of feudal-imperialist robbery, was unable to cut his production to counter the rapid fall in prices on agricultural goods. The reasons were as follows:

—Colonial agriculture consisted of fragmented small parcels of land, where it was impossible to organise a general cut in production.

—Constant costs (rent, taxes, interest) were not directly dependent on the area cultivated and accounted for 60-70 per cent of the value of the output.

—Against the background of a constantly growing agricultural overpopulation, virtual bondage of the peasants to the land, rising unemployment in the towns, weak proletarianisation, and strong pauperisation among the peasantry, the labour power of the direct producer and the members of his family could only be used, and even then not to the full, on his own small holding.

—The collapse of the monoculture production of industrial crops that no longer found a world market, which was accompanied by a serious underproduction of foodstuffs, engendered a tendency towards a change in agriculture and a transition to cultivation mainly of low-quality food crops.

This trend in the colonial-agrarian crisis countered the impact of that towards a cut in production, as is shown by the changes in the sown area under the chief food and industrial crops (Table 36).

Table 36

Changes in the Sown Area Under the Chief Food and Industrial Crops,
million acres

Province	1928/29	1929/30	1930/31	1931/32	1932/33	1932/33 as % of 1928/29
			Rice			
Madras	11.0	—	11.7	11.6	11.5	104.5
Bombay	3.3	—	3.7	3.5	3.2	97.0
Bengal	21.4	20.2	20.6	22.1	21.7	101.4
United Provinces	7.1	—	6.8	6.7	6.1	85.9
Punjab	—	—	—	—	—	—
Burma	12.5	12.8	13.0	12.5	12.6	100.8
Bihar and Orissa	14.3	—	13.9	14.1	13.0	90.9
Central Provinces and Berar	6.1	—	6.8	7.0	7.0	114.8
Assam	4.4	—	4.5	4.5	4.5	102.3
Total, together with other regions	82.1	80.0	82.7	84.0	82.0	99.9

Province	1928/29	1929/30	1930/31	1931/32	1932/33	1932/33 as %% of 1928/29
Wheat						
Madras	—	—	—	—	—	—
Bombay	3.1	—	2.8	2.9	3.0	96.8
Bengal	0.1	0.1	0.1	0.1	0.1	100.0
United Provinces	7.2	—	7.7	7.6	7.8	108.7
Punjab	11.2	11.3	10.6	10.9	9.7	86.6
Burma	—	—	—	—	—	—
Bihar and Orissa	1.2	—	1.2	1.2	1.2	100.0
Central Provinces and Berar	3.3	—	3.1	3.6	3.5	106.1
Assam	—	—	—	—	—	—
Total, together with other regions	32.0	31.6	32.0	33.8	32.6	101.9
Cotton						
Madras	2.3	—	2.1	2.3	1.9	82.6
Bombay	7.3	—	6.3	6.2	6.1	83.6
Bengal	—	—	—	—	—	—
United Provinces	2.8	—	2.5	2.5	2.2	78.6
Punjab	0.4	—	0.4	0.2	0.3	75.0
Burma	—	—	—	—	—	—
Bihar and Orissa	—	—	—	—	—	—
Central Provinces and Berar	4.9	—	4.8	4.6	4.1	85.7
Assam	—	—	—	—	—	—
Total, together with other regions	25.8	25.9	23.8	23.5	22.3	86.4
Jute						
Madras	—	—	—	—	—	—
Bombay	—	—	—	—	—	—
Bengal	2.7	2.6	1.6	1.6	1.6	93.3
United Provinces	—	—	—	—	—	—
Punjab	—	—	—	—	—	—
Burma	—	—	—	—	—	—
Bihar and Orissa	0.1	0.1	0.1	0.1	0.1	100.0

Province	1928/29	1929/30	1930/31	1931/32	1932/33	1932/33 as % of 1928/29
Central Provinces and Berar	—	—	—	—	—	—
Assam	—	—	—	—	—	—
Total, together with other regions	3.1	3.3	1.9	1.9	1.9	61.3
			Groundnuts			
Madras	3.5	—	3.6	2.7	3.4	97.1
Bombay	1.3	—	1.6	1.5	1.6	123.1*
Bengal	—	—	—	—	—	—
United Provinces	—	—	—	—	—	—
Punjab	—	—	—	—	—	—
Burma	—	—	—	—	—	—
Bihar and Orissa	—	—	—	—	—	—
Central Provinces and Berar	—	—	—	—	—	—
Assam	—	—	—	—	—	—
Total, together with other regions	6.0	5.7	6.6	5.6	6.9	115.0

* The growth in the sown area under groundnuts was a result of the formation of the Unilever international monopoly association on the basis of a merger between British and Dutch vegetable-oil trusts, which bought up the raw material at monopoly prices and organised a speculative rise in prices in 1932/33.

Chapter Eight

The Levying of Colonial Tribute During the World Economic Crisis of 1929-1933

The development of the world economic crisis in India, as a British colony, and the influence of the crisis in India's economy were revealed in the boldest relief in the state of Indian finances, in the budget of the Anglo-Indian government, and especially in its monetary policy as a means for robbing the peasantry. British imperialism enjoyed an absolute monopoly in the sphere of money circulation and credit, disposed of the colonial budget and possessed all the levers for levying colonial tribute. It was compelled to make a number of complex manoeuvres in order to ensure the uninterrupted pumping out of colonial tribute under the difficult economic conditions obtaining in the country and the changed balance of forces between the various imperialist powers on both the world and the Indian home market. The political situation in India also reflected on the Anglo-Indian government's policy in the sphere of finance, and demanded a modification of the forms for levying colonial tribute on the peasants. A number of major monetary measures introduced by the Anglo-Indian government were implemented in an extremely confused and veiled form.

Monetary Policy Under the Gold Standard

The chief monetary unit, means of circulation and payment within India was the silver rupee, the value of which was determined by the gold value of silver or, the same thing, the price of silver calculated in terms of gold.

The economic crisis, which also told in the tremendous drop

in the price of silver, had a number of new consequences for the colonial currency.

The worldwide production of silver stood at 174 million ounces in 1920, 262 million in 1929, 244 million in 1930 and 200 million in 1931, 75 per cent of the total being a by-product of the mining of zinc, tin and copper. A rise in the extraction of these metals led to an increase in the production of silver, and vice versa. An overproduction of silver, as of any other commodity, should result in a considerable drop in its value. The sharp drop in the value of silver on the world market is confirmed by the following data:

Year	*Cents per ounce*	*Pence per ounce*
1913	61	27
1926	62	31
1928	58	26
1930	38	14
1931	28.6	14
January 1932	29	19
February 1932	30	19

According to calculations by Indian bourgeois economists, the Indian peasantry owned about 4,230 million ounces of silver. This figure serves as a point of reference showing that the drop in the value of silver on the world market reflected catastrophically on both the more prosperous strata of the peasantry and especially on the poorest and middle strata, with their silver mostly in the form of women's jewelry.

The sharp drop in the value of silver on the world market naturally made the Anglo-Indian government concerned over the fate of the Indian silver rupee, especially since the drop in budget revenues, the regular budget deficits over a number of years running, the huge outlays on putting down the revolutionary movement, the mass non-payment of taxes, the fall in the freight and commodity turnover in the country, the sharp contraction of foreign trade and revenues from it and, finally, the cut in production itself led to an oversaturation of the money market with devalued rupees and, inevitably, to inflation.

The Anglo-Indian government was striving during this period to utilise all means at its disposal to, at least temporarily, avoid inflation. Above all, it reduced the money supply in the country, with a certain degree of temporary success. The scale of the cut in money circulation in India is indicated by the following data:

Year	*Million rupees*
1926/27	2,877
1927/28	410
1928/29	190
1929/30	3,241
1930/31	2,629

Government accounts of the state of money circulation underestimated the scale of the cut in the country's money supply, but could not conceal this process, reflecting the government policy of attempting to avoid inflation. The quantity of banknotes in circulation was:

Month, year	*Thousand rupees*
March 1930	1,722,300
June 1930	1,637,272
September 1930	1,714,682
December 1930	1,613,403
March 1931	1,583,070
June 1931	1,533,083
September 1931	1,484,031
August 1932	1,755,821

At the same time, the government was exporting silver to China. The Indian press criticised the government in connection with the large sales of silver, for purchasing silver cheaply from the peasants through the merchant-moneylender network and selling it at a high price in China (through the Hong Kong-Shanghai Banking Corporation) and thereby reaping substantial profits. The sale by India of demonetised silver constituted:

Year	*Million ounces*
1927	9.2
1928	22.5
1929	35.0
1930	29.5
1931	35.0

Out of the 277.1 million ounces of silver, demonetised throughout the world, India's share was the greatest.

In July 1930, the government issued an internal loan of 300 million rupees at 6 per cent per annum. This was one way of reducing the money supply in circulation. Another, considerably more serious means was the sale of short-term Treasury Bills. A special tax also played its part in pumping money out of the population. Here we must include increased import and export duties, excise on a number of consumer goods (salt, paraffin, and others), and particularly special sorts of indirect taxes, which ultimately became an additional burden on the mass taxpayer—the peasant. It is not by chance that indirect taxes in particular grew sharply during this period. The government could not resort to additional direct taxation as successfully as it had done previously. The political situation in the country, obviously, exerted a decisive impact on the forms and methods of government policy implementation. The veil of indirect taxation was required. Moreover, since it reflected in a rise in import duties, individual groups of the Indian industrial bourgeoisie, especially textile manufacturers, had a vested interest in this.

One lever used to influence money circulation in the country was the maintenance of a high bank rate. Throughout the period of deflationary policy, it stood at seven per cent. This aspect of government policy came under particular attack from the national bourgeoisie, for it led primarily to a credit squeeze for local industry, reflecting imperialism's anti-industrialisation policy. The national bourgeoisie, especially those connected with the textile industry, were quite vigorous in their attacks on this credit squeeze policy.

The mobilisation of silver through taxes, both indirect and direct, the wringing of the last silver or paper rupee out of the direct producer, the internal loan, the sale of short-term bills in exchange for rupees, and the high bank rate were all introduced in an attempt to avoid inflation. This is a brief description of the government policy in relation to the Indian rupee on the money market within the country. It should also be mentioned that this policy, which obviously led to the ruin and impoverishment of the peasant masses and to a contraction of the home market more than ever before, allowed the Anglo-Indian government, on the one hand, to mobilise to some extent the silver money circulation in the country and, on the other, to concentrate a substantial quantity of silver in its own hands. Government stocks of silver stood at:

Month, year	*Thousand rupees*
March 1930	28,510
June 1930	34,799
September 1930	58,311
December 1930	53,930
December 1931	64,626
June 1932	80,175
September 1932	107,777

In this way, within India the government was pursuing a deflationary policy. From the formal-logical point of view, this sort of policy should have led, if not to a rise in prices, at least, to a brake on their fall. Yet, nothing of the kind happened, primarily because the government was also pursuing a policy of devaluing export colonial raw materials within India on the basis of an artificially high rupee exchange rate in relation to the pound sterling. Before the gold standard was abolished, this was achieved as follows. Under the 1927 law, which reflected nothing but the arbitrary power of the colonial monopolists, possessing the decisive levers in the economy and politics of the country they were robbing, one rupee was exchanged for 18 pence and vice versa.

At the Indian producer's expense, the British importer received 12.5 per cent additional exchange premium as a result of the artificially high rupee exchange rate.

In addition, the monetary policy pursued by British imperalism in India reduced to the extreme the competitiveness of Indian raw materials on the world market, blocked its penetration into the foreign market, raised the competitiveness of raw materials and foodstuffs from the British dominions (Canada, Australia, New Zealand, South Africa), kept turning India into the object of furious dumping of agricultural output produced on the basis of the capitalist mode of production. The overproduction of colonial raw materials in India was backed up by a constant, unchanging monetary policy that led to an even greater saturation of the home raw material market, to a blockade of foreign markets and, consequently, to a further drop in the value of raw materials within the country. In this lay the possibility for British imperialism of reaping abundant colonial superprofits.

In India's export trade, Britain occupied a far from monopolistic position. Its share was roughly a fifth of India's total exports; neither was Britain's share in the exports of India's chief raw materials and foodstuffs anywhere near monopolistic (Table 37). This monetary policy was pursued precisely in order to obtain 20 per cent of the raw materials exported by India cheaply, and receive additional profits from the import of its own goods.

Table 37

Britain's Share in Indian Exports
%

Year	Tea	Raw Jute	Jute goods	Cotton	Oil-bearing crops	Cereals	Pelts and hides
1929/30	85	25	6	6.6	16	2	26
1930/31	84	17	5	6.5	15	9	52

It was one of the firmest guarantees of colonial superprofits. There was no need to monopolise the sphere of direct raw material exports from India, but in order to levy colonial tribute and adjust all foreign trade to the pumping of valuables out of the colonies, out of the countryside there, it was essential to monopolise the sphere of money circulation and monetary policy. British finance capital in India was represented by a network of banks, purchase and marketing firms, all sorts of agencies for the purchase of raw materials—a network that was extremely ramified and monopolistic. Within India, the entire or almost the entire market for raw materials was controlled by British finance capital, which naturally had no desire to allow its competitors from Japan, North America, and Germany to acquire these raw materials cheaply. This meant however, that, by pursuing a methodical and consistent policy of devaluing Indian raw materials within India itself, British finance capital had a monopoly in reaping the economic results of this policy, sharing it with no one but the merchant, moneylender and comprador strata of the local bourgeoisie. In this, its raw material monopoly was accomplished through its finance and currency monopoly. In this, the direct producer, above all the peasant, was subject to a methodical and consistent policy of robbery in the form of colonial tribute. Consequently, the monetary monopoly acted as an instrument and mechanism for accomplishing the raw material monopoly, though the positions of British imperialism itself in India's actual raw material exports were far from outstanding and were losing ground by the year.

The monetary monopoly, as the medium through which the raw material monopoly was accomplished, was one of the pivots of British imperialism's colonial rule in India. Here, too, lay the kernel of the dissent between Britain and its imperialist rivals, on the one hand, and between it and the national bourgeoisie, striving to reap these huge profits themselves, on the other. The criticism levelled by the national bourgeoisie at the monetary monopoly of British imperialism in India was "popular" in character and was grounded primarily from the angle that the British monetary policy would act as a brake on the expansion of the home market and the development of industry. There can be no doubt that this sort of monetary policy had the most destructive effect on the state of the home market, on the peasantry's effective demand and the possibility of industrial development. It was a monetary-credit expression of imperialism's anti-industrialisation policy in relation to India's productive forces. It was a means for keeping India in the position of an agrarian-raw material appendage of Britain.

The prices of Indian raw materials on the home market were usually below the world prices for raw materials produced in capitalist countries. This did not, however, reflect high productivity and the presence of a highly developed agriculture in India. On the contrary, it was an indication of poverty, of very great exploitation, reducing the direct producer's share in the price of his output to less than a semi-starvation level of existence and allowing, on this basis, the commodities produced under semi-feudal conditions of production an opportunity to compete at times with ones produced under capitalist conditions. It could do so, however, only at the cost of systematic famine and the extinction and ruin of the direct producer, and the degradation of agriculture.

The question is, why British imperialism needed to raise the prices of Indian raw materials on the world market by employing its monetary monopoly. First, in order to reduce their competitiveness against the agricultural produce of the British dominions. Second, in order to devalue them even more on the home market. Third, in order to sell the raw materials, purchased cheaply on the Indian market for its own industry, at higher prices (though still below world ones), the potential purchasers of the Indian raw materials being its imperialist rivals. It should be mentioned that the crisis years were marked by Japan, then an importer of Indian cotton and a number of other Indian agricultural goods, beginning to acquire, though not without a fierce struggle with the British monopoly, its own purchasing trade network in India; even so, it did not enjoy the same advantages as British imperialism. This prompts the following conclusion: the monetary monopoly of British imperialism in India was geared to fixing monopoly low prices for colonial raw materials for itself and monopoly high ones for the same raw materials for the other imperialist countries competing with Britain.

Did Indian national capital reap any substantial benefits from the policy of a sharp devaluation of raw materials on the home market? No! There is a simple explanation for this. Rail, sea and river transport and all means of communications were a British monopoly, and the tariff policy pursued was such that the national bourgeoisie was largely deprived of the benefits deriving from the cheap raw materials on the home market, and paradoxes were engendered. For example, it was more economical to bring coal to Bombay from South Africa than from the mines of Bihar and Orissa, cotton from the USA than from the Central Provinces, jute goods from Scotland than from Calcutta, oil and petrol from the USSR and the USA than from Burma, and wheat from Australia and Canada than from the Punjab.

The rates charged for rail, sea and river freight, and the aggregate of small, but extremely important colonial methods brought the prices of Indian raw materials up to world levels and often even higher for local national capital, forcing it to purchase raw materials even from the British dominions. Only in the light of this policy can we understand the geographical scattering of national Indian industry, its direct transition to sources of raw materials and the market, this being a process that had begun long since and now gained greatly in intensity as a result of imperialism's monetary policy during the period of the crisis.

The contradiction between imperialism and the national bourgeoisie on this issue was extremely fierce and protracted. At the same time, this position taken by British imperialism in the sphere of Indian finances reserved it the room for manoeuvre in relation to the local bourgeoisie, made it more flexible, allowed it to supposedly "favour" India with certain negligible concessions in rail and sea freight tariffs, and the like, concessions for the sake of which the Indian bourgeoisie repeatedly compromised with the colonialists.

The comparatively extended deflationary policy prepared the ground for the inflationary policy that the Anglo-Indian government adopted after the abolition of the gold standard. These preparations were reflected in the following:

I. In addition to reducing the paper money supply, the government slowly, little by little and extremely cautiously removed the stocks of gold coins and ingots from the country. Here are some data on India's gold reserves:

Month, year	*Thousand rupees*
March 1930	322,735
June 1930	322,762
September 1930	322,764
December 1930	317,415
March 1931	237,590
June 1931	202,270
September 1931	71,928
December 1931	45,645

At first gradually and then sharply, the government sent India's gold reserves to Britain, this process gaining momentum as Britain's currency slipped. This was a measure geared to delaying the financial collapse of the pound sterling at the colony's expense. What is more, the bourgeois-nationalist press in India ignored this outflow of gold from the country's treasury throughout 1931.

2. India's gold reserves were gradually replaced by growing reserves of silver. The metal reserves and metal security increased through the stocks of silver and the quantity of silver coins. The percentage of the metal reserves in circulation was as follows:

Month, year	%
March 1930	80.81
June 1930	88.36
September 1930	85.83
December 1930	94.04
March 1931	93.36
June 1931	97.06
September 1931	93.91
August 1932	71.84

Thus, the gold was removed and sent to Britain, to be replaced by devalued silver stolen from the peasantry. This was the basis of the increase in the metal security for circulation. Such a policy contained all the signs of the inflationary policy the government desired. Why, then, did the Anglo-Indian government not set out on inflation from the beginning of the crisis and the drop in the value of silver? The temporary delay in the introduction of the inflationary policy was engendered by the need: a) to concentrate the mass of silver in the government's hands in order to replace the gold reserves with it; b) to reduce the paper and money supply in the country, for, since no deal had yet been made with the national reformist bourgeoisie (1930 and the first half of 1931), a depreciation of it would have been fraught with very unpleasant consequences; c) to conclude a number of sterling loans on the London market, for which purpose both time and proof of the "stability" of Indian finances were required.

The decisive factors delaying the introduction of the inflationary policy lay, of course, chiefly in the sphere of the class struggle. It should be recalled that almost throughout 1930 and the first six months of 1931, there were fierce class conflicts that, in a number of places, grew into armed rebellions. In this political situation, it was impossible to introduce a policy of sharp inflation and, moreover, a number of preliminary conditions for the implementation of such a policy had not yet been prepared. The economic horizon of the open transition to the lines of inflation was the abolition of the gold standard in Britain.

The period of deflation had, at the same time, certain specific features related to the transfer of colonial tribute. It saw a whole series of sterling loans, concluded by the Anglo-Indian government on the London money market, loans that consisted essentially in the advance of capital to put down the revolutionary movement and ensure the uninterrupted pumping out of colonial tribute. These loans were supposed to be paid back shortly, at the expense of the Indian people, over and above the "normal" colonial tribute usually levied on them. Here are some relevant data:

When advanced	Size of loan £ million	Interest rate	Repayment period, years
February 1930	6	6	1932—33
May 1930	7	6	1933—35
October 1930	12	6	1935—37
February 1931	18	5.5	1936—38
May 1931	10	6	1933—34
April 1932	10	5	1942—47

Consequently, over two years, £63 million were borrowed on the London market. In addition to these loans, in January 1928 a sterling loan of £7.5 million was concluded and in January 1929—one of £10 million.

The following two facts deserve attention: 1) the loans were essentially short-term, with repayment coming due in the next few years; 2) the loans brought in an unprecedented interest rate for the crisis years, and precisely at a time when the bank rate in all the world's chief banking centres, including London, was only 2-3 per cent. It should be mentioned that the nationalistic press met the government communiqué on the loans with criticism.

This criticism stopped sharply when the British colonialists advanced the Indian bourgeoisie an internal loan of 30 million rupees at 6 per cent per annum. This loan, like the London ones, was covered in literally a few minutes. The London stock exchange reacted to the May 1930 loan of £7 million thus: in 19 minutes the loan had been underwritten to the tune of £90 million instead of the required £7 million. The loan promised what were enormous profits under the crisis conditions.

During the crisis, the parasitic nature of the export of capital to the colonies was graphically illustrated by the example of India. The export of capital to India from Britain was (in £ millions).

1927	1928	1929	1930	1931
0.5	8.3	9.5	25.1	22.2

Almost 100 per cent of the capital exported to India was used for non-productive purposes as an advance on the colonial tribute, a fact that became more and more significant. It meant the reproduction of the colonial monopoly on an even more parasitic basis, as well as the reproduction of the class and economic contradictions in an even more acute form. The class struggle in the country and the attempt to subdue the growing forces of revolution showed this increasingly parasitic role of imperialism with even greater clarity. The export of capital to India during the years of the crisis coincided completely, both quantitatively and qualitatively, with the government loans concluded in London.

After borrowing £63 million in the City and giving it the opportunity to make £10-12 million in just interest on this (some loan bills were sold at £95 for an actual £100 value), the government paid this money into the British Treasury as colonial tribute. India never even saw the money. On the authority of the Anglo-Indian government, the City, having made substantial profits, transferred these £63 million from its own pockets to that of Britain's state Treasury. The transfer of colonial tribute was thus accomplished. India now had to pay this transfer sum, however much it might cost its toiling masses. The crisis, which disrupted the usual transfer mechanism and lowered India's active balance of trade, which had reduced Britain's share in India's export-import trade to the extreme and disrupted India's balance of payments and settlement of accounts with Britain, forced the Anglo-Indian government to resort to operations that would ensure the transfer of colonial tribute to Britain. These were:

1) A deflationary policy during the crisis made it possible to concentrate silver in the hands of the government in order to replace India's gold reserves with silver. The policy of pumping Indian gold out to Britain as colonial tribute in order to support the pound sterling continued under the conditions of the gradual inflation of paper money, but demonstrated a number of new features.

2) A step-up in the borrowing of money on the London market to the same ends—to cover the colonial tribute, accomplish its transfer when the mechanism of this operation, so expensive for the Indian people, had been disrupted by the crisis.

How exactly was the disruption of the transfer mechanism of colonial tribute manifested? Only analysis of India'a balance of trade during the crisis allows this question to be answered. India's usually active balance of trade, which served, as it were, as the material basis for the payment of colonial tribute, fell sharply during the three years of crisis. In 1929/30 it stood at 715.3 million rupees, in 1930/31 at only 590.3 million and in 1931/32—326.7 million rupees.

The active balance of export-import trade in goods alone (excluding gold, silver and other valuables) fell by over 50 per cent. The material basis for paying off the metropolis had narrowed greatly as a result of the crisis. If the total colonial tribute, which reached £35-40 million a year, had fallen in proportion to the drop in the active side of the balance of import-export trade, the usual transfer mechanism would not have been disrupted and the active balance of export-import trade in commodities would have been sufficient to cover the colonial tribute. But the fact is that the size of this colonial tribute not only did not drop proportionally, it actually rose, for a substantial sum of payments resulting from the policy of transferring the consequences of the crisis from Britain to India, especially the Indian countryside, was added to the usual colonial tribute levied on India and the Indian peasantry. Thus, we have two diametrically opposed processes: on the one hand, a sharp drop in the active balance of the export-import trade in commodities and, on the other, an increase in the colonial tribute.

Even so, the transfer of colonial tribute had to take place, and it did take place. The material basis for this was provided by the export of gold as such, rather than the usual export of commodities. Data on the balance of export-import operations in gold reveal precisely this. In 1929/30 India imported 142.2 million rupees' worth of gold and in 1930/31—127.5 million rupees' worth, while in 1931/32 India was already exporting 579.7 million rupees' worth of gold. From April 1 to September 3, 1932, the export of gold from India reached 239.4 million rupees. Consequently, India's total gold exports exceeded 800 million rupees or £60 million.

Official government data showed, just as the officials of the Anglo-Indian government asserted, that India's visible balance of trade had gone further into the black: it rose from 527.8 million rupees in 1929/30 to 905 million rupees in 1931/32. This visible balance included, however, over 550 million rupees' worth of exports in the form of gold, not commodities. For the export of commodities, India received valuables or commodities that fully maintained the non-equivalence of exchange. In exchange for the gold sent to Britain, it now received sterling valuables. Minister of Finances Schuster said at the time that the government held strong positions in relation to the gold balance.

Pursuing this policy, in exchange for the unprecedented gold exports, the Anglo-Indian government concentrated in circulation an unprecedented quantity of sterling valuables. In 1930, the Indian Treasury had at its disposal 338,496 thousand rupees' worth of sterling valuables and in 1931—103,847 thousand, but the figure for 1932 was 579,932 thousand rupees.

The abolition of the gold standard in September 1931 and the start of the extensive export of gold from India meant that Indian money circulation began to be filled with falling foreign valuables instead of real gold. Gold flowed in enormous quantities from the colony to the metropolis and the plunder of the colony intensified.

Monetary Policy After the Abolition of the Gold Standard

After the abolition of the gold standard of the pound sterling and the drop in the latter's value by 30-35 per cent, all the key problems of British imperialism's currency policy in India naturally appeared in a new light and new measures were required. To illustrate all the complexity of these problems, it is enough to point to just one of them, that of the British capital invested in India. The Anglo-Indian government sought and found a solution to some of them.

The chief problem facing the Anglo-Indian government was to maintain the previous correlation or parity between the Indian rupee and the British pound, which had now lost its gold basis. The solution to this problem was, of course, predetermined in Britain's favour. At the time when the members of the British House of Commons were voting for the gold standard to be abolished, the Secretary of State for Indian Affairs sent a telegram to the Viceroy in India concerning the need to tie the rupee to the pound. As soon as the gold standard was abolished, the Anglo-Indian government passed special legislation confirming the unchanged correlation between the rupee and the pound. The rupee, which had previously been indirectly tied to gold, was separated from it completely, while remaining tied to the falling pound. The tying of the rupee to the pound meant that neither the pound nor the rupee could rise or fall in relation to gold without affecting the other. The sterling value of the rupee remained unchanged, and the motivation behind the trade between Britain and India was not shaken.

British imperialism's monetary policy in India, which pivoted on maintaining an artificially high rupee exchange rate in relation to gold and led to Indian raw materials being ousted from the world market and being devalued within the country as a means for carrying out financial and accounting operations in India's foreign trade links with the rest of the world and as a mechanism for accomplishing the raw material monopoly for the purpose of ensuring colonial superprofits, remained "unshaken", thanks to this measure taken by the Anglo-Indian government.

This manoeuvre by British imperialism entailed a further drop in the competitiveness of Indian raw materials on the world market. It thus created even more favourable market conditions for the raw materials and foodstuffs produced in the British dominions and opened India's doors to dumping. Now, the British importers received an additional import bonus, over and above their "normal" rate of 12.5 per cent, and this largely paralysed the effect of import duties raised on a number of goods entering India.

At the same time, this manoeuvre (this probably being its chief essence) protected British capital invested in India against devaluation corresponding to the devaluation of the pound, for the parity between the rupee and the pound remained the same, though their real values had fallen. The value of the pound sterling had fallen by 30-35 per cent, while that of the rupee had fallen by exactly the same amount. The exchange rate between the rupee and the pound did not, however, alter or even became somewhat higher, and colonial tribute was paid not according to value but the exchange rate. This meant that India, as an exporter, would receive even less for its exports as a result of the maintenance of the old, artificially high exchange rate, while Britain, as the importer, would, as a result of the same policy, receive even more for its imports. The losses of the former were the gains of the latter. The robbery of the colony, the simplicity of which was concealed by intricate accounting operations, continued with ever greater intensity.

On April 5, 1932, the real gold content of the rupee was

13.9 pence, while its sterling exchange rate was almost 18.5 pence, i.e., 4.6 pence or 30-35 per cent higher than its gold content. The greater the difference between the real value of the rupee and its outward sterling exchange rate, the more the colonial peasantry lost on their exports of raw materials, the more they paid as a bonus to the imperialist importer. Such a situation, when the real value of the silver rupee in terms of gold fell together with the value of the pound or even lower, while the rupee exchange rate not only did not fall, but actually rose above the artificially high, enforced exchange rate, seemed incomprehensible and paradoxical at first glance. Superficial observers of these specific economic processes, which hit the colonial peasantry hardest, explained the scissors between the actual and constantly falling gold content of the rupee and its rising outward exchange rate as inevitable, or they even suspected economists, when they announced a certain rise in the rupee exchange rate alongside the drop in its real value, of taking the same position as Samuel Hoare, Secretary of State for Indian Affairs; straight after the abolition of the gold standard, he announcd an economic revival in India and the beginning of the country's escape from the crisis.

Briefly, this bold and risky manoeuvre on the part of British imperialism in India can be assessed only as a means for speeding up, in a camouflaged form, hidden from the eyes of the people, the transfer of the consequences of the crisis from Britain and the dominions on to the shoulders of the Indian peasants and workers. This was the class sense of British imperialism's policy. It acted primarily as a means for ensuring the continued pumping of colonial tribute out of the country, whose economy had been shaken to its foundations by the economic crisis developing on the basis of the old crisis of the entire colonial economy.

Let us throw some light on certain aspects of this problem. An article by one Indian economist states that, if the exchange rate between the rupee and the pound rose or fell (the latter would happen if the rupee were not tied to the pound), in the first case Lancashire and, in the second, Bombay would gain unilateral advantages over the other on the Indian market. Thus, British imperialism supposedly proved to be so "merciful" and "disinterested" that, by maintaining the former parity between the two currencies, it prevented harm coming to either Britain or India—such was the conclusion drawn by this article. But this is only the way things seemed on the surface. The very maintenance of the former rupee-pound parity, when the currency of one of the countries involved was bankrupted, still gave British imperialism, rather than the colonial peasant, the advantage.

The position of the Indian national bourgeoisie on this issue was simple enough. They wanted the abolition of the gold standard to entail the abolition of any enforced link between the rupee and the pound, the abolition at least of their former parity. The Executive Committee of the National Congress announced in its communiqué that the government was tying the rupee to the pound instead of leaving it alone and allowing it to find its own level in relation to gold.

Thus, the national bourgeoisie demanded a break away from the pound and the abolition of the existing rupee exchange rate. The economic motives behind these demands were obvious, and we have already outlined them in the section on the monetary policy before the abolition of the gold standard. The national bourgeoisie stood for the spontaneous market adjustment of the value of the falling silver rupee to that of gold, since this would make real value of the rupee correspond to its outward pound exchange rate. This would close the channel by which British importers received an import currency bonus and would make Indian industrial goods more competitive with British goods on the Indian market and, by reducing the artificially inflated prices of Indian raw materials on the world market and thereby somewhat increasing their competitiveness, would allow the national bourgeoisie to increase their profits. The Indian peasant would gain nothing from this, of course.

One more point deserves attention. Japan is known to have occupied a substantial place on the Indian market, especially that for the export of cotton and import of cotton goods. Britain's inflationary policy after the abolition of the gold standard of the pound sterling had to have an unfavourable effect on the trade between Japan and India, by raising the competitiveness of the country that had started pursuing the inflationary policy, i.e., Britain. This worried Japan. It also worried the Bombay capitalists, in case Lancashire returned even partially to the coarse fabrics market. The abolition of the gold standard of the yen and the imposition fo an embargo on the export of gold from Japan restored, however, the former balance of power between these two competitors on the Indian market.

The advantages of both Bombay and Lancashire over Japan were destroyed when the latter rejected the gold standard, the yen exchange rate fell and more or less reached the level of the pound sterling. The Bombay capitalists were quite pleased about the abolition of the gold standard of the yen, since this measure counteracted the attempts made by Lancashire to regain at least some of its positions. Soon, however, and precisely when Japanese competition—the dumping of cotton fabrics and artificial silk fabrics—was backed up by the falling yen exchange rate, the Bombay capitalists demanded raised import duties against Japan.

The Anglo-Indian government's monetary policy after the abolition of the gold standard was also marked by the beginning of open inflation on India's money market. Under the conditions of falling production, the crisis on the home market, the sharp drop in freight and commodity turnover, and budget deficits unprecedented in Indian history, between September 30 and December 31, 1931, the Anglo-Indian government increased the amount of money in circulation in the country from 1,484,840 thousand rupees to 1,793,031 thousand. The Indian Treasury's gold reserves were cut over this time from 71,928 thousand to 45,645 thousand rupees. The metal reserve of money circulation fell from 93.91 per cent to 72.14 per cent, and on March 31, 1932 stood at only 66.78 per cent, i.e., its lowest level. Inflation set in. The British imperialists paid for the raw materials and gold they exported from the country with paper money and falling sterling valuables. This was the background against which the export of gold from India began.

The export of gold allowed the Anglo-Indian government, first, to restore the active balance of trade, second, to pay off the sterling loan and, third, to expand the country's money circulation. These were the three arguments used by the government to substantiate the "beneficial" role of the export of gold from India.

The Anglo-Indian government's official and semi-official

press encouraged the inflationary policy and the export of gold, and tried to soothe the public on this count. It wrote that the export of gold had affected only a tenth of India's gold reserves, accumulated over just the previous thirty years, while India possessed almost as much gold as the USA, which had exported even more than a tenth of its reserves. The export of gold should not, according to the press, have caused the slightest concern, but rather should have been welcomed as a factor called on to bring the world out of its state of economic depression and to lead to a drop in the price of gold, which would push commodity prices up.

The magazine *Capital* took the following stand on this issue: the amount of gold exported was a negligible part of India's gold reserves; long before the British authorities had concentrated power in their own hands, long before the East-India Company had been formed to trade with India, gold had been accumulating in considerable quantities in the country and people well-informed on trade matters believed that, although there were no exact statistics available, India's gold reserves stood at 660 million tolas,[1] or 20 billion rupees. A large part of this gold was inactive in the country. People who bought gold at a price of 19-21 rupees a tola one month previously, would now get 30 rupees for it. The magazine even asked the following questions: How could these people be prohibited from or hindered in earning legal profits on their savings? Why should they not use their life-savings, accumulated at a low price, and sell them at considerably more favourable prices?

The same magazine claimed that, although the total value of the gold exported from India was 500 million rupees' worth by the end of March 1932, 150 million rupees of this consisted of profit from the sale of this gold at a substantially higher price than that at which it was purchased on the Indian home market. During this period, the British press in India overflowed with articles on the size of India's gold reserves. The most contradictory and, at the same time, the most fantastic figures were presented. All the authors were in a hurry to prove that India was an inexhaustible source of gold and that the value of that already exported was an insignificant part of its gold stocks, which equalled those of the USA.

The main theme of all these articles was that the gold stocks were in the hands of the Indian rural population, who brought their gold to the market but not in big enough quantities, and that they should be forced to increase the sale of their gold, which lay motionless in the countryside.

Let us, however, return to the question of inflation. Prof. Thomas of Madras University believed that the government was in no condition to accomplish money transfers to London. When, though the export of gold began, the situation improved so much that it was able not only to pay off the 15-million sterling loan, but also satisfy the demands made by the Secretary of State for Indian Affairs for the current financial year; sterling valuables were paid off in India in rupees, which entailed an expansion of the money circulation by 510 million rupees over just four months; this expansion consisted of 430 million in sterling valuables and 80 million government securities (Indian), borrowed from the Imperial Bank of India. For the exported gold, India received sterling valuables that, in turn, were exchanged for rupees. Paper-money circulation in India expanded by precisely the amount of the gold exported. Consequently, paper-money inflation required sterling valuables to be purchased in exchange for the exported gold. Real valuables left the country, to be replaced by falling sterling valuables and paper rupees.

Thus, the export of gold from India, which became particularly rapid after the abolition of the gold standard, was inevitably accompanied by the beginning of an inflationary policy, the first signs of which, as necessary preconditions, were clearly visible even during the period of deflation, before the gold standard was abolished. Is it, however, true that the export of gold was itself a profitable enough operation for those who bought up gold on the Indian home market and exported it to Britain on the world market? For an answer to this question, let us turn to the changes in the price of gold on the world market in 1931 (shillings and pence per troy ounce):

	Peak	Medium	Trough
January	85—1.25	85—0.05	84—11.40
March	84—11.5	84—10.94	84—9.25
May	84—11.5	84—10.32	84—9.25

	Peak	Medium	Trough
July	84—11.5	84—11.19	84—10.13
September	114—9.0	91—2.70	84—9.75
October	108—6.0	106—9.44	103—8.0
November	117—11.0	110—8.95	108—2.0
December	126—10.0	122—5.60	118—9.0

The price of an ounce of gold jumped up sharply over the last four months of 1931, i.e., the period when Britain was followed by over thirty countries in abolishing the gold standard. The demand for gold on the world market rose extraordinarily. Its export was prohibited from all countries that had abolished the gold standard, and only India, whose falling currency was deprived of any real gold back-up (the Indian currency was supported only by silver and falling sterling valuables), exported huge quantities of gold to Britain.

The export of gold was carried out mainly by the banking system of British finance capital in India and the Anglo-Indian government itself, through the Imperial Bank of India. While, therefore, the export of gold could, like any other commodity-money operation, bring substantial profits, based on the difference in prices, the direct seller of the gold could hardly, given the fixed purchase price, earn anything from this operation, for the price at which he sold his gold was set at a level to ensure that not he, but the exporter of the gold, reaped the profits. If one is to believe the data published in the Anglo-Indian press, at a fixed purchase price of 21 rupees 3 annas for a tola of gold, the sale of a tola of gold to Britain for 29 rupees 6 annas would bring the exporter a profit of 8 rupees 3 annas a tola, or 38 per cent.

To say nothing of exported gold itself as a form of colonial tribute, its export from India, i.e., the process of its realisation on the British market, brought in tremendous profits for the crisis period, since the export was carried out by British finance capital operating in India. These profits were based primarily on British finance capital's monopoly position in India, so expressed nothing but additional profits, unprecedented under crisis conditions. The upper echelons of the Indian financial bourgeoisie also, naturally, got rich from the export of gold. This stratum, on the one hand, being connected with British banking in India and, on the other, possessing its own quite ramified network of agents on the money market, concentrated in its own hands a considerable quantity of gold, which was exported through the British banks or, less frequently, independently. In both cases, however, it brought the Indian financiers substantial profits. It should not be thought that the fixed price of gold precluded speculation on India's money market. Quite the opposite. It fostered unprecedented speculation and actually nourished it.

The conclusions drawn by Chunilal Mehta, a big capitalist, at a meeting of the Bombay stock exchange may be set out as follows: the value of gold did not rise, while that of the rupee fell; in relation to export-import prices, the value of gold remained the same; the purchasing power of gold, expressed in terms of commodities, remained unchanged; the export of gold raised the rupee exchange rate and, consequently, prevented a growth of commodity prices, increased the government's opportunities for maintaining its policy of a high rupee exchange rate; gold was leaving the country and being replaced by paper money.

The eminent bourgeois economist Sarkar announced at a meeting of the Bengal Chamber of Commerce that the export of gold from India over only four months had reached a third of the amount mined annually throughout the world and that the majority of the exported gold was going to Europe. Moreover, the European purchasers of gold were paying the Indian exporters with pounds, while the government of India was buying these pounds of them for rupees, leaving the pounds in London and thereby paying off its £15-million loan. He then drew attention to the fact that the Indian public was demanding an immediate embargo, while the commercial organisations and chambers of commerce were protesting against the government's encouragement of the enormous and steady outflow of gold from the country. This same Chamber of Commerce did not, however, forget, in case the government ignored its protests, to ask for an increase in the fixed purchase price of gold, so that its purchase and concentration in the hands of the biggest British banks in India might leave the local bourgeoisie some profit.

After the adoption of the resolution requiring an embargo on the export of gold and the purchase of gold on the open market with the purpose of forming gold stocks for the future reserve bank of India, A. R. Bhat, a Deccan merchant, noted that the gold coming on to the market as a result of the existing management system allowed the government to increase the country's gold reserves to such an extent that there would be enough not only for organising a reserve bank, but also for paying off India's foreign obligations if necessary. He recommended the government to begin buying up gold on the open market.

As a result, the Federation of Indian Chambers of Commerce adopted the following resolution:

1. The Federation is observing with acute interest the protracted and significant export of gold, which has reached 550 million rupees and demands that the government of India put an immediate embargo on the export of gold from India, since the substantial and protracted pumping out of this precious metal poses a serious threat to the future reconstruction of Indian finances.

2. The Federation demands that the government buy up gold on the open market at real market prices, set daily on the market, for the purpose of accumulating gold reserves which would allow the future Indian government to organise a reserve bank with the necessary gold stocks at its disposal.

In this way, the Indian bourgeoisie loudly condemned the government's monetary policy and demanded that an embargo be imposed on the export of gold, but some of them, secretly, to avoid being suspected of betraying the national interests, sold gold on the world market, for this operation promised incredible profits. At the same time, the Indian bourgeoisie wanted an abolition or at least an increase in the fixed price of gold, the purpose being to get rich from purchasing gold within India, on the open market, and then selling it to British finance capital.

The inflationary policy that replaced the deflationary one and was constantly being criticised brought the bourgeoisie none of the things it wanted. The bank rate was just as high, and the credit squeeze as an expression of the anti-industrialisation policy of imperialism in the sphere of Indian finances continued. The gold continued to be exported. Most of the profits from the export of gold did not fall into the hands of the local bourgeoisie inspite of their wishes. The monopoly enjoyed by British finance capital made itself felt with full force.

On this point (the finance problem as a whole), the contradictions between the national bourgeoisie and imperialism gained in intensity. Imperialism enjoyed considerable room for manoeuvre here. It could make concessions, though not on the major issues of financial policy, but only on partial and secondary ones. The 18-pence rupee exchange rate was a powerful weapon in the struggle to find a way out of the crisis at the expense of India and its toiling masses, so no matter what the Indian bourgeoisie demanded, it was not abolished, of course, for it was one of the decisive supports of imperialism, one that acquired growing significance during the crisis. The possibility of concessions, as a cut in the bank rate, in the tariff for individual railway lines and routes, the issue of additional internal loans on comparatively profitable terms for the Indian bourgeoisie, was not excluded. Insistence on the central points and concessions over the partial and secondary ones, constituted the financial policy pursued by British imperialism in India.

As for the problem of setting up a reserve bank, independent of the government, judging from how this issue was posed during the four crisis years, and from the negotiations between representatives of the Indian bourgeoisie and British imperialism, the establishment of a bank would have been unlikely to undermine British imperialism's financial monopoly in India, for it would have retained only formal independence from British finance capital. In reality, however, a number of reins would have been used to keep it under control. The Anglo-Indian government did everything possible to drag out the negotiations on this, and reserved its own right to decide the issue, in order to use it as a trump card if a new edition of the Ghandi-Irwin "Delhi Pact" was required. Without a corresponding political equivalent, British imperialism would not agree to the establishment of this bank.

The Anglo-Indian government's policy led to a further rise in retail prices, for the value of the paper rupee was already demonstrating a considerable fall. The scissors between wholesale and retail prices were widening. Consequently, the rift between town and country was widening, too. Exploitation of the mass consumer—the peasant—became even more intensive. The commodity scissors between the metropolis and the colony grew ever wider.

India was faced again and again, year after year, by the need to transfer colonial tribute. The hope of covering it through a possible growth of the active balance of trade was unfounded. This exacerbated the economic situation in the country even more. The 1932/33 economic year saw a passive balance of commodity trade from one month to the next, this being a new feature for the Indian economy, testifying to a further intensification of the economic crisis. Consequently, the export of gold as a particular form for extracting colonial tribute under crisis conditions was inevitable. Not only the peasant and the worker were pauperised, but also the petty urban bourgeoisie, the artisan, small shopkeeper and junior official. The crisis deepened and grew. The contradictions and disproportions in the colonial economy were reproduced on a new basis and appeared in an even more acute form, painful for the toiling masses. The feudal merchant and moneylender exploitation of the rural masses gained in strength.

* * *

The material in this book allows us to conclude our analysis of India's agrarian problem by stating the indubitable fact that the Indian countryside was an original symbiosis of the feudal survivals that prevailed there in the 1920s and 1930s and the leading commodity-capitalist structure of the economy, which were in a state of mutual penetration, under the tremendously powerful political, economic and—we can say without presenting any of the essentially obvious proofs—military monopoly of British imperialism. In this last aspect, it acted primarily in the role of an occupying force, ensuring the plunder of the colony.

After World War I, India's development definitely shifted to general European capitalist lines.[2] Colonial-feudal capitalism began to dominate its agrarian economy. This was capitalism of a special sort, on the one hand, inherent in its overall laws in all countries that began to make the transition from feudalism to capitalism and, on the other hand, special in that it was developing in a typical colonial country, whose economy, the labour of its people and the entire pattern of economic structures, social classes and strata were to a decisive degree oppressed by foreign imperialist rule. The economic and social processes of transition to capitalism were deformed in India, and in this they differed greatly from the same processes on a free, independent and spontaneous basis in the countries of Europe and in Russia. All this provides the grounds for stating that, in as far as we are considering India and its agrarian economy at that time, it really did bear all the features of colonial-feudal capitalism.

Notes

Foreword

[1] M. K. Kudryavtsev, *The Commune and Caste in Hindustan (From the Life of the Indian Village)*, Moscow, 1971 (in Russian); V. I. Pavlov, *The Socio-Economic Structure of Indian Industry. The Historical Preconditions for the Genesis of Capitalism (End of the 18th to the Mid-19th Century)*, Moscow, 1973 (in Russian); V. I. Pavlov, *A Typology of the Genesis of Capitalism in Asia and Africa—Problems of Socio-Economic Formations,* Moscow, 1975 (in Russian); V. Pavlov, V. Rastyannikov, G. Shirokov, *India: Social and Economic Development (18th-20th Centuries)*, Moscow, 1975; V. G. Rastyannikov, "Problems of Capitalist Development in the Countryside of the Modern Orient" in *The World Economy and International Affairs,* No. 5, 1974 (in Russian); V. G. Rastyannikov, *The Agrarian Revolution in the Multistructured Society. The Experience of Independent India,* Moscow, 1973 (in Russian); A. P. Kolontaev, *The Lowest Forms of Production in the Countries of South and Southeast Asia. Specifics of Their Evolution,* Moscow, 1975 (in Russian); A. P. Kolontaev. "The Development of the Commodity Economy and the Problem of the Disintegration of the Indian Economy" in *Commodity-Money Relations in the Indian Economy,* Moscow, 1976 (in Russian); G. K. Shirokov, "The Evolution of the Commodity Economy in Colonial India" in *Commodity-Money Relations in the Indian Economy,* Moscow, 1976 (in Russian); L. B. Alayev, "On the Question of the Role of the Labour of the Landless in the Agriculture of the North-Western Provinces of India in the 19th Century" in *Countries and Peoples of the East,* Ed. 14, "India—the Country and Its People", Book 3, Moscow, 1972 (in Russian); L. B. Alayev, *The Social Structure of the Indian Countryside (The Territory of Uttar-Pradesh, 19th Century)*, Moscow, 1976 (in Russian); E. N. Komarov, "The Content and Chief Forms of the Evolution of Agrarian Relations in India at the End of the 18th and in the 19th Century" in *Problems of the History of India and the Countries of the Middle East,* Moscow, 1972 (in Russian); A. I. Chicherov, "Questions of the Theory of the Multistructural Socio-Economic System and Certain Problems of the Typology of

Social Development Processes in the 18th and Early 19th Centuries" in *Essays on the Economic and Social Structure of India,* Moscow, 1973 (in Russian); A. I. Chicherov, "On the Question of a Description of Commodity-Money Relations in India on the Eve of Its Colonisation" in *Commodity-Money Relations in the Indian Economy,* Moscow, 1976 (in Russian); V. V. Krylov, "Specifics of the Development of the Productive Forces and the Reproduction Process in the Developing Countries" in *The Economy of the Developing Countries: Theory and Research Methods,* Moscow, 1979 (in Russian); V. V. Krylov, "Traditionalism and Modernisation of the Countryside of the Developing Countries During the Scientific and Technical Revolution" in *The Agrarian Structures of the Countries of the Orient. Genesis, Evolution, and Social Transformation,* Moscow, 1977 (in Russian); V. P. Danilov, L. V. Danilova, V. G. Rastyannikov "The Chief Stages in the Development of the Peasant Economy" in *The Agrarian Structures of the Countries of the Orient. Genesis, Evolution and Social Transformations,* Moscow, 1977 (in Russian); E. G. Belyaev, O. E. Belyaeva, "On the Struggle Between the Imperialist Countries for Markets and Sources of Raw Materials in India (1932-1939)" in *Questions of World History,* Ed. 2, Cheboksary, 1974 (in Russian); H. Grinich, "On the Question of the Place of the Peasantry in the System of Imperialist Dependence, Exploitation and Backwardness" in *The Agrarian Question and the Role of the Peasantry at the Current Stage of the National Liberation Revolution,* Prague, 1978 (in Russian); *The Developing Countries and the "Green Revolution"* (Collection of Articles), Moscow, 1974 (in Russian).

Chapter One

[1] Karl Marx, "The British Rule in India", in Karl Marx, Frederick Engels, *Collected Works,* Vol. 12, Progress Publishers, Moscow, 1979, p. 131.

[2] Karl Marx, "The Future Results of British Rule in India", Karl Marx, Frederick Engels, *Collected Works,* Vol. 12, p. 217.

[3] M. M. Kovalevsky, *Communal Landownership: The Reasons, Course and Consequences of Its Disintegration,* Part I, Moscow, 1879, pp. 152-55 (in Russian).

[4] Karl Marx, *Capital. A Critique of Political Economy,* Vol. III, Progress Publishers, Moscow, 1977, pp. 790-91.

[5] See U. Roslavlev, *The Agrarian Crisis in India,* Moscow, 1932, pp. 10-11 (in Russian); B. H. Baden-Powell, *The Land Systems of British India,* Vol. 1, Oxford, 1892, pp. 340-46.

[6] See Yu. V. Gankovsky, A. M. Gurevich, "The Land Tax Rate in Colonial India" in *Peoples of Asia and Africa,* No. 6, 1978.

[7] Karl Marx, *Capital,* Vol. III, p. 334.

8 *Ibid.*, p. 617.

9 *The Agrarian Question and the Peasant Movement. Handbook*, Vol. 4, Moscow, 1937, p. 109 (in Russian).

10 U. Roslavlev, *op. cit.*, p. 16.

11 *Ibid.*, p. 17.

12 *Agrarian Problems*, Moscow, No. 3, 1928, p. 113 (in Russian).

13 On the significance of the land system introduced in India by the British authorities during the period of its colonisation see: Karl Marx, "The War Question.—Doings of Parliament.—India", Karl Marx, Frederick Engels, *Collected Works*, Vol. 12, pp. 214-15.

14 *Agrarian Problems*, No. 3, 1928.

15 Karl Marx, *Capital*, Vol. III, p. 803.

16 *Ibid.*, pp. 794-802.

17 The most important English-language works on the land system in India and its evolution from the period of colonial seizure to the mid-1930s include: K. B. Saha, *Economics of Rural Bengal*, Chuckervertty, Chatterjee & Co., Ltd., Calcutta, 1930; B. H. Baden-Powell, *The Land Systems of British India*, Vols. 1-3, Oxford, 1892; John Briggs, *The Peasant Land Tax in India*, Longmans, Green, London, 1830; Romesh Dutt, *Economic History of British India*, Vols. 1-2, Kegan, London, 1902; R. C. Dutt, *Famines and Land Assessments in India*, Paul Trench, Trübner & Co., London, 1900; G. Keating, *Rural Economics in the Bombay Deccan*, London, 1912; R. Mukerjee, *The Foundation of Indian Economics*, Longmans, Green, London, 1916; W. H. Moreland, *India at the Death of Akbar*, Macmillan, London, 1920; J. C. Sinha, *Economic Annals of Bengal*, Macmillan, London, 1927; Radhakamal Mukerjee, *The Rural Economy of India*, Longmans, London, 1926; R. Mukerjee, *Land Problems of India*, Longmans, Green, London, 1933; S. Gopal, *Permanent Settlement in Bengal and Its Results*, London, 1949.

Chapter Two

1 V. I. Lenin, "The Last Valve", *Collected Works*, Vol. 18, Progress Publishers, Moscow, 1973, p. 249.

2 *The Revolutionary Movement in the Colonies. Thesis on the Revolutionary Movement in the Colonies and Semi-Colonies, adopted by the Sixth World Congress of the Communist International, 1928*, Modern Books Limited, London, 1929, p. 16.

3 See *Agrarian Problems*, No. 3, 1928, p. 85.

4 *Ibidem.*

5 *Ibid.*, p. 178.

6 The drop in the numbers of debt slaves and agricultural labourers was a result of their mass deaths between 1919 and 1921 from famines and epidemics. According to official data, about 12 million people died from famine and epidemics in 1921.

[7] P. P. Pillai, *Economic Conditions in India,* George Routledge and Sons, London, 1925, p. 114.

[8] See *The Agrarian Question and the Peasant Movement. Handbook,* Vol. 4, pp. 112-16.

[9] 1 maund = 37.3 kg.

[10] V. I. Lenin, "The Agrarian Programme of Russian Social-Democracy", *Collected Works,* Vol. 6, 1977, p. 114.

[11] *Royal Commission on Agriculture in India* (henceforward *RCAI*), Vol. VIII, Evidence taken in the Punjab, HMSO, London, 1927, p. 261.

[12] V. I. Lenin, "The Agrarian Programme of Social-Democracy in the First Russian Revolution 1905-1907", *Collected Works,* Vol. 13, 1978, p. 296.

Chapter Three

[1] *RCAI,* Vols. I-XIII, HMSO, London, 1927; Report. Government of India Central Branch, Calcutta, 1928; Abridged Report, Bombay, 1928.

[2] *RCAI,* Vol. VI, Evidence taken in the Central Provinces, pp. 304, 306, 307.

[3] His own estate was in the Wardha district, 30 miles from Nagpur, and included two villages. In his words, the farm was worked with the help of "servants", i.e., essentially the labour of landless peasants who had become his debt slaves.

[4] 1 khandi = 780 lb.

[5] The minimum unrated income of the moneylender was, at that time, 12,000 rupees a year.

[6] *RCAI,* Vol. VI, Evidence taken in the Central Provinces, pp. 307, 313, 315.

[7] *Ibid.*, pp. 404, 406.

[8] *Ibid.*, p. 6.

[9] *RCAI,* Vol. IX, Evidence taken in the North-West Frontier Province, pp. 73, 74, 77, 79.

[10] *Ibid.*, pp. 4, 11-12.

[11] *Ibid.*, pp. 91, 94.

[12] *RCAI,* Vol. III, Evidence taken in the Madras Presidency, pp. 436, 442.

[13] *Ibid.*, pp. 553-54.

[14] *RCAI*, Vol. VIII, Evidence taken in the Punjab, p. 587.

[15] *Ibid.*, p. 618.

[16] *Ibid.*, p. 799.

[17] *Ibid.*, p. 809.

[18] *Ibid.*, p. 841.

[19] *RCAI,* Vol. VII, Evidence taken in the United Provinces, pp. 600, 605.

[20] *RCAI,* Vol. II, Evidence taken in the Bombay Presidency, pp.291-92.

[21] *Ibid.,* p. 337.

[22] *Ibidem.*

[23] *RCAI.* Vol. IX, Evidence taken in the North-West Frontier Province, p. 120.

[24] *RCAI,* Abridged Report, Bombay, 1928, p. 141.

[25] *RCAI,* Vol. III, Evidence taken in the Madras Presidency, p. 265.

[26] *RCAI,* Vol. VII, Evidence taken in the United Provinces, pp. 553-54.

[27] This once again confirms the point often repeated in Soviet literature, that the ryotwari system, introduced into India by the British in the middle of the first half of the 19th century and usually proclaimed by British economists as an ideal, supposedly ensuring the flourishing of the small land parcel under the favourable impact of direct fiscal and tax links with the government avoiding intermediary landlord links, had essentially, by the 1930s, turned into the usual landlord landownership system.

[28] See *RCAI,* Vol. VI, Evidence taken in the Central Provinces, pp. 321, 322, 324.

[29] *Ibid.,* pp. 388, 393.

[30] *Ibid.,* pp. 431, 433, 438-40.

[31] *Ibid.,* pp. 485, 487, 489.

[32] *RCAI,* Vol. VIII, Evidence taken in the Punjab, pp. 495, 499.

[33] This is on the condition that the usual price paid by the peasant for land in the regions of canal irrigation in the Punjab equalled 600 to 2,000 rupees an acre.

[34] *RCAI,* Vol. VIII, Evidence taken in the Punjab, pp. 374, 376, 378.

[35] *RCAI,* Vol. VII, Evidence taken in the United Provinces, pp. 133, 136, 137, 139, 149, 150-52.

[36] *Ibid.,* pp. 234-44.

[37] In its summary report, the Royal Commission on Agriculture in India wrote: "India is still pre-eminently the land of the small holder. Large-scale farming, even in the altered conditions of today [this refers to the recently passed laws on rent, making it easier for the landlords to evict tenants—*R.U.*] though open to many is practised by few. The large landholder, and there are many such, leases his land on rent to a number of petty cultivators." (*RCAI,* Abridged Report, p. 12).

[38] The Royal Commission explained this fate of barbarous exploitation of the vast majority of the Indian peasantry and their virtual bondage to the land as follows: "The crowding of the people on the land, the lack of alternative means of securing a living, the dif-

ficulty of finding any avenue of escape ... combine to force the cultivator to grow foods wherever he can and whatever terms he can." The Banking Committee recognised this as being correct, formulating it thus: "In India agriculture is, with most cultivators with uneconomic holdings, more a mode of living than a business." (*RCAI*, Abridged Report, p. 433; *The Indian Central Banking Enquiry Committee*, Vol. I, Part I, Majority Report, Calcutta, 1931, p. 53).

39 V. I. Lenin, "The Agrarian Programme of Social-Democracy in the Russian Revolution", *Collected Works*, Vol. 15, 1982, p. 159.

40 V. I. Lenin, "The Agrarian Programme of Social-Democracy in the First Russian Revolution 1905-1907", *Collected Works*, Vol. 13, p. 345.

41 *The Revolutionary Movement in the Colonies...*, p. 18.

42 V. I. Lenin, "The Agrarian Question in Russia Towards the Close of the Nineteenth Century", *Collected Works*, Vol. 15, pp. 73, 74.

43 *Ibid.*, p. 85.

44 *Ibidem.*

45 V. I. Lenin, "Political Notes", *Collected Works*, Vol. 13, p. 443.

46 V. I. Lenin, "The Agrarian Programme of Social-Democracy in the Russian Revolution", *Collected Works*, Vol. 15, p. 179.

Chapter Four

1 N. M. Pal, *Some Social and Economic Aspects of the Land System of Bengal*, The Book Company, Calcutta, 1929, p. 21.

2 V. I. Lenin, "The Agrarian Question and the 'Critics of Marx' ", *Collected Works*, Vol. 5, 1977, p. 121.

3 See N. M. Pal, *op. cit.*, p. 28.

4 K. B. Saha, *Economics of Rural Bengal*, p. 85.

5 *Ibid.*, p. 104.

6 V. I. Lenin, "The Development of Capitalism in Russia", *Collected Works*, Vol. 3, 1977, p. 205.

7 K. B. Saha, *op. cit.*, p. 100.

8 *Ibid.*, p. 103.

9 *RCAI*, Vol. IV, Evidence taken in Bengal, p. 426.

10 N. M. Pal, *op. cit.*, p. 113.

11 *Ibid.*, p. 73.

12 See *Census of India. 1931*, Vol. V, Central Publication Branch, Calcutta, 1933.

13 K. B. Saha, *op. cit.*, p. 116.

14 *RCAI*, Vol. IV, Evidence taken in Bengal, pp. 323, 328.

15 *Ibid.*, p. 433.

[16] K. B. Saha, *op cit.*, p. 145.

[17] *RCAI*, Vol. IV, Evidence taken in Bengal, p. 426.

[18] K. B. Saha, *op. cit.*, pp. 138-39.

[19] *Ibid.*, pp. 114, 117, 133.

[20] N. M. Pal, *op. cit.*, p. 135.

[21] See K. B. Saha, *op. cit.*, p. 242.

[22] *Ibid.*, pp. 222-23.

[23] *RCAI*, Vol. IV, Evidence taken in Bengal.

[24] *Ibidem.*

[25] *Ibidem.*

[26] *Ibid.*, §§ 23277-23278.

[27] *Ibid.*, p. 66.

Chapter Five

[1] *The Indian Central Banking Enquiry Committee*, Vol. I, Part I, Majority Report; Part II, Minority Report, Calcutta, 1931.

[2] The Banking Committee noted that the part of the income remaining at the disposal of the peasant family after all payments had been made either did not suffice to support it or was zero.

[3] *The Indian Central Banking Enquiry Committee*, Majority Report, p. 59.

[4] *Ibid.*, p. 74.

[5] *Ibid.*, p. 75.

[6] The Banking Committee's report stated that people who usually dealt with those moneylenders were so ignorant and so terror-stricken that they scarcely dared file a complaint against them. Cases of suicide were known as a result of the terrorism of Pathans.

[7] *The Indian Central Banking Enquiry Committee*, Majority Report, pp. 75, 76.

[8] *Ibid.*, p. 76.

[9] *RCAI*, Vol. VIII, Evidence taken in the Punjab, p. 746.

[10] This applies to the time before the crisis. The 1929-1933 crisis made substantial changes in the activities of the local urban bankers, arousing their interest in concentrating silver and gold in order to sell it at a profit in connection with government's monetary policy, the sharp price fluctuations for gold and silver and the policy of exporting gold from India. The buying up of gold and silver on the Indian money market and their export to Britain testified to the further ruin of the countryside, above all of the peasant masses, as well as to new forms of colonial tribute.

[11] *RCAI*, Vol. VI, Evidence taken in the Central Provinces, pp. 266, 326.

[12] *RCAI*, Abridged Report, pp. 388-89.

[13] *RCAI,* Vol. III, Evidence taken in the Madras Presidency, pp. 55-56.

[14] *RCAI,* Vol. V, Evidence taken in Assam, p. 58.

[15] *RCAI,* Vol. IX, Evidence taken in the North-West Frontier Province, p. 70.

[16] *RCAI,* Vol. II, Evidence taken in the Bombay Presidency, p. 314.

[17] *RCAI,* Abridged Report, p. 434.

[18] *The Indian Central Banking Enquiry Committee,* Majority Report, p. 700.

[19] MacDougall wrote that if the output per acre in terms of wheat had been raised to that of France, the wealth of the country would have been increased by £669,000,000. If the output had been in terms of English production it would have been raised by £1,000,000,000 per year. In terms of Danish wheat production the increased wealth to India would have been £1,500,000,000 per year. But he admitted that this was impossible.

[20] *The Indian Central Banking Enquiry Committee,* Majority Report, pp. 719-20.

[21] *The Indian Central Banking Enquiry Committee,* Minority Report, p. 22.

[22] *Ibidem.*

[23] *Ibid.,* p. 24.

[24] *Ibid.,* p. 30.

[25] Up to 1929, the land tax stood at 350 million rupees. Manu Subedar proposed, by the way, that the tax debt be levied on deferred terms, in equal parts.

[26] *The Indian Central Banking Enquiry Committee,* Minority Report, pp. 42, 43.

[27] *Ibid.,* pp. 49-50, 57.

[28] *Ibid.,* p. 58.

Chapter Seven

[1] Karl Marx, *Capital,* Vol. II, pp. 811-12.

[2] *Ibid.,* p. 325.

[3] See G. I. Safarov, *The Problems of the National Colonial Revolution,* Moscow, 1932 (in Russian).

Chapter Eight

[1] 1 tola = 11.644 g.

[2] V. I. Lenin, "Better Fewer, but Better", *Collected Works,* Vol. 33, 1976, p. 499.